A Short Course in Christian Doctrine

Also by the same author and published by SCM Press

A Short Course in the Philosophy of Religion

A Short Course in Christian Doctrine

George Pattison

scm press

British Library Cataloguing in Publication data

A catalogue record for this book is available
from the British Library

0 334 02978 3

First published in 2005 by SCM Press
9–17 St Albans Place, London N1 0NX

www.scm-canterburypress.co.uk

SCM Press is a division of
SCM-Canterbury Press Ltd

Printed and bound in Great Britain by
William Clowes Ltd, Beccles, Suffolk

Contents

Acknowledgements

The heart of this book reflects the teaching I gave over several semesters in the theology faculty of the University of Aarhus. I am therefore chiefly grateful to all who made it possible for me to have the experience of teaching there and who helped in innumerable ways in the teaching process – fellow teachers, TAPs and, of course, the students themselves. The two deans of the faculty, Peter Widmann and Carsten Riis deserve special thanks for supporting the bold venture of placing their students into the hands of an Anglican with a rather uneven grasp of the Danish language. Otherwise it would be invidious to single out individuals, except that I should mention that for one semester I shared the teaching programme with Johannes Nissen, and some traces of that collaboration are found in the book. I shall always remember those two years with warmth and gratitude. Thanks are also due to Christopher Adams for help with indexing. As on a number of previous occasions, I am, naturally, grateful also to the editorial staff at SCM Press for their confidence in the project and their support in executing it.

To the Theology Faculty of the
University of Aarhus, with gratitude

Introduction

The basic shape of this short course reflects the introductory course in practical theology that I gave in the theology faculty of Aarhus University. That this now emerges as a short course in *doctrine* is in itself a significant pointer to my understanding of Christian theology. For once the centrality of communication as the mode and not just the idea of Christian doctrine has been grasped, many of the traditional lines of demarcation between the theological disciplines start to crumble. These lines are, of course, historically relative. Their current definition reinforced by the academic concepts of the nineteenth century (e.g. Schleiermacher's *Short Outline of Theological Study*), owes most to the practices of knowledge embodied in the book culture of early modernity. This is a theme associated with the work of Walter J. Ong, whom I shall be discussing further in Chapter 6. Ong – to my mind brilliantly – has shown how a combination of the logical theory of Petrus Ramus and the new technology of book production led in the seventeenth century to a reconceptualization and a reorganization of the nature and practice of teaching and learning. Among other things, this involved a taxonomic division of the fields of possible knowledge and a hardening of the boundaries separating these fields. It is not to decry all of the advances made possible by this new approach to knowledge to observe that we are now coming or have already come out of the intellectual epoch shaped by the exclusive primacy of the book and that this shift calls for a reconsideration of the whole structure of our studies. The growing demand for what have been called 'interdisciplinary' studies is one reflection of this situation, although the name itself also perpetuates the idea that the classical disciplines are or should be one's starting-point. But if theology, at least, is led by the questions that arise for faith in the life and practice of believers and believing communities, then it is clear that disciplines and the methods associated with them have to be led by those questions and not the other way round. We have to think first about the matter to be thought, rather than determining what is to be thought from the perspective of given procedures, no matter how powerfully institutionalized. In this regard, my chief regret concerning this book is that I do not have a sufficient grasp of biblical studies to bring the perspectives offered by this discipline to the questions I am addressing, because I have no doubt that they are extremely relevant.

Nevertheless, the reworking of a course in practical theology as a course in doctrine has had some impact on the content. Those who participated in the course will recognize many things, but not everything, and there are other things that have been significantly reduced or even dropped. Most noticeable in this regard is the introduction of a chapter on Christology (Chapter 4), and the compression of material relating to homiletics, pastoral theology, pedagogy and spirituality (material that, in the nature of the case, made up a significant part of the practical theology course) into a subdivision of Chapter 5. I have also added sections on the ethical and political dimensions of doctrine that, in the Danish Lutheran context, could not easily be incorporated into the practical theological curriculum, although they would maybe be more readily assimilated to it in the Anglo-Saxon environment.

Having said all this, I should immediately add that this is not primarily a book for the academy but for the Church, for those concerned with the practice of Christian communicative action rather than its theoretical analysis (though that division too is doubtless open to question). My aim is not to argue for or to defend my case, but simply to present it: to set out, as well as I can, a view of what is happening in Christian doctrine. There are therefore many points at which scholars will find the case under-argued or dangerously exposed to one or other contrary view. In the classroom, where the book originated, many of these questions could be dealt with in live dialogue. To have gone into such questions here, however, would be to have burdened the text with a multitude of in-crowd discussions and ponderous notes, and to have diverted attention away from the central vision I am attempting to offer. In some cases I have dealt with these background issues in other of my published works, in other (more frequent) cases others have dealt with them more adequately than I can ever hope to do, and in yet other cases I hope to return to them in future work. At the same time, what I have said about this being a non-academic book and the very nature of the view I present here means that if there is a real 'key' or supplement to this text, it is my own practice in preaching and in prayer and, even more importantly, in what I have received from participating in lived contexts of preaching, worship, prayer, pastoral concern and existential dialogue. To the extent that readers will have had analogous experiences, they will themselves be able to give depth and life to this sketch.

1

From Saving Knowledge to Communicative Action

From Classical Creeds to Communicative Action

When, as a young adult, I first began to get seriously interested in Christianity, my parish priest gave me a book he thought might be helpful. It was a book that explained Christian doctrine in terms of the doctrinal debates that culminated in the creeds or statements of belief that were thrashed out in the great Church councils of the fourth and fifth centuries AD and that have remained a constant point of reference for Christian belief ever since. These creeds stated in succinct terms what it was that Christians ought to believe regarding God and, in particular, God's being as Father, Son and Holy Spirit, together with a number of core statements about the Church and its role in mediating Christ's saving work. Even under the pressure of later splits in the Church, as in the Protestant Reformation of the sixteenth century, these creeds retained a definitive role in all the mainstream Protestant churches, Lutheran, Calvinist and Anglican. Having once been 'made', Christian doctrine now became the measure of what was and what wasn't 'Christian', of what – and who – did or didn't belong in the Church.

Not only did the content of these particular creeds remain unchallenged in Christianity's great historic upheavals. No less important was the fact that, except among some extreme Protestant groups such as the Quakers, the idea of a 'creed' and its normative function was virtually unquestioned. The Reformers – and their Catholic counterparts – were, of course, well aware that times change and that the message, though unchangeable in itself, needed to be adapted to the circumstances of the early modern world. Print, literacy and the widening horizons of knowledge, together with the particular social, political and psychological crises of the age, all called for the faith to be restated. In response, the sixteenth and seventeenth centuries witnessed a massive output of new credal-type formulations, such as the Augsburg and Westminster Confessions on the Protestant side and the decrees of the Council of Trent on the Catholic side, as well as the proliferation of teaching programmes ('catechisms') designed to train the ordinary believer in the language and culture of faith. One popular publication of this era bore the title *The Sum of Saving Knowledge*, a title which epitomizes the assumptions underlying much of the doctrinal debate of the times. If a person is to be saved, it seems to say, then there are certain things that he or she has to know. These things can be summarized in a form that (a) everyone within a given Christian community can agree on and (b) makes them accessible to the averagely educated person. These assumptions were scarcely new. In the creed known as the Athanasian Creed, dating (perhaps) from the fifth century and enshrined in the articles of the Church of England as a criterion of orthodoxy, we read that 'Whosoever will be saved, before all things it is necessary that he hold the catholic faith; which faith except every one do keep whole and undefiled, without doubt he shall perish everlastingly.'

Christian doctrine, then, would seem to be the sum of the knowledge that a person has to believe to be true if he or she is to be saved and to enjoy the fellowship of the Church. But is it true that Christianity requires us to believe certain things about God, ourselves and the world if we are to be saved? Is such a way of considering the matter even helpful? Does it not immediately trap us into all those confusing questions as to just what each particular clause means and how, in any case, is what the creeds actually say to be squared with what we know of the world through science, history or everyday experience? Isn't it just this way of seeing things that has led some people to regard Christianity as the art of believing six impossible things before breakfast?

Saying that the creeds remained normative in all the mainstream churches might seem to imply that doctrinal development simply stopped in AD 451, the date of the last great credal council (the Council of Chalcedon). This is not entirely accurate. Apart from the ongoing process of defining new areas of doctrine not covered by the great councils (such as the nature of Christ's presence in the Eucharist or the role of Mary), modern theology has undertaken a series of attempts to revisit the classic creeds themselves. Particularly in the movement known as liberal Protestantism the ideas of the Trinity and of the divinity of Jesus came to be regarded as reflecting the world-view of earlier times and, in more radical developments, even the idea of God was sometimes said to be surplus to modern requirements. Most of the liberals still accepted that the idea of some agreed common statement as to what it was that Christians believed was desirable and even essential if Christianity was to continue to exist, but, as their opponents pointed out, the kind of minimalist creed that liberals could agree on was far too thin and abstract to inspire the kind of heroic sanctity, joyous worship and cultural creativity to which historical Christianity had given rise. In Christian theology itself, the last 20 years have seen something of a reversal of the nineteenth- and twentieth-century liberal mainstream in terms of a very robust reassertion of the Trinitarian nature of Christian belief and of a number of classic themes from ancient and medieval thought.

It would be foolish to get into the ever-popular but ultimately idle game of guessing where the future lies and whether it will be liberals or conservatives who have the final say, if, indeed, there ever will be a 'final say'! The question I want to address here is a rather different one. As I listen now to one side, now to the other, I feel that something rather important is being overlooked. Orthodox, liberal, radical and neo-orthodox agree in defining their differences in terms of *what* it is they believe. But, I suggest, *what* we believe is only the tip of the iceberg of what is actually going on in a believing life. As theologians have long recognized, there is an important ambiguity in the word 'faith' itself, for 'faith' can either be understood objectively, as when a creed is said to define '*the* Christian faith' or *what* it is that Christian believe, or it can be heard more subjectively, as the faith a person has, the quality of their believing (thus the title *Christian Believing* given to the Church of England's Doctrine Commission report of 1976). The distinction itself is nothing new, but the admission of a subjective dimension has mostly been seen as supplementing the objective, credal idea of faith. Faith as *what* is believed has remained the yardstick by which the quality of an individual's believing is measured, and not vice versa. Too much emphasis on the subjective 'believing' has generally been seen as a weakening of the common faith of the Christian community. But is this either/or entirely helpful?

Let us try to approach the matter in another way. This book is about Christian *doctrine*, but what does the word 'doctrine' itself mean? It is a word derived, with minimal alteration, from the Latin *doctrina*. It is also virtually synonymous with another English word 'teaching' and, indeed, 'teaching' is sometimes used to translate *doctrina*. 'Teaching', however, allows us to notice something that is obscured for non-Latin readers by the word 'doctrine'. For 'teaching' – like faith – can be seen either in objective or subjective terms. When we see a book with a title like 'The Teaching of the Buddha' we expect to find in it an account of what the Buddha taught. When a student at a teacher-training college speaks about 'teaching practice', however, it is the subjective aspect that is meant, the actual practice and experience of the activity known as 'teaching'. We can therefore treat the word 'teaching' either as a noun or as a verb, either as a 'what', a thing or a substance of some sort, or a practice, an activity, a doing.

Now, I do not wish to claim here that all nouns are ultimately reducible to verbs or that language in general is better understood as expressing the turbulently interactive 'verbal' process of life, of doing and being-done-to, acting and suffering, rather than as a conglomeration of labels attached to static objects. I do find such an approach attractive, but to justify it as a general thesis about language would involve a long and uncertain philosophical detour. I do, however, think that it will help us to see important aspects of Christian doctrine if we think of the word 'doctrine' itself in verbal terms. For if we do so, then doctrine becomes something rather more than a fixed body of 'saving knowledge'. It becomes the expression of a willed and passionate movement of life.

To look at it like this draws attention to the subjective quality of faith, the faith that believes – but it also helps us to avoid a limitation to which an overemphasis on the subjective aspect can give rise. For if I define faith simply in terms of what *I* believe, then it can easily become something quite arbitrary. Why should I not believe whatever I like, however crazy, if faith is determined by my subjective input and nothing else? But to speak of doctrine as the activity of teaching, is also to speak of it as something occurring in a situation where the individual is never alone in some utterly subjectivized universe. 'Teaching' is something that can only happen when there are at least two people involved. Teaching arises from and only really lives in a relationship. This relationship can, of course, be variously configured: as an authoritative top-down process of instruction, perhaps, or as a dialogical effort in problem-solving.

Both in this chapter and subsequently I shall return to the different kinds of relationship that 'teaching' can imply. The point here is merely to underline that whatever actual form it takes, teaching is a fundamentally relational concept, a social process extended through time. Even where the content of the teaching is fixed – as, let us say, in the teaching of Euclidean geometry – the relationship between teacher and pupil is an important and developing reality without which learning can scarcely occur. Of course, one could argue that precisely the truths of geometry are truths of a kind that we could, in principle, learn for ourselves, since they subsist in formal relationships that do not depend on any accidental historical or human knowledge.

Socrates, famously, used an uneducated slave-boy to show that any rational being has an innate capacity for grasping such truths. Yet, as the story itself (and the whole body of Plato's writings, in which Socrates plays so crucial a role) shows, the slave-boy would probably never have discovered this capacity all by himself. It took the initiative of the teacher to make him realize it, even if the teacher only taught him what, in one sense, he already knew. And if the living, relational process of teaching can be important for such an abstract discipline as geometry, it is likely that it will be proportionately more so when what is being taught involves the learner's whole view of life or sense of self. Whatever else may be said about it, this, at least, is surely the case with Christian faith: that it engages our whole view of life and sense of self. The truth of faith, then, cannot but become entangled with the interactive and interpersonal processes and relationships by and in which it is taught and learned. To introduce yet another word: Christian faith, Christian teaching, lives in and as *communication*.

The idea of communication, though it has a certain late twentieth-century ring to it, is not strange to classical Christianity. In the New Testament itself Christ is spoken of as the 'Word' or the 'image' or 'icon' of God, both crucial terms in the vocabulary of communication. Throughout the Bible questions of communication are constantly present and we are shown that God is adept in using such varied communicative media as rainbows, thunderstorms, earthquakes, plagues, asses, 'the still, small voice' and the whirlwind, as well as the words of prophets, poets, singers, commentators, letter-writers, stones and the voices of children. The Bible itself as a book, or a collection of books, is a very specific form of communication. Later ages have added visual art, architecture, music and drama to Christianity's arsenal of communicative forms, as well as many reflections on the nature and needs of the Church's communicative task. In the English-speaking world, at least, those who express and nourish their faith by sharing in the ritual known as Holy Communion or the Eucharist are referred to as communicants. Several of the most influential twentieth-century theologians, including both the Protestant Karl Barth and the Catholic Karl Rahner, have also – in very different ways – made ideas of communication central to their vision of the God–human relationship.

But taking our cue from the idea of communication is not only justifiable in terms of its internal theological credentials. It is also a key aspect of our own contemporary world. Several theological generations ago, Paul Tillich insisted that theology should always be 'answering theology', that is to say it should always respond to the most important issues and insights of the contemporary word. Later

Tillich formalized this into his 'method of correlation', according to which the theological answers are to be correlated to the questions that shape contemporary culture. In the immediate post-war period, when Tillich was producing his best-known work, these were the kinds of questions associated with existentialism, abstract expressionism, Bergman movies and the atom bomb. It was, as Tillich put it, the question of meaning, given voice in the existentialists' anguished declaration of life's ultimate meaninglessness. It would not be hard to argue the case that, in a similar way, questions of 'communication' are central to our own culture. IT and the explosion of the internet, cable television, the mobile phone and, at another level, the geometrically expanding awareness of the processes of DNA as a communications system of unique (some would say all-encompassing) sophistication and importance – these and many other phenomena reveal ours to be a time intensely conscious of communication as a primary form of human existence. Some commentators say that even war has become just an event on television. In an age such as this, it seems, we 'exist' only in so far as we are produced by and participate in the onward and outward flow of information.

This situation has its utopian advocates, for whom a phenomenon such as the advent of the internet is a major step forward in liberating us for an absolutely democratic, absolutely open global society. How could an Iron Curtain fall over Europe today, when people are so incessantly and unstoppably in communication with one another? But there are at least as many who see in the exponential growth of communications systems an all-out assault on stable social relationships and psychological formation, who experience the proliferation of cable-TV channels and the omnipresence of the mobile phone as symptoms of a massive dumbing-down, that may or may not be being manipulated by dark forces behind the scenes (usually global capitalism). In either case, we have become aware that the way in which we communicate with one another is at least as important as what we communicate. If the famous slogan 'the medium is the message' is just a bit too glib, it highlights an important lesson that most of us intuitively understand.

The philosopher Jürgen Habermas – to whom we shall return shortly – has distinguished between those forms of communication that are aimed at communicating information or knowledge and those that are aimed at understanding.[1] The former may be appropriate when it is simply a matter of transmitting scientific facts or arguments or explaining technical processes, but this by no means exhausts human beings' communicative practices. We also have the need to express our feelings about things, and, no less importantly, we need to be able to argue over whether some proposed action is morally justifiable. One can only talk about 'understanding' in the full sense of the word when these other dimensions are taken into account over and above the merely factual or technical. Like many other commentators, Habermas believes it to be a major problem of our time that the scientific and technical modes of discourse have been developed at the cost of the other modes, and that social justice and personal fulfilment demand that these too are taken into account.

The argument is not hard to follow. Let us imagine a doctor dealing with a patient preparing for a major operation. Once the patient is unconscious on the operating table, he or she is, of course, nothing more than the object of a purely technical, scientifically regulated, action. An extreme example of this would be the treatment of the front-line rescue workers of Chernobyl, who were so heavily radiated that no direct human contact between doctors and patients was permitted, but in a less dramatic way the same situation is repeated daily in countless operating theatres. The surgeon's own training will primarily be oriented towards acquiring the knowledge and the skills appropriate to this objectified situation. However, it is also generally accepted that the patient needs – if possible – to be informed about all aspects of the operation, how it will affect his or her lifestyle, and – ideally – to have time to talk through how he or she feels about it. In some situations there may also be a question as to whether, no matter how technically unproblematic, the operation is morally justifiable. Religious believers in particular may have reservations about abortion, blood transfusion, artificial conception, genetic intervention, etc. Of course, many people have experienced that, alongside being grateful for the technical proficiency of modern medical practice, they have also been frustrated, angered and frightened by their doctors' failure to treat them with an appropriate consideration, to allow them to voice their anxieties, or to help them talk through what the treatment they are receiving means for their lives. Hospital practice has, happily, become much more aware of these dimensions in the last 20 or soyears, though old-style horror stories of lack of appropriate information occasionally resurface.

The point – Habermas's point – is simply that it is not enough merely to regard our problems, in this case sickness, as susceptible to scientific and technical solutions. Even if the treatment of a rare type of cancer, for example, necessarily involves an irreducibly technical element, and even if that element is the hinge on which the success or failure of the whole treatment turns, it is not enough. This will be yet

more true if we think of psychoanalysis or some other form of psychotherapy, where the patient's own acceptance of a particular way
of understanding the situation is pivotal to any successful outcome.[2]
A surgeon can operate no less successfully on a patient who is completely ignorant of medical science than on a fellow surgeon, whereas
it is no good for an analyst or a therapist being able to diagnose a
client's problems, if the client is not willing or able to appropriate that
diagnostic understanding for him- or herself. Naturally, the understanding at which the client arrives may not be articulated in the
same technical vocabulary as the diagnosis offered by the therapist,
but without some such understanding on the client's part the whole
process is left hanging in thin air.

The same pattern recurs at the social level: it is profoundly unsat-
isfactory that governments or corporations are all too prone to set in
motion projects that, they assure us, will be good for the economy,
etc., without taking into account the multiple ways in which these
schemes will impact on local communities, the natural and historical
environment, and other relevant (but hard to quantify) factors. The
expert view is not enough: it has also to be socially acceptable – and
for this to happen everybody affected by the project has to be part
of the discussion. In Western democracies this need is now generally
acknowledged, though many would question whether the consulta-
tive processes actually offered in concrete situations involve 'real'
consultation or are just a sop to refractory pressure groups. Whatever
one's view of this question, genuine communicative action, to use
Habermas's expression for the optimal communicative situation, is
never merely one-way. It is interactive and open, and the outcome is
dependent on the whole process of communication itself.

How might we relate such reflections to the question of Christian
communication, Christian doctrine?

Whatever role we ascribe to the classic creeds, it is not hard to see
that the communication of Christian doctrine must involve more than
the kind of teaching and learning involved in learning a scientific
theory or a technical practice. Even if there is some analogy to the
kind of process a medical student must go through with regard to
the study of physiology and the acquiring of clinical skills, there is a
closer analogy to the process through which a person comes to qualify
as an analyst, or, for that matter, successfully to complete a course of
therapy. Later I shall draw attention to the limits of this analogy too,
but the point to be emphasized here is simply that one cannot become
an analyst or live through analysis without one's self, one's feelings,
values, aspirations and anxieties being central to the whole process. I
myself am at stake every step of the way.

Christian Midwifery

In the nineteenth century, the Danish Christian thinker Søren Kierkegaard drew attention to a similar distinction between what he called disinterested and concerned truths, the latter being the kind of truths in which the teacher and learner themselves are inevitably and necessarily involved, in which one cannot take a detached view, because the question on which the whole thing turns is the question of oneself, one's own identity and, as Kierkegaard put it, one's own eternal happiness. Kierkegaard's thought is seen by many commentators as marred by an overemphasis on the subjective element in knowledge. He, or one of his pseudonyms, certainly did proclaim that 'subjectivity is truth', and this is often taken as a sign of his extreme individualism. Without denying either the subjective or the individualist aspect of Kierkegaard's view of life, however, the fact remains that he was one of the first Christian thinkers really to grasp the centrality of the question of communication. The role he gives to communication therefore implies a limit to the adequacy of any merely individualistic account of faith. His attack on the impersonal objectivity of systematic philosophy or 'science' was not simply a battle fought on behalf of subjectivity and passion. It was also intended to draw attention to the situation that faith lives and moves through an open-ended process of communication, a process in which we need to be aware of the 'how' as well as the 'what' of knowledge. In this spirit he remarked at one point that whereas theology had in the past had primarily defined itself in relation to philosophy, that is, as a form of knowledge, it should in future take more note of rhetoric, in other words, learn to see itself as being about reflection on the 'how' of communication.

It was in keeping with this insight that, at one point, Kierkegaard planned a series of lectures (which he never, in fact, had the opportunity to give) on 'the dialectics of ethical and ethico-religious communication'.[3] The fragmentary and unfinished notes for these lectures are, I suggest, one of the unnoticed turning-points of modern Christian thought, and at least as important as his other much-discussed contributions to theology (some of which we shall touch on later). They are, of course, notes and, as such, repetitive, often unclear and, generally, unfinished. They do not give answers, let alone tell us in any detail how the job is to be done. What they do, however, is to point to a number of key issues that any serious reflection of Christian communication will do well to take into account.

Kierkegaard begins by making a fundamental distinction between science and art. The problem with the modern world, he immediately adds, is that it has forgotten this distinction and, in giving pre-eminence to science, teaches as science what really belongs to art. By art, it should be said, he does not mean any of the fine arts, such as painting, poetry or literature, but art in an older, Aristotelian sense, art as a practical skill (as, perhaps, in the art of archery or flower-arranging or, even, the art of government). Though generally lamentable, this confusion is fatal when it comes to ethics. For ethics is not about having a correct theoretical view of the world. Ethics is about right action. But surely, one might ask, one has to know what is right before one can do it? Isn't ethics, especially Christian ethics, the application in practice of truths, principles or world-views that have already been proved true at the theoretical level? Kierkegaard wouldn't agree. Like a number of other leading moral philosophers, including Kant and Habermas, he would argue that moral or ethical truth is something to which every individual has equal access. Clearly, when it comes to matters of theoretical or scientific truth, it is quite reasonable to claim that one person knows more than another or that there can be experts. But there can be no experts in ethics. For an action is or becomes ethical to the extent that I engage in it on the basis of a free decision motivated solely by the belief that it is right.[4] If I do the right thing under duress, or without really being aware of what I am doing, such an action, whatever its results, is scarcely moral. Even more than successfully completing a course of therapy, acting morally requires me to be fully engaged in what I do. Ethical teaching, therefore (this is Kierkegaard's argument), has to be teaching that in some way arouses and engages the learner's readiness to act. In doing so it crucially presumes that the learner is someone capable of such action. The learner must be a potential moral agent, that is, a member of the universal moral community to which the teacher also belongs.

One example Kierkegaard uses to illustrate this point is the relationship between a drill-sergeant and a raw recruit. No matter how rough the sergeant's treatment of the recruit, the whole process of training depends on the assumption that the recruit has it within him to become a soldier. What the training aims at is the realization of this potential. Perhaps the example is not so good in relation to a modern, technological army, but Kierkegaard has other examples, such as learning to swim, that do not involve anything other than the learner's own mind–body unity. Of course, the person who learns to swim learns something they did not know how to do before, but what they learn is not the theory of swimming, indeed they might be altogether ignorant of why it is that human bodies can float in water: what they learn is, simply, to swim. And to do that, they themselves must do it. Teaching ethics is teaching what Kierkegaard calls a 'should-can', that is, help-ing the learner to become aware of standing under a certain obligation and of their capacities for responding to that obligation. It is learning how to engage myself with my life and my world in a certain way. And everybody has this potential.

This has a number of important implications. First, the one who 'teaches' does so in only a qualified sense. He is, as Kierkegaard's chief model for a genuine ethical teacher, Socrates, said of himself, a midwife, someone whose work consists in bringing to birth what is already stirring in the learner. In these terms, the teacher does not have any kind of authority in relation to the learner. He cannot tell him what he should do, since that would be precisely to overrule the learn-er's freedom, which it is the whole object of the exercise to arouse. He is not 'above' the learner, but on a level with him. No matter how skilled in his maieutic (midwife's) art, the teacher serves rather than manages the learner.

But, second, the teacher too is a member of the moral community, and it would be a glaring contradiction if in seeking to arouse the moral concern and engagement of others he neglected his own duty to live morally. This puts ethics on a very different footing from any kind of 'science'. In the case of an abstract science such as geometry, the personality of the teacher is neither here nor there. In the case of a humanistic discipline such as history, a history teacher does not have to be a great politician or military leader in order to be able to teach about the rise of women's suffrage or Napoleon's campaigns. Even in the case of the arts, it is possible to teach art appreciation with-out oneself being competent in any actual art. But, in ethics, to teach that one should always do the good while not doing it or not even attempting to do it is to confuse matters utterly. We are, of course, all familiar with the dyed-in-the-wool smoker who says to a young person, 'Listen to me, the best way to stop is never to start.' Perhaps if the speaker is far gone in the course of a smoking-related illness or if their breath, teeth and tobacco-stained fingers are sufficiently repul-sive, the testimony might have some admonitory effect, but otherwise it is more likely simply to function as yet another proof of the incurable hypocrisy of the middle-aged.

A third important feature of ethical teaching stressed by Kierkegaard is that it always occurs in a quite concrete situation. Or, to put it another way, the concrete situation in which the teaching is given fundamen-tally affects the meaning of the whole teaching/learning event. To recur to the example of swimming: it is one thing to teach swimming on dry land, by lying the learner over a chair and teaching him or her the correct strokes, but it is something else for the learner to do this in the water, and something else again to do it in a turbulent sea over 70,000 fathoms of water, rather than in a 1.5 metre-deep learning pool. Kierkegaard's point here is not the relativistic point that the good means different things in different contexts, but simply the pedagogical point that if the situation is not taken into account, then whatever is learned will not really engage the learner's whole personality. It will remain abstract, superficial or irrelevant.

There is a nice illustration of this in Berthold Brecht's play *The Mother*.[5] One of Brecht's most propagandistic plays, it involves a group of communists seeking to establish revolutionary cells amongst the factory workers. Most of the latter are illiterate, so the first task of the communists is to teach them to read and write. They start with what they think will be easiest, words and phrases like 'The cat sat on the mat.' However, progress is slow to non-existent. Puzzled, they ask the workers what is wrong. At this point the 'mother' springs to her feet and explains that the trouble is that what is being taught is simply irrelevant to the workers. They don't want to be able to write sentences like 'The cat sat on the mat', they want to be able to write words like 'class-consciousness' and 'revolution'. One doesn't have to share Brecht's politics to take the point. The teacher – and this pre-eminently means the teacher of morals or ethics, though something similar might be said of teaching in more 'objective' disciplines – has to begin at the point where the learner finds him- or herself. One cannot just talk about morality or the good in abstraction: they must be relatable to the learner's actual circumstances.

All this is, clearly, said about ethics or morals. And thus far many moral philosophers, including, as I have already indicated, Kant and Habermas, could go along with Kierkegaard. For Kant it is the very definition of a human being that he or she is a moral agent, capable of acting according to the dictates of practical reason. Habermas's thought relates more to the concrete circumstances of social and political life, but in his insistence on democracy, consensus and the common sense of everyday life, he too affirms that ethical concern and action are the equal concern of all responsible human beings. Though we live in a world of experts, it is precisely one of the goals of ethically engaged communicative action to make sure that the knowledge and technical applications possessed by these experts are subordinated to goals and values that we all have an equal right to help formulate.

As a moral philosopher, Kierkegaard could well stand alongside Habermas in terms of his sense for the need to combine a reflection on the good, the ultimate concern of ethical thinking, with a matching reflection on the forms in which the good might be communicated to and made present to the world. Both would also agree that this need is not only rooted in the human condition as such but is exponentially heightened by the weight of scientific-technical discourse in industrial and post-industrial societies, a weight that threatens to stifle something essential to the humanity that science and technology themselves seek to serve. That, both the philosopher and the religious thinker would say, is a defining characteristic of the particular moral situation in which we find ourselves today.

We have been focusing on the question of how to communicate ethical freedom and have done so with the particular problems raised for such freedom by our contemporary technological society. Perhaps we have unconsciously reflected the tendency in our society to more or less conflate such terms as 'Christian' and 'moral', either in the sense that being a Christian means having an especial concern for issues of morality or that being engaged in moral reflection is already halfway to being religious. Kierkegaard, at least, would readily concede a significant convergence or even overlap, hence the title of his lectures – 'ethical and ethico-religious communication'. But the question of the possibility and fate of freedom in the modern world is not exhausted by the question of a purely moral freedom. There is also the question of creativity.

Admittedly, Christian theology has been generally less interested in engaging with the aspiration towards creativity than with questions of ethics. The reasons for this are complex, and are likely to include a deep-rooted sense that whereas the ethical is a hallmark of Hebrew and, therefore, of biblical faith, our fascination with human creativity belongs more to the pagan culture of ancient Greece. Art, and the artist's desire to create beautiful works, are not, of course, the only forms in which the question of creativity is likely to arise, but it is probably no accident that art remains the sphere in which we find it easiest to talk about creativity, even if we also extend the idea to creative cooking, creative gardening or even creative living. For whether we think of art in terms of such crafts as pottery, dressmaking or carpentry, or as, simply, 'fine art' (as in painting, music and poetry), it seems that the artist gives supreme testimony to the human capacity for bringing something altogether new into being. But it is just this that has attracted the suspicion of many religious believers, who see in it the seeds of a Promethean rebellion in which the artist tries to rival God's exclusive power to create in an absolute sense. The inflation of the artist's skill in moulding and shaping the God-given materials of earthly life to something resembling absolute creativity is indeed encountered in some forms of Romanticism and modernism. However, it would be unjust to condemn the human aspiration to create merely by referring to the more fantastical declamations of a Nietzsche. On the contrary, it could be argued that the Christian doctrine of creation, according to which human beings were made in the image of God the Creator, *requires us* to value human creativity as a part of our birthright.

One of the few Christian thinkers to address this question directly was Nicholas Berdyaev. Dismissing the charge that creativity was to be identified with presumptuous self-assertion on the part of the creature, Berdyaev wrote that 'Creativeness is a mark of man's Godlike freedom, the revelation of the image of the Creator within him.'[6] And, he added, '*In creativeness the divine in man is revealed by man's own free initiative, revealed from below rather than from above.*'[7] Intriguingly, Berdyaev further suggests that in creating a being endowed with such creative potential God also freely chose to limit his own knowledge of what such a being might do and, in this connection, it is precisely the silence of the Bible on this matter that he finds supremely telling. 'The Creator does not wish to know what the anthropological revelation will be,' he writes, 'God wisely concealed from man His will that man should be called to be a free and daring Creator and concealed from Himself what man would create in his free courageous action.'[8]

With or without such theological backing, however, the aspiration to creativity is a no less potent focus of human concern than the aspiration to moral freedom. And, as I have indicated, it typically centres on the kinds of symbolic actions that we group together in the word 'art'. But here too we encounter a paradox with regard to teaching creativity. For, like moral freedom, truly creative artistic work must be something for which the learner already has a potential. Yet, as in the case of moral freedom, we sense that this is a potential that is often unrealized, and that unless the learner's potential is unlocked, creativity will be stifled and its energy diverted into routine and conformity to external rules. Here too, it would seem, the learner needs the help of a midwifely hand.

Berdyaev also bore witness to the situation that creative freedom no less than moral freedom is threatened by the social, intellectual and material pressures of contemporary technological society. In his lifetime these pressures were primarily coming from the legacy of the nineteenth century's industrial revolution, as manifested in such phenomena as the factory system, the routinization of work and the machinization of war, Soviet communism and the atom bomb. Today the forces at work are subtler, the tensions more complex. But whether it is with regard to the displacement of creative values in education in favour of tests and targets or the transformation of the arts into the 'culture industry', we are still tempted to conclude that the technological criteria of quantifiability, predictability and manageability are systematically eroding the springs of creative action. The art critic Robert Hughes's jeremiad over the crushing effect of market forces in the contemporary art world is only one particularly potent expression of this feeling. How, in such a world, can we reclaim a creativity we believe to be integral to our being human?

Through God Alone can God be Known

Much, in a sense all, of what has been said thus far could also be said of the religious. But the situation is also transformed when the focus moves from ethics and creativity to what believers would say is the fundamental reality of our God-relationship. For religion is not concerned simply with the good, something in which all human beings might be presumed to have an equal stake and in relation to which all might be assumed, at least in principle, to have an equal competence. Religion is also concerned with God, with what exceeds all the powers of human thought and action. In encountering God, we come up against the limit of our human possibilities: 'It is he that hath made us and not we ourselves.'

At this point, with a good or ill grace, philosophy generally withdraws from the field. A philosopher like Habermas would say that if we claim to derive norms for human action from something that exceeds human reason on the basis of our participation in some traditional faith or form of life, we must recognize that these norms are only valid for those who participate in the tradition. We must, therefore, learn to distinguish what we thus believe on the basis of a traditional faith from the sphere of rational moral reflection, a sphere that, Habermas claims, is essentially universal and concerns all rational agents, all human beings. Although he comes at the question from the opposite side, as it were, a religious thinker such as Kierkegaard is no less concerned to make such distinctions. The problem with the modern age, he stated, is not that it is too rational but that it has confused what can and what cannot be reduced to reason. It is damaging to religion itself to believe that it can be effectively communicated where there is only the general common sense of the age for guidance. His strategy, we might say, is one of give unto Caesar the things that are Caesar's, since my relation to God cannot be measured by the same yardstick as my grasp of engineering or my participation in a political debate about the freedom of the press.[9] And although religious discourse shares many of the same features as moral discourse – both of them require me freely to commit myself as the concrete individual I am – learning to be religious involves something more than learning to be moral. What is this 'more'?

For a start, it will involve understanding myself, my situation and my decisions in the light of my relation to God. For Kierkegaard, as for Christian teaching generally, this means a relation that is fundamentally personal. Even if God is not a person in exactly the same way that you or I are, whatever God is, God is not less than personal. Christian faith usually affirms that this personal being is presented in a definite form in the human life of Jesus who both offers us and claims us for a personal relationship. We shall at a number of points return to what this might mean, but for now I wish only to point to how this distinguishes the exercise of Christian communication from the general situation of ethical communication. But it is not at first obvious that adding the word 'personal' does in fact take us beyond the sphere of morality. Hasn't it been emphasized several times, that in learning to act morally I have to engage myself as the real, actual free agent that I am? And in acting morally, don't I also necessarily relate to the others to whom or for whom I act as moral agents, as persons, on the same footing as myself? Isn't the recognition of the other's moral equality with myself integral to being moral? As Kant famously put it, in acting morally I treat the other as an end in their own right and not as a means to my ends. In other words, acting morally requires us to recognize the other person as a person. Learning to activate my moral potential is, therefore, personal, in at least one important sense. Kierkegaard would not disagree. But his point in the lectures on communication is not about what it means to practise morality or to be a Christian any more than it is about defining morality or Christianity. His aim is rather to raise the question as to *how one learns to become moral* and *how one learns to become, first, religious and, then, Christian.* As I have emphasized, it is about *the process of communicating faith*, about *how to teach it and how to learn it*, and only in this sense is it about *doctrine*.

Now, ethics and religion are alike in that, in the last resort, I never really learn them from another human being. The real work of learning is work I can only do myself, by exercising my freedom, by believing. However, this means something slightly different in each case. Thus, in relation to ethics, the teacher-midwife is happy to disappear and, as it were, leave me to myself. This does not mean that once I have learned how to be a moral agent I have no debt of gratitude to the teacher who helped me to this 'knowledge'. And it certainly doesn't exclude the possibility that I may have more than a little need of refresher courses from time to time. But the primary thing is not my relation to the teacher, it is my acquiring the courage to use the freedom that I already potentially had. For Christianity, however, the personal relation to God is in itself integral to the whole continuing learning process. The role of the human teacher may – must – be provisional and recedes into the background as the learner takes responsibility for their own life. But the God-relationship necessarily endures beyond the initial moment of awakening. If it is in and through this relationship that I not only learn who I am but am what I am, the relationship continues to be a condition of my being just that: who I am.

It has often been said that when Christianity came to the North European Germanic and Scandinavian lands, the idea of faith became strongly influenced by the supremely important role of personal trust between a chief and his followers in these societies. This was something different from the legal relationship between citizens and the State (as in Rome or in later European history), being a freely chosen commitment to just this person as one's acknowledged liege-lord. Whatever the historical facts, the idea illustrates the point (which Kierkegaard also makes in his lectures and elsewhere) that if learning to be ethical hinges on the idea of freedom (namely, the freedom of the learner), learning to be Christian hinges on the relation to the one in whom one believes or on the believing relationship itself. Importantly, this is not the human teacher. 'Through God alone can God be known.' God is the first and last teacher of faith and God is more than a 'Socratic' teacher. God is a teacher I not only learn from, but also the one on whom I depend for life itself. At the same time, it is true, Kierkegaard insists that the highest relationship between the human beings involved in the communication of religious faith remains Socratic, just as in ethics. No matter how grateful I may be to my human teachers, no matter how deeply I may wish to honour them by following the particular example they have given me in terms of Christian ethics, lifestyle, etc., they are not the ones who really taught me what being religious was about. I could only ever really come to know this through the God-relationship itself.

There is another difference between ethics and religion that is crucial for Kierkegaard's understanding of the dynamics of communicating Christian faith. Although this is not something emphasized very much in the lectures on communication themselves, it is something to which other Kierkegaard texts, such as *Practice in Christianity*, do pay attention. Moral philosophers are inclined to speak in the name of what courts of law used to refer to as 'any reasonable man'. A human being's concern for the good, in other words, is something that belongs to every human being qua moral agent, which, if we follow many moral philosophers, is much the same as saying every human being. A human being is human precisely by virtue of the rational freedom that makes morality possible. In terms of the image of Socratic midwifery, the moral teacher regards every human being as potentially a moral agent. The art is simply how to turn this potential into a living reality. Deep down, all of us have an urge to do the right thing. We have, in other words, a good will or a will to do the good. Moral philosophers are not, of course, ignorant of the fact that there may be human beings, such as infants, who are not mature enough to be addressed as free, rational agents, and others who, through illness or some psychological condition might be incapable of living up to the moral requirement. Nevertheless, these cases do not fundamentally threaten the philosopher's assumption in favour of the good will. We still, quite spontaneously, treat infants and the severely mental ill as human beings and make decisions on their behalf according as to how we would wish to be treated in their situation, 'as if' they were capable of making such choices for themselves. Such cases do not affect the philosopher's basic assumption that a person is intrinsically capable of understanding and enacting the good.

In the Christian view of life, however, human beings are regarded as fallen. The story of Adam and Eve eating the fruit of the tree from which God had forbidden them to eat, and their consequent expulsion from the Garden of Eden, highlights with profound simplicity the insight that human beings cannot be relied on to will the good. Even when the will of God has, as in this case, been plainly revealed, they are fully capable of doing the opposite. Dostoevsky would argue against the utopian humanism of the nineteenth century that even if we could create a perfect society on earth, one in which every human being had the maximum happiness and the maximum opportunity for positive social behaviour, sooner or later someone would come along who would just put their hands on their hips and say 'No!', if for no other reason than to show his independence of everybody else.[10] The philosophers' assumption about everyone being basically persuadable in terms of rational freedom just doesn't hold. There are points where freedom and reason drift apart. In words that would become compelling for such later theologians as Augustine, Luther and Calvin, the Apostle Paul spoke his inability to do the good that he wanted to do, and of his compulsion to do the bad thing that he didn't want to do (Romans 7). We don't have to hold to the extreme interpretation of these words that would make them mean that no human being ever or anywhere was in a position freely to will and to do the good in order to see the problem. All we need to allow for is the possibility that some human beings sometimes lack or are prepared to defy their own will to do the good. Once we allow for this, the philosopher's assumption that we can treat all human beings as if they were rational free agents falls to pieces. For who can know which human beings have the right view as to the good? If 'the vision of Christ that thou dost see is my vision's greatest enemy', who is to adjudicate? God, we might say – yes, obviously, but who can know the mind of God? Even a child knows that, whatever else there is to be said about God, God is in some sense not like us. There is a difference between Creator and creature, to speak in biblical terms, that involves a fundamental asymmetry. God is 'other', 'greater', or, as was said previously, 'he that hath made us and not we ourselves'. Whereas we might always be presumed to be capable of recognizing a moral action or a truly creative work of art when we see one, can we be presumed to be capable of recognizing God, if and when God enters into the field of our experience? Can we possibly know who God really is, or what God wants? 'God' is that which eye has not seen, nor ear heard, nor the heart of man conceived. Can we presume that our social and moral goods coincide with God's idea of goodness?

In a situation in which the task proposed is to accept and to live from within the God-relationship, but where (1) the God-term of the relationship by definition transcends our capacities of knowing and (2) our human will to respond positively to God is, at the very least, questionable, the problem of communicating faith is raised to a level of difficulty much greater than that involved in communicating ethical truth or creativity. Who can do such a thing? 'Through God alone can God be known' – yes, but who's to know when, where and to whom God has been made known? Surely God's presence in the world, God's self-communication to human beings will be problematic. God will never be knowable like other objects of knowledge, not even like the good. God will be present among us as if incognito, necessarily and always ambiguous, unable to be caught in the spiralling web of human symbols, 'clouds and darkness are his dwelling-place'.

From a certain point of view – that of philosophy perhaps – this might seem to mark the point of no return for any kind of discourse about religion. Such discourse, it seems, is just going to lose itself in endless, paradoxical self-contradiction and equivocation. If it is to claim the attention of those who are not paid-up believers it can only be because, in its own way, it expresses something we deeply feel about ourselves. In Habermas's terminology (and what I am outlining here seems to be his own positive view of religion) it is 'expressive' or 'dramaturgic' – in other words, it has the same kind of truth as poetry and art. In word, symbol and ritual action it gives us to sense the mystery, the aura or the holiness that, in our best moments, we glimpse in life, though these qualities will always elude definition and analysis. In these terms, religion provides important testimony to the meaning of being human, but it neither informs us as to what the world is really like, nor can it be a vehicle for defining norms that hold for all members of society.

Christianity seems to require something 'more' than this 'poetic' view of religion. For although it claims that God does indeed dwell in clouds and darkness, it also claims that God has been revealed and made known – communicated – to us. Other religions also have ideas of revelation, and even within Christianity there are various views as to what revelation involves. However, to the extent that it claims that the supreme or sole focus of revelation is 'Christ and him crucified', it becomes clear that we cannot imagine revelation as being like the moment in which the quizmaster reveals the answer to the £1,000,000 question or the Hollywood host announces the Oscar winner. If the man who died on the cross is the defining moment of God's self-communication, then it is clear that paradox, affront and incomprehensibility are plainly advertised features of the message. Kierkegaard returns to this scandalous element of early Christian preaching when, in *Practice in Christianity,* he emphasizes the idea of Christ as 'a sign of contradiction'. It is striking that in terms of understanding Christian doctrine more in terms of Christian communication than Christian theory, it is precisely the communicative category 'sign' that Kierkegaard places at the centre of his discussion. In other words, he is not so much thinking about God's presence in Christ as a problem of historical or metaphysical or saving knowledge, but as a communicative event or action, a word addressed to us that we are now called to decipher and make our own. But, as the expression 'sign of contradiction' itself shows, this is a communicative action of infinite internal difficulty that is likely to throw the recipient of the message into a situation of painful uncertainty.

One way of alleviating this painful uncertainty is to appeal to authority. Around the beginning of the twentieth century Roman Catholic apologists frequently described the differences between Catholicism and Protestantism in terms of the question of authority. The problem with Protestantism, it was said, is that it entirely lacked any principle of authority, having made human reason, and especially historical science, the measure of divine revelation. The inevitable result is the anarchy of out-and-out individualism, with everyone deciding matters of right and wrong for themselves. Church and society dissolve into a multiplicity of arbitrary choices. This charge could not entirely be made to stick in the case of Kierkegaard. Although suspiciously individualistic, he seems to have been very insistent on the question of authority. Finally, he says, the claims of Christianity rest only on the authoritative or apostolic proclamation of them as true. This is what is to be believed, says the apostle: believe – or be offended. From the humanist and liberal Protestant point of view Catholicism and (in this regard) Kierkegaard seem to be going against the grain of one of the most fundamental of all modern values, the principle of autonomy. According to this principle, it is the chief task of human beings to acquire the moral and intellectual maturity to think, judge and act for themselves, and not to place themselves in the hands of any external authority in matters in which they can or ought to be able to judge for themselves. Is the appeal to authority, then, simply an inalienable element of the scandal of the Christian message, the bald rebuttal of the modern human being's claim to autonomy?

Neither nineteenth-century Catholicism nor Kierkegaard were ashamed to present it in this way, but I think we can see some reason in what a humanist might regard as their shared madness. For the question of authority is inherently and intimately tied to the personal nature of the Christian communication, that it is an act or a process of communication calling the one we might name the recipient into a personal relationship. The link does not depend on any particular verbal formulation, but it is usefully approached by considering the word 'authority' itself. It is a word closely related to the word 'author', and what is an author? An author is someone we think of as being the originator of the text that goes by their name. Dickens is the author of what only Dickens wrote and, arguably, of what only Dickens could have written. There is a first-hand relationship between an author and his words. Likewise in the Gospels, when it is said of Jesus that he spoke 'not as the scribes and Pharisees, but as one with authority', the point being made is that there is a first-hand relationship between Jesus and his words. He is the originator of what he says. He is 'in' his words. To find a text authoritative is, then, to find in it the original word of its author.

To say that what we hear in the founding texts of the Christian community is such an original and creative voice may seem to offer a non-authoritarian way of affirming the authority of the Christian claim, but isn't it still the case that for those who haven't heard it for themselves this word is going to be experienced as heteronomous, as the word of another, a word that can never be theirs in the way that it was the original author's? To make somebody else's word our rule of life is surely to forego the possibility of ever becoming truly autonomous, a dynamic borne out by the ultimate mediocrity of too many followers of great geniuses! The very power of the original voice seems to rob those who surround him of their freedom to think and act for themselves.

Since the eighteenth century this problematic relationship between autonomy and heteronomy has been one of the most significant underlying themes in the social and intellectual debate about religion and belief, and it continues to inform contemporary discussion. Habermas, as we have seen, insists that the only legitimate means of deciding questions of normativity, right and wrong, is through the use of the basic common-sense reason that is equally available to all human beings qua moral agents. Religious traditions, he concedes, may have their role in the overall shaping of human life, in expressing human beings' feelings about themselves, their worth or dignity, but they can never decide which norms our society should enshrine in its laws. To do so would be to impose a false heteronomy on the freedom of the public sphere. It was also a major theme in the thought of Paul Tillich. Tillich was modernist enough to insist that over against every attempt of the Church to impose limits on the free exercise of reason, the principle of autonomy had to be defended. Science, democracy, artistic freedom and the other defining features of modernity all faced deep-rooted opposition from religious authorities, but in every case the rights of autonomy have been vindicated. But, and for Tillich it is a very big 'but', autonomy itself lacks substance or depth. A world of autonomous agents, autonomous values, of autonomous intellectual disciplines or artistic practices, is an empty, abstract, superficial world, engendering the kinds of nostalgic anxieties that can make the most rational states succumb to the most sudden 'throw-backs' to crude authoritarianism, as Tillich saw happening in the Third Reich. If rational democratic societies are to develop staying-power, they have to offer their members more than the abstract formulations of the drive to autonomy, but not by reimposing some kind of authoritarian yoke. Tillich's answer was what he called the principle of theonomy, the law or direction provided by God. What was the difference between this and heteronomy? Simply that, for the individual concerned, the 'law' was not experienced as something imposed from the outside but as meeting and answering and even arising out of his own inner needs, aspirations and experiences. Whereas a heteronomous faith is a faith held only on the authority of others – Church, Bible, parents or society – a theonomous faith is a faith in which the individual has had a first-hand encounter with the sources of faith, which is to say, with the God with whom, in faith, we find ourselves in a glad and liberating relationship. 'Through God alone can God be known.' But how does this solve the problem of the 'authority' that Kierkegaard deems to be inextricable from the Christian proclamation? If the apostle or the preacher tells me I must believe in Jesus if I am to be saved, and that he can offer no proof for this other than his own word that it is so, how can this be anything other than an attempt to stop me functioning as a free and responsible agent?

Perhaps Kierkegaard, as he so often seems to do, is overstating his case. After all, doesn't he also say, even in some of his most radical passages, that ultimately the Socratic relationship is the highest that can exist between any two human beings? Neither Paul nor the Pope nor Martin Luther nor my parish priest can give me faith if I do not choose faith for myself. What, then, is happening if I accept their word as authoritative? On Kierkegaard's account it cannot be that I am seduced or overawed by any of their human attributes. Neither the splendour of the papal court nor the earthy humour of Luther, neither the skilled use of art or rhetoric, nor any show of force, nor the almost invisible pressures and allurements of a subtle parochial fisher of men, can really make me accept a word as a word of God. Or, if I accept it because of its beauty, out of fear, or because I am manipulable, then what I have submitted to is a distorted human power relationship and not God: it is not theonomy.

Let us go back a step. What is it, actually, that the Socratic teacher does for the student? He cannot give him faith, but (1) he can, nega-tively, show that some of the objections that have been made against faith do not hold (not all, because even the Socratic teacher cannot remove the possibility of offence) and he can show that some of the phenomena that sometimes claim to be forms of faith can scarcely be such because of their patently all-too-human character; (2) positively, he can draw attention to the aspects of the learner's situation that might be relevant for the decision of faith, and he can show that the decision for faith is the responsibility of the learner himself. Tillich would go further than Kierkegaard in this regard and would add the personal witness that 'thus have we seen and experienced, in our way and in our situation', a testimony that cannot, of course, be simply transferred from the situation in which the teacher found faith to that of the learner. The teacher does not himself become authoritative in this process, he is not the 'author' or source of what is being talked about. At the same time the process itself offers the possibility for the learner to hear the word around which the discussion turns as an authoritative word, a word of God. In this moment, the Socratic teacher becomes – for the learner – an apostolic witness. Even so, as apostolic witness, he also remains the Socratic teacher, who willingly steps to one side and leaves the learner to the God-relationship that the word of faith has opened up. The learner does not lose or suppress his self for the sake of another. He finds himself in God. If, within the God-relationship, he then finds the relation to the teacher restored, it is restored in different terms. For the learner is no longer a learner and the teacher no longer a teacher. Now there are no more teachers and learners, but a community of friends, capable of levelling with each other about the things that matter the most.

'In my end is my beginning,' as the poet said, and there is a real and important sense in which the idea of a community of friends, the 'end' at which the discussion seems to have arrived, is in another sense, its beginning. Having begun with the question as to what Christian doctrine actually is, and having identified the paradoxical aspect of the God-relationship that sets a seemingly insuperable obstacle in the path of any human being who might presume to be competent to serve as a teacher of the things of God, I have argued that our incompetence as teachers does not absolve us from the care we spontaneously have for one another in our common, shared humanity. In the obligation of this care, I suggest, lies the possibility of our becoming, *as friends,* each other's Socratic teachers, through whom – if God wills – the word of salvation can be heard and learned as what it is, and our human friendship find its depth in the friendship of God. This, as I understand it, is the hope, the method and, at best, the outcome of Christian doctrine, the communicating of faith to faith.

2

The Movement of the Mystery

Three-in-One and One-in-Three

In Chapter 1, I attempted to see Christian doctrine as an active process of teaching and communication rather than a body of supernatural facts, a 'sum of saving knowledge'. In the light of the situation that what is at stake in this communicative action is, for each of us, the very meaning of our lives, I introduced Kierkegaard's idea of Socratic midwifery as a model for Christian communication. For the distinguishing mark of this type of communication is precisely its concern for the integrity of the recipient of the communication. Indeed, we cannot really speak of 'recipients', since in order to understand what is being communicated we must each be fully active in making the message our very own. Yet if Christian communication shares certain basic features of the communication of such human values as moral freedom or creativity, it also goes further since it (1) involves a God who, in every conceivable way, infinitely surpasses our powers of understanding and (2) questions whether we really want to know what it is that God is communicating to us. Even if we can say that what God seeks to communicate to us is, in the final analysis, our very selves, it may be that we have different ideas from God as to the kinds of selves we'd like to be.

Throughout this discussion we took our bearings from human realities, human aspirations and human possibilities, even if, at the end, we thus found ourselves being pointed beyond what we know ourselves to be capable of. From our human point of view, the revelation that might fulfil our longing for God will, therefore, always appear as something unexpected, miraculous even: a communication from 'another place' and the opening up of possibilities we'd never even imagined. There would therefore seem to be a limit to any attempt to base Christian doctrine purely on what we currently know or experience of ourselves and our world, a theology 'from below', as some have described it.

But do we have any other way of approaching it? In an absolute sense, perhaps not, but what I want to attempt in this chapter is to turn the question round. It is to ask: what would God have to be like in order to set in motion the communicative event that gives us the freedom that, in our aspirations towards goodness and creativity, we are ever seeking and ever missing; or: what would God have to be like to enter into the kind of relation to us that wouldsustain us in and lead us through the patterns of failure and mis-understanding that thwart the realization of these, our best aspirations?

A complete 'theology from above', a God's-eye view of the divine–human relationship, is, almost certainly, not possible for beings such as we are. All we can offer – what Christian doctrine offers – is a way of looking at and thinking about our situation that helps us make sense of those moments in which we seem to experience something like a revelation, moments in which the word suddenly resounds 'as if with authority', moments in which we can believe that 'with God all things are possible' (Mark 9.23). There is therefore a sense in which a 'theology from above' can only ever be hypothetical, the best way we have of making sense of our experiences in religion this side of the time when 'we shall know as we are known' (1 Cor. 13.12). It is, then, in this hypothetical, imaginative mode that I shall now revisit the ground covered in the previous chapter, but this time, as it were, 'from above'. Instead of addressing the question as an issue of human communication and human communicative possibilities, I shall attempt to show some of the ways in which the Christian idea of God is itself profoundly shaped in terms of communication, so that God is thought of as being in God's deepest being a self-communicative God. The focus is no longer on the questions that lead us towards God but on what we see or believe we see in God.

What we see in God: and I shall begin quite literally with seeing, with a vision of God, a painted image, an icon. It is, in fact, one of the best known of all of the icons of the Eastern churches, The 'Old Testament Trinity', painted by the Russian monk, Andrei Rublev, in the fifteenth century. It has appeared on the covers of many theological books in recent years and, in reproduction, is to be seen in innumerable churches and clergy studies. To the extent that such a thing is possible for a work of art, it is a painting that has become a theological commonplace, a Christian classic.[1] Like many icons, it is associated with a particular feast in the Church's year, namely Pentecost, the second day of which is kept in the Russian Church as the feast of the Trinity. The scene is based on the rather mysterious story told in Genesis 18 of Abraham being visited by three men, whom he plied with hospitality and who, subsequently, prophesied that his wife

Sara, though beyond the age of childbearing, would conceive and have a son within a year. It is a long-standing Christian tradition to interpret the scene as a revelation of God the Trinity to Abraham, thus underlining the point that the doctrine of the Trinity is not an artificial theological construct but a statement about the real, living character of God. Rublev's icon shows the three as winged angelic figures, seated around a table on which is a plate with meat on and a cup, hinting at both Passover and eucharistic associations. One, robed in pink, is seated to the viewer's left, a second, robed in purple, is seated in the middle, behind the table, and the third, robed in green, is on the right. Commentators have disagreed as to which of the figures represents which of the persons of the Trinity. We might take the one on the left to be the Father, since, if we follow the practice of reading pictures from left to right, the left marks the point of departure and therefore the figure on the left has to be the one who has the best claim to be source or origin. Or is it the one in the middle, robed in the purple of authority, and also larger than the others and dominating them in terms of the vertical construction of the painting? Or is the purple robe to be interpreted as the same purple robe as that in which God incarnate, Jesus Christ, is generally portrayed in East and West?

But perhaps the point is that it doesn't matter. The icon does not represent the Trinity in such a simplistically allegorical way. More important than the manner in which each of the three figures is represented separately is the dynamism of the movement between them. The inclination of their heads, the positioning of their hands, the way they are seated, and the play of the colours in which they are variously robed – all these show, as well as any work of painting ever could – just what it might mean for God to be three-in-one and one-in-three. Each is what it is in and through its relation to the others. It is the unity of a dynamic movement, of a conversation or even a dance. To use a long out-of-use theological term that has recently re-entered the vocabulary of Western theology, it is a picture of the divine *perichoresis*, a Greek term that challenges exact translation but that highlights the mutual indwelling of the three divine persons in the one being of the divine life. The word itself can, inevitably, be interpreted in subtly different ways. It can be understood primarily verbally, as an active process in which each actively enters into and opens itself to the others. Or it can be construed as a noun, an unchanging structure of relationship. Something like this distinction is made by the Swiss theologian Karl Barth, who did much to bring about the renewed interest in Trinitarian theology in modern Protestantism. Barth notes that *perichoresis* has been translated into Latin both as *circumincessio* (passing into one another) and as *circuminsessio* (being in one another, as in 'the court is now in session'), terms that have subtly different connotations. Barth himself makes plain that he is rather suspicious of the former, since it seems to imply some kind of change or development in time, and Barth doesn't like the idea of God being 'in' time in any way. Whatever else God is, insists Barth, he is eternal, above and beyond any possible temporal categories. Therefore he prefers *circuminsessio*, God 'in session' or just 'sitting', which emphasizes the unalterability of the mutual internal relationships of the eternal Trinity.[2]

Clearly, as I have already stated, we do not know what it is like for God to be God. There can be no question here of presuming to a knowledge we simply cannot have. That said, there might nevertheless be grounds for disagreeing with Barth at this point. Admittedly, every word said about God will bear the impress of God's freedom in relation to all our mental conceptions and images, but, in so far as we can say anything about God, there is no obvious reason why it is necessary to deny *some* analogue to time and history in the divine life. How can we in fact avoid doing so if we also wish to speak of God as living or dynamic? Is the insistence on God's timeless eternity really intrinsical to Christianity's historical witness, or is it perhaps the application within theology of what is in fact a very human – and very understandable – sense that time and history are, in some way, part of the problem to which God is the answer? Our experience is that time means change and change, after the initial novelty has worn off, means decay. To be creatures of time is to be creatures subject to change, dissolution and, finally, death. But if that is generally true of our human experience, can we simply assume that it is true also for God? Do we really honour God less by speaking of God as living in a dynamic, forward or progressive movement, than by repeating the mantra about changelessness or timelessness? Sometimes the great religious vision of the Greek philosophers, a vision in which the created universe emanated or flowed out of God, has been described as the vision of a frozen waterfall. Everything comes from and returns to God in an eternally completed cycle in which nothing new ever really happens. But wasn't it part of the impact of Christianity to unfreeze the waterfall, to bring movement into the universe, and to open the gate to novelty? With characteristic boldness Berdyaev, for one, affirmed that the divine life 'in a deep and mysterious sense is history, historical drama and mystery'.[3] Whichever way we decide this question, Rublev's icon presents us with a picture of a God who is relational through and through, who lives, who 'is', in a movement of personal self-communication. This God lives in and as and out of and through the conversation that binds the three figures into a single composition, and, as the meat and wine set out on the table suggest, this God is, simply, 'communion', pure communication, the communication not merely of ideas but of life and being.

One thinker who took seriously and arguably initiated the modern interest in the analogy of history in the divine life was the German philosopher G. W. F. Hegel. Whether Hegel was a genuinely Christian thinker has been much debated, and critics from Kierkegaard onwards have attacked him for turning theological issues into logical puzzles. This criticism is not entirely unfair, but it is not entirely fair either. On any account, Hegel both took up some of the classical themes of Christian doctrine and, at the same time, radically transformed the way in which they were understood. This is not least true of his view of the Trinity. The critics have complained that Hegel seemed to 'deduce' the necessity of God being Trinity and, indeed, the necessity for God to create the world, from some kind of logical formula. Hegel might have put it slightly differently. He might have said that he was merely trying to show how the three themes of God as Trinity, of the world as God's creation, and of human history made no sense if they were merely regarded as disconnected facts without any coherent pattern or reason linking them. His job, as a philosopher, was simply to explicate this pattern, but more in the sense of tracing and elucidating it than deducing it in some sort of algebraic way. And, ultimately (a Hegelian theologian could argue), he could only do this because it was a pattern rooted and grounded in the inner dynamic of God's own life. The challenge is at least worth considering, so let us look more closely at this difficult but rewarding thinker.

Fundamental to Hegel's thought is the idea that really to know something is not to be able to offer an abstract definition of it but to know everything about it, to be able to track it through every twist and turn of its development and to know how it relates to the whole field of other entities that constitute its world. This is central to his idea of 'phenomenology', namely, that to know something is to know it in accordance with the way it manifests itself in life. The same is true of objects themselves. An object that exists all by itself, independent of all other objects, existing for itself alone, would not be the highest conceivable object, as some previous philosophers thought. On the contrary it would be somehow lacking, reality-poor, we might say. A person who stands apart from society imagining himself to be too elevated to engage in the everyday struggle of life may imagine that he is a very grand figure, but from Hegel's point of view we should not see him as superior to the crowd, but as isolated and, in Hegel's often-quoted phrase, an 'unhappy consciousness'. A thing becomes *real*, Hegel insisted, by the fact that it enters into relations with other things, and the more relations it has, the more real it is. This will therefore be supremely true of God. The real sovereignty of God is not that God is simply 'One', over and above and apart from the world. God is God and not a human idea precisely because God is free both to be One *and* to enter creatively into a maximal number of possible relationships.

If, then, we think of God solely in terms of bare unity, we will never be able to do justice to all the things that Christian doctrine (for example) has wanted to say about God. As opposed to a God who was simple unity, Hegel suggests that the truly free, truly creative God would best show that freedom by being able to bring into being, to produce (or, in the language of the creeds, 'to beget') a being equal in power, majesty and freedom. And, if we have once allowed for two equal divine persons, then, says Hegel, we must also allow for a relation between them in which their unity is reaffirmed, otherwise one of them would have ceased to be divine. That they are different does not mean that they have become alienated from each other since they are held together in a continuing and dynamic relationship. This relationship is the Spirit, which, Hegel says, is equally God, since it is the Spirit that sustains the other divine persons in the unity of the divine life. Without the Spirit the whole thing would fall apart. The perfect symmetry and circularity of this threefold relationship – as in Rublev's icon – thus expresses a difference amongst equals.

However, the process doesn't stop there. For if we believe that the fullest expression of divine freedom is to hold in unity the maximum of difference, then we might question whether a Trinity of divine persons, living perfectly in harmony with each other for ever and ever, would really be free. For God's freedom really to be expressed as what it is, says Hegel, God must allow there to be a world, a non-divine creation must come into being, and, further, within this non-divine world there must be creatures who are so different from God that they can choose to reject God for the sake of being godless. And yet, for God really to be God, even this difference must be reconcilable, and God must be able to enter into the non-divine world, into the evil that these free creatures have set in motion, and so restore the world to unity with God's own being. Berdyaev gives Hegel's rather abstract way of saying this a more dramatic colouring. He writes:

[T]he creation of the world by God the Father is a moment of the deepest mystery in the relation between God the Father and God the Son. The revelation of the divine mystery in the depths of the divine and spiritual life, of the inner passionate divine thirst and longing for an other self, that other self which may be the object of a great and infinite love on the part of God, and that infinite search for reciprocity and love on the part of the other self, determines for the deep Christian consciousness the very principle of movement and process. The inner tragedy of the love felt by God for His other self and its longing for reciprocal love constitutes the very mystery of the divine life which is associated with the creation of the world and of man.[4]

Apart from Berdyaev's allusion to a possible tragic dimension in the divine life itself, this may seem at first glance like a fairly straightforward restatement of the story told in the creeds. The difference is that whereas earlier theologies seemed to regard the creation of the world as something essentially external to God, since God could equally well have chosen not to create as to create, Hegel, Berdyaev and many other modern Christian thinkers portray the creation and the familiar story of the fall and redemption as, in some way, the manner in which God gives expression to his own inner being. The world is not God. It is by definition other than God. It exists over against God and, in the history of human creatures, it has chosen to disconnect itself from God. But equally the world is not an artefact, having the same sort of relation to God as a table to a carpenter. The world is a form, a manifestation, a mirror, in which God's own way of being can, if viewed with the eye of faith, be discerned. To reformulate a well-known phrase, the world is the continuation of the divine Trinity's internal conversation 'by other means'.

If, then, it is possible to represent the divine life as a threefold self-communication held in the unity of an insoluble communion, faith can also see the world in terms of God's self-communication, a self-giving, that is both a giving-away and a holding in communion. In saying 'the world', of course, it is not a matter simply of nature at its most beautiful, when, for a moment at least, even the most prosaic 'non-religious' person is likely to admit a certain awe and to entertain the idea that there is some creative mystery behind it all. The world here means, has to mean, the world that includes and is indeed defined by human action in history, the good and the ill. But the pattern of divine self-communication/communion is sustained and repeated even in relation to what is ill, so that all the ill that 'man has made of man' can become the occasion for the most intense insight into the divine life.

As Berdyaev's mention of tragedy suggests, there are important questions that need to be asked about what all this means for our understanding of evil and particular evils, such as the Holocaust, that seem to mock any power of restoration and communion. For if God's own being is somehow expressed in the world, doesn't it follow that God is also, somehow, 'in' the evil that seems inseparable from our experience of life in the world? In this short course I shall not attempt to answer this question in a philosophical manner,[5] though I do hope to show how the practice of Christian doctrine, the communication of Christian faith, hope and love, may find its way into the places where what we call evil is at its most intense, in the experience of human beings. It may be relevant to add, however, that if we can rethink our idea of God in thoroughly communicational terms, there are significant implications for our idea of evil. For evil would then seem to have an intrinsic affinity with situations of non-communication, situations in which communication is refused or distorted. This seems to fit with our experience. In Hannah Arendt's famous account of the trial of the Nazi war criminal Adolf Eichmann, she described how Eichmann told the court of meeting up with a Jewish inmate of Auschwitz with whom he had collaborated some time before on arranging the transportation of Jews out of Germany ('an old friend', Eichmann calls him) and telling about the meeting in terms of a friendly chat, man to man. Perhaps even more than some of the unbelievable cruelties perpetrated in that time and place, the anecdote illustrates the utter distortion and failure of communication that lay at its heart, as if there could really be a friendly man-to-man chat between a powerless 'musselman' and one of those with ultimate responsibility for the systematic killing of millions (the prisoner was, in fact, killed some time afterwards). In situations of evil, both perpetrators and victims fall out of communication with each other, with the world, and, thus, into utter emptiness.[6] Isn't it precisely the terror of Edvard Munch's famous painting of the scream that we just know that no one can hear it, and that precisely such a silent medium as painting can convey this inability of pain to come to expression with so much greater pathos than the loudest shrieks of a theatrical Philoctetes? In relation to the characterization of evil in terms of non-communication, it is relevant to recall that, for the Bible, the devil is precisely defined as 'a liar, and the father of lies', in other words, as the ultimate corrupter of communication who makes what is believed to be communication to be no such thing and thus effects the destruction of faith in communication itself. And if, as I have suggested, communication also involves movement, it is again no coincidence that the description of Satan in Dante's hell is precisely that of a being frozen into eternal immobility, unable to speak and unable to change.

From Communication to Participation

Looking at God's way of being as essentially communicative has a number of other implications and applications that are important for the basic construal of the divine–human relationship. The Bible states that human beings were made in God's image. But if God's being is communicative being then it will be precisely in our own communicative capacities and actions that we most clearly mirror the divine image. Often the divine image has been identified with human reason and this in turn has been understood in terms of our capacity for contemplating timeless truths, that is, our aptitude for knowledge. It has also been identified with our essential freedom. Neither of these excludes the idea of communication, but perhaps this is, ultimately, the more adequate idea. For while we can imagine a rational being that existed in splendid solitude contemplating its eternal truths and that neither lacked nor sought any kind of relationship with others, a communicative being would also intrinsically be a rational being, but of a kind that expressed its rationality by continually engaging in understanding, interpreting and seeking truth through dialogue with others. Similarly, we could imagine a being that had freed itself from all the conditions that beset the majority of humankind and that exercised that freedom without regard to others. Yet this would be a hollow kind of freedom, a 'freedom from' that did not have any positive content or meaning. A communicative being, on the other hand, would be a being that related itself freely to the other with whom it was in essential communication and, through that relation, its freedom would acquire a definite content.

Many aspects of our existence point to our essential communicativeness. Not the least of these is our capacity for language. Indeed, some philosophers have in the past defined human beings as the animals possessed of language, the speaking animals. While it is debatable whether animals are, in fact, completely without some analogue to language, it is undoubtedly true that we are deeply linguistic beings. Even our capacity for reason is dependent on language, or other shared symbolic systems such as that of mathematics, if we are to think at all. Thus the Greek term *logos*, often translated as 'word' (as in 'In the beginning was the Word') could also come to mean 'reason' or 'idea'. But in case that tempts us back into thinking of language itself as being no more than a moving image of timeless truths, it is perhaps more fruitful to emphasize precisely the communicativeness of language in the fine, continuous, close-knit, ever-developing context-dependent practice of language in human beings' day-to-day, minute-by-minute intercourse with one another. The contemporary Catholic theologian Oliver Davies has argued for an understanding of human language that would reflect the inner divine discourse that we glimpsed in Rublev's icon. He calls this a pragmatic understanding of language, since it is precisely language *in use*, creating meaning through a constantly changing pattern of linguistic practices, that best captures both the freedom and the intimacy of the divine being as 'Word'. It is in our life as pragmatic language users, he argues, that we 'envoice' the circumincession of the threefold divine being. If language does not of itself exhaust what it means to be communicative (and the fact that we began this section by looking at a picture indicates one other vitally important way of communicating), it has perhaps an unparalleled range, depth and openness to development that fit it to serve as the epitome of our divine communicativeness.[7]

This pragmatic way of looking at language also emphasizes that language does not exist as a self-enclosed 'autopoietic' system, something that could function all by itself without any human input. Language has many uses, as the philosopher Wittgenstein illustrated by referring to it as a toolkit containing many very different tools for many very different kinds of jobs. We don't evaluate the language use of a PhD student in biochemistry in the same way as that of a poet or that of a five-year-old reporting on his day at school. That we are able to distinguish between such differing 'language games' almost without thinking is itself a remarkable testimony to language's scope and power.

Whatever else language may be capable of, one thing it does do, when functioning as communication, is to bring us into communication with one another, to open us up and hold us open to each other, to express how we are towards each other and to be a decisive instrument in bringing us closer to one another or separating us. As the Jewish thinker Martin Buber said, we live in and through two basic words: I-It and I-Thou. That is to say that although we could not exist without relating to the world as a world of objects and objective forces (I-It), we cannot, being the beings that we are, live in it without also seeking, finding and being granted a sense of life as deeply and powerfully personal, an encounter with an unfathomable and infinite 'Thou'.[8] The world is only partially disclosed through all the 'its' we have to deal with, the quantifiable tasks, little or great, that constitute so much of our work and (inevitably and properly) our relationships. But the world also has a personal dimension that escapes easy definition but that is indicated by thinking of communication as communion. Of itself 'communication' does not necessarily imply a personal relation. Computers can communicate with computers, and do so very efficiently. Communion, however, implies something different. It implies the intimacy, the mutual understanding, the *perichoresis*, the passing-into-one-another, of personal life. This interweaving of communicativeness, communion and the personal has important implications for the way in which we think (1) about the divine life and (2) about the relationship between the divine and the human. Let us, briefly, look at these.

The Divine Life

With regard to the divine life, theologians of the Eastern churches have made some sharp criticisms of the Western understanding of the Trinity.[9] They point out that when the creeds were translated from their original Greek into Latin, some unfortunate choices of words were made. Anyone with experience of translating, even from one living language into another, knows how imprecise a science it is, and that every translation is also an interpretation. What, then, is the issue here? The Western creed says of the Trinity that it involves three persons and one substance, the latter translating the Greek term *ousia*, a word translated in the more recent versions of the creed as 'Being' (though given the philosophical difficulties surrounding the term 'Being', this doesn't really get us out of the briar patch!).The term 'sub-stance' means, literally, what stands underneath something, thus suggesting the idea of the reality behind the appearance. Thinking of three persons and one substance, then, could give the impression that each of the three persons, the Father, the Son and the Spirit, is 'divine' only by virtue of participating in the common divine 'substance'. That could lead us to think of there being some divine essence, some quality of 'Godness', that was more fundamental than the personality of each of the three persons. It was an analogous problem that led existentialist philosophers in the middle of the twentieth century to assert that 'existence precedes essence'. What they meant was that whereas it might be possible to define the substance of a natural form such as a fish or a tree in terms of substance or essence, since a tree just has to be a tree and obey all the laws of its species and genus (as does a fish), human beings are what they are in and through the exercise of freedom. To be sure, nature imposes certain physical and behavioural limits on my freedom. I cannot simply step off the earth onto the moon. But in the things that really decide the kind of human being I am, good or evil, let us say, I am not determined by any essence or substance: 'we are the sum of our actions', said Jean-Paul Sartre, and these actions are the outcome of free choices for which we hold ourselves and one another accountable.

To think of God as being God by virtue of a divine substance would, on this view, be to think of him more by analogy with a fish or a tree than a human being. If, on the other hand, what is most human about us is the way in which we live or exist as freedom, so too will God's Godness be an analogue of our best ideas of personal freedom – even if it is also infinitely freer than anything we know as freedom! At the same time, thinking of there being three divine persons and one divine substance could seem to imply that being a person was something that, in itself, lacked substance, that it was somehow a deficient mode of being. This, we might add, is precisely the tendency of Sartre's idea of freedom: it is freedom altogether without substance, an 'upsurge of nothingness' in the midst of the solidity of the world, as Sartre himself puts it. Such freedom is self-avowedly arbitrary and unconstrained and claims the right to do whatever it freely chooses to do. But if Christians want to insist on God's freedom as being sovereign, a freedom that cannot and must not be limited by anything less than God's own self, they do not think of this freedom as arbitrary. Nor shall we, say the Orthodox, so long as we hold on to the original Greek meaning of the creed. For the choice between a sub-personal divine substance and an arbitrary, motiveless freedom is a false one. One reason for this is that, curiously enough, not only does the Latin *substantia*/substance translate the Greek *ousia*, but the Latin *persona*/person translates the Greek *hypostasis*, which, like *sub-stantia*, means literally 'standing underneath', that is, what stands under something to hold it up and sustain it in being. In Greek, then (though not in Latin or in English!) it is the three persons who 'stand under' and sustain the divine being rather than themselves resting on some pre-existent quality of 'Godness'. The freedom of the persons is thus the ground and support of the divine being, which, therefore, never exists other than in a manner permeated by the qualities of personal life.

These admittedly abstract considerations give added depth to the image of the three divine persons engaged in their perichoretic conversation. For it is no longer just a matter of their sitting round the table, as it were, and communicating with each other about whatever it was they felt they needed to talk about. The matter of their communication *is* their being, their life itself. It is the divine being or existence itself, that is being sustained, kept going, and, quite simply, 'existing' by virtue of this divine conversation. Divine communication is self-communication, communication of the divine being, held open and sustained as a threefold 'Thou'; it is the communication of the personal truth that *is* God's way of being.

The Relationship between the Divine and the Human

What, then, would it mean to assert that we, mortal creatures of dust that we are, are also in some way part of this conversation, that the whole event of creation and of ourselves emerging through it is an expression of the same originating impulse that gives life to and sustains God's own Trinitarian way of being? Wouldn't it mean that being in communication with God, whatever else we may want to say about it, can never be just a matter of God divulging occasional pieces of information about himself, as some accounts of revelation seem to imply? Instead, to be communicated to by God is in some measure to be offered a share in God's own way of being, it is the opportunity to participate in God's own life.

At the end of the last chapter we reflected on how the mutual communication characteristic of friendship could become an occasion for us, as individuals, to become recipients of the divine self-communication. Now we might add that our essential communicativeness, our capacity for moving towards one another in the grace of personal communication, may already be a reflection of the divine image in which, according to the Bible, we were created. Consequently, the exercise, deepening and fulfilling of this communicativeness may not only be a way whereby we are brought closer to each other, but also a way of being drawn ever more intimately, ever more consciously and freely into the inner circle of the divine conversation itself. It is, in other words, to discover our human communication of personal truth as a revelation, reflection or symbol of the divine word. True personal communication always already, in some sense, involves God. This, I believe is close to the heart of what the Eastern Church means when it speaks of our destiny as being *theosis* – divinization: the idea that what God is calling us to is nothing less than the possibility of sharing in the divine life itself. To Western ears, the idea sounds radical and, maybe, verging on the blasphemous. But perhaps it is only underlining something we are familiar or half-familiar with from such phrases as 'having fellowship in Christ', 'being one in the Spirit', 'God with us', 'our conversation is in heaven', 'walking with God' or having God 'in our hearts'. For how can we have fellowship with Christ, or be one with Christ in the Spirit, or walk with God or have God in our hearts if there were no kinship between ourselves and God? Isn't just this the point of the New Testament's insistence that Christ was the first-born of many brothers and sisters, that we are called to the glorious liberty of the children of God, that we will come to know as we are known? Is this not the crux of the matter when Jesus says to his disciples that he calls them disciples no longer, but friends?

It is also important to remember what was said about the relationship between person and substance in the divine way of being. *Theosis* does not mean that we get a new essence or substance, that we stop being human beings or get an injection of 'Godness'. It means that in our most decisive personal being we come to know ourselves as we are in and through the relation to the personal God. To share in God's way of being is not to become gods. It is simply to exist in a defining, free and freeing *relation* to God. In discussing the question of introspection, the Russian philosopher Mikhail Bakhtin remarked that there is in fact no internal boundary to the self, no point at which I can stop and say 'Ah! Now I've gone all the way through and know myself from back to front.' For, as he put it, no matter how deeply I look within, I always find myself regarding myself with the eyes of another.[10] In other words, who we are is, ultimately, inseparable from the most intimate relations we have with others. We are not first of all a nice rounded-off ego that then, somehow, has to establish relations with other egos (who are, of course, similarly groping about in the darkness of the external world). We are first of all beings-in-relation and this quality of being-in-relation is inseparable from what it means to be a person. This is true within the orbit of our basic human relationships. We discover who we are by discovering how, in our heart of hearts, our actions and reactions relate to the essential others of our lives. A similar insight underlies the whole project of psychoanalysis: what we regard as our stable, everyday ego or self is not some primitive datum but the provisional outcome of a long and ongoing process of encountering, reacting to and acting upon others.

What a theological extension of Bakhtin's saying would add is that this process both mirrors the pattern of relational self-being summed up in the term *perichoresis* and also, in its own deepest reaches, expresses or opens out into that same inner divine conversation. To come to know who we truly are is to come to know ourselves as we are in and as participants in the divine conversation, and, as partakers in that conversation, finding ourselves being partakers of the divine way of being, namely this being-as-conversation itself. Really to be part of a conversation, of course, means more than just listening in. It means taking part, and those who take part in something are just that, part-takers, partakers, and, through the grace of the conversation itself, contributing to the 'new thing' that it is continually bringing to pass. In this active taking part, which is something more than merely 'participating' in a divine essence, we become *in our human way* divine.

Grace and Mystery

Let's not get above ourselves. For a start, as I have tried to stress, the external form of this process of becoming divine is not necessarily startling or exotic. It is perfectly compatible with what the Danish poet-priest N. F. S. Grundtvig called 'a simple, cheerful, active life on earth',[11] or one might think of Brother Lawrence and his sense of the presence of God among the pots and pans of his kitchen.[12] And, more fundamentally, we have to remember that even on the rationalistic version of this story as told by Hegel *we* did not initiate the dynamic movement that first opened up the conversation that we come to find ourselves existing as. Maybe one could say of God in Hegel's theology what God said of human beings in Genesis: it was not good for God to be alone. But if God, in some sense, needs the fulfilment and the enrichment that come through bringing many to glory, we, for our part, have a deeply engrained impulse in us that wants to acknowledge God as source, originator, creator or, in the language of traditional theology and piety, 'Father'. This priority is not impaired if, in the course of the conversation, as sometimes, maybe often, happens in human lives the 'Father' also becomes transformed into a friend. Indeed, perhaps it would only be from the perspective of friendship that we could come to know the true 'priority' owing to fatherhood.

Putting it another way: if, by grace, we come to be participants in the divine conversation, we nevertheless sense that although we are welcomed into that conversation with (so to speak) open arms, there is a dimension to its history that will always and necessarily lie outside our experience. Just as for any child there is that in its parents' life that it will never come to know, no matter how much it is told about the family history, so too there is a depth in the divine conversation that will always elude us. Another analogy would be our ordinary human experience of love. I can know all the psychological, social and personal reasons why my partner is well-suited to me. Dating agencies even have such things worked out as a fine art. Yet for those who fall in love, it is always something astonishing and inexplicable. Why just this person? Why her? Why him? Why now? 'Had it been some other day, I might have looked another way, and I'd have never been aware, but as it is I'll dream of her tonight and every night.' In biblical and theological terms the divine way of being is by definition a mystery, and it does not cease to be so because we ourselves are now becoming a part of it.

That 'mystery' does not belong to the external aspect of the divine life alone, as if it was only from our limited and finite view that God was mysterious and that as we get to know God better the mystery will gradually give way to light, is indicated by many of the formulations of the New Testament. Certainly the New Testament is familiar with the idea that there are divine 'secrets' that are hidden from human eyes for a while until they are ready to be revealed. This is the whole idea of an 'apocalypse', the revelation of what has been hidden. But there is also a sense that there is something indissolubly mysterious about the message itself. Take the parable of the sower, in which Jesus tells the disciples that while the parable is incomprehensible to those outside the chosen circle, 'to you it is given to know the *musterion*, the mystery, of the Kingdom of God' (Mark 4.11). This could be read in terms of the parable-form of Jesus' teaching serving as a kind of incognito or veil, hiding divine truths from the eyes of the uninitiated, but it could also be read as pointing to the mystery of the message itself: that, in the parable's own terms, communication *can* occur, that the good seed and the good heart can be conjoined in such a way as to bring forth fruits that overpass all possible expectations and *that just that possibility is itself the mystery*. The theme that mystery is not an impediment to be removed but the very matter of the Christian proclamation can also be read in several formulations from the writings of Paul, as when he describes himself as householder over God's mysteries (1 Cor. 4.1). In the Letter to the Colossians he defines Christ as God's mystery (Col. 2.2), and in the Letter to the Ephesians, he speaks of his own task as being to make the mystery of the gospel known (Eph. 6.19).

The theme of mystery, which rather disappeared from sight in the Protestant theology of the nineteenth century, made an unmistakable comeback in the twentieth. The tone was set by Rudolf Otto's phenomenological study *The Holy*, in which Otto emphasized that mystery was an integral part of human beings' descriptions of their encounters with God, as in Isaiah's account of his prophetic call. When God appears to human beings, it is always a matter of fear and trembling, of the *mysterium fascinosum et tremendum*, or what Otto called the numinous, namely, what lies beyond the reach of any possible rational explanation.[13] The theme was taken up in the movement of theology known as dialectical theology initiated by Barth. In the early chapters of his massive *Church Dogmatics* Barth took pains to stress that even when God reveals himself or 'speaks' to human beings (the idea of revelation is the linchpin of Barth's own theology) there is an unavoidable dimension of mystery. Why? Because if the event of revelation is to be an event within human lives, something we are able to hear and take part in, then it must be expressed in human words that are a part of the general language of humankind. Revelation, as Barth puts it, has a necessarily 'secular' dimension. In other words, the Bible as the Word of God is also a book of human words that can be studied and analysed and explained in the same way as any other body of human words – historically, grammatically, philologically, etc., etc. It will *always* be possible to read and to hear these words as 'nothing but' just another slice of human history and culture. As human words they belong in the collective public sphere and are open to examination and criticism by all comers. Yet, for believers, they are also words of revelation, words of life, words that communicate the mystery of God's being. All of which means precisely that the truly divine meaning of these words remains mysterious even in being expressed as a human word-event.[14]

Paul Tillich, a theologian who generally took a very different line to Barth, nevertheless said something fundamentally similar when he stated that 'Whatever is essentially mysterious cannot lose its mysteriousness even when it is revealed.'[15] Miracle and ecstasy are intrinsic marks of revelation, he wrote, since divine revelation is always the gift of a 'more' that rational and logical categories and, indeed, common sense, cannot deal with. Tillich furthermore connects the idea of mystery with the idea of the personal: it is, he says, precisely because what claims our attention, what gives itself, in divine revelation is personal that the concepts and categories of philosophy and formal thought will necessarily fall short of the mark and the media of human language will be transformed from their normal usage into symbolic expressions of what can never be stated right out.

If the return of mystery to modern theology was a typical feature of the generation of Barth and Tillich, it was, of course, very much the matter of a 'return', of the rediscovery of what had, in the earliest times, been a fundamental theological theme. Catholic theology had never felt the same embarrassment about the term,[16] but, again the example of the Eastern Church is especially instructive. There theology itself is conceived not so much in terms of a 'science' (as we have increasingly come to think of it, under the pressure of the modern university system), but as 'mystagogy', as a deepening initiation into the mystery of faith.[17] And, while the Eastern Church was not embarrassed to speak of *theosis* or divinization, this was matched with an equal insistence on the apophatic element in all thinking about God, meaning that none of our words or concepts can ever adequately express God's way of being and that, in the mystical moment itself, even such concepts as 'Father' or 'Being' must be left behind. In the Middle Ages in the West there was a similar emphasis, not only among the upper echelons of the theological elite, but also in texts that spoke directly, in the vernacular, of a 'cloud of unknowing' that encompasses all those who truly seek to draw near to God.

The French Catholic philosopher Gabriel Marcel made an important distinction with regard to the idea of mystery when he differentiated between a mystery and a problem.[18] A problem, he asserted, can, in principle, be solved. Such problems are those of mathematics, science and, at least to some extent, history. There is at least some point in attempting to answer the question 'Why did Napoleon invade Russia?' even if, perhaps, Napoleon's own reasons were proved, in the event, to be unsound. A mystery, however, can never be cleared up in this way. I can go through all the reasons why I love my partner and still not get to the bottom of the reality of what it is I am foolishly attempting to explain. The distinction is easy enough to understand, but, Marcel argued, it is constantly overlooked in philosophy and, not least, in thinking about religion. Both from the side of philosophers and from the side of believers themselves, mysteries are constantly being treated as if they were problems. When churches forbid (or attempt to forbid: they rarely succeed any more!) discussion of points of faith, such as the historical investigation of the Bible, they are imposing the limitations of a mystery onto what is actually a problem. Conversely, when philosophers insist that there must be a clear-cut 'answer' to, let us say, 'the problem of evil', they are overlooking the mysterious dimension of all fundamental religious questions. The problem is where to draw the line. On the one hand, it is clear that a rationalistic explanation of the Bible will, in the last resort, never prevent some readers from finding in it a word of God, while, on the other hand, the mystery of evil does not mean that we should simply submit to the brute facts without thought or reflection. Aristotle once remarked that to think critically is to learn to distinguish between what does and what doesn't require rational explanation, a remark that is relevant in the present context.

This insistence on the necessarily mysterious aspect of revelation is, once more, an important check against interpreting the notion of *theosis* in any self-aggrandizing way. No matter how deeply we journey into the mystery of God's being-there-for us, we shall never achieve any kind of knowledge that would qualify us as experts. The most travelled knight-errant of faith knows as much (that is, as little) as the beginner. If there is anything to 'learn' here it is, chiefly, a matter of unlearning the presumption that we have aptitudes or rights in the matter. If we are ever more fully being welcomed into the infinite mystery of the divine conversation, it is not because we are clever, or interesting, or brave, or beautiful. The only final 'because' is, as the New Testament put it, God first loved us.

I have several times used the human analogy of love, and, fundamentally, it is precisely the belief that God is love (and, therefore, a being who is self-related and other-related) that requires theology to insist on the mysterious element in God. It is not the mystery of, say, an unfathomable philosophical concept such as 'Being' that is in play, though it is not inappropriate to ponder the mystery of being as an introductory element in thinking about God (or, with Tillich, 'the shock of non-being'). It is rather the mystery of love, of the experience of our being as having been brought into being by and for love, and owing itself as love to love. As John Zizioulas says of the apophatic theology of the Eastern Church, 'The principal object of this theology is to remove the question of truth and knowledge from the domain of Greek theories of ontology in order to situate it within that of *love* and communion.'[19] And within the word 'love' here are also to be heard all the other key words of this discussion: freedom, the personal, relation, conversation, being and mystery itself: 'Rise to adore the mystery of love,' commands the hymn, in words that epitomize the call made to us from the heart of the loving God.

From Rublev to Grünewald

This all sounds wonderful. Perhaps a little too wonderful. Hasn't something rather important been left out, namely, that the world as we know it is not plausibly describable as an expression of love? Don't we have to say that if God's call to love, to live ourselves into the divine conversation that is love, nevertheless still resounds in our world, it is a call that, for the most part, is refused, or misappropriated, or distorted in any one of innumerable frightful ways? I began this chapter with a picture, Rublev's icon of the Trinity. I offered it as one of the supreme pictorial expressions of what might be meant by the divine conversation that is the Trinitarian life. Another picture, no less well known, no less 'canonical' in modern theology than Rublev's, confronts us with the other pole of the ellipse that the dynamics of Christian doctrine encompass. It is a late medieval picture of the crucifixion that belongs to a complex altarpiece painted for the hospital church of St Anthony in Isenheim, and it was painted by one Matthias Grünewald.[20] Even after a century in which artists have portrayed the crucifixion in the prism of such horrors as those of the First World War's Western Front or the Nazi concentration camps, and when television images of death and mayhem have become familiar parts of daily life, Grünewald's painting remains an amazingly powerful representation of a reality in which love is all too often refused. Showing the image to a class, without warning, at the end of a long, lyrical exposition of Rublev, I have heard an audible gasp of collective shock. Yet the basic construction of the picture is conventional enough: Jesus hangs on the cross, with Mary, John and Mary Magdalene on one side and John the Baptist on the other. Formally, it is not so different from many other paintings of this over-familiar scene. Where it differs is in the unflinching manner in which it confronts the sheer cruelty of death by crucifixion. The limbs and face are distorted in pain, the body is flecked with blood and discoloured from loss of blood and the final exhaustion preceding death. It is, almost, a picture devoid of any possibility of redemption, a picture of a violent, sadistically conceived and brutally enacted murder. The reality of the human situation, we are tempted to think. As such, it is also a picture of non-communication. Each of the three figures – the dying man, the grieving mother, the bereft disciple – is locked into the isolation of their respective agony. And the terrible thing is, that this picture no less truly defines Christian faith pictorially than that luminous conversation beneath the oaks of Mamre.

We are, I suggest, compelled by Christian doctrine itself always to take both pictures together. The one is a window into heaven, an image of pure communication, theology from above, the other mirroring the world as it all too often is, and, as such, the ineluctable meeting point of our theology from above with life as it is experienced here below. So great is the force of this second picture – and of comparable pictures of suffering, violence and death – that even if we are lucky enough never to have encountered anything quite so gruesome in our own experience, we have to acknowledge that the whole way in which we see the world in general is changed because of it. We cannot escape the revelation that this is what the world is like. As Dostoevsky's sceptical Ivan Karamazov put it in challenging the faith of his younger brother Alyosha, we don't need horror stories of massacres, we only need the tears of one child to bring the whole edifice of a harmonious world order crashing down around our ears. There only needs to have been one crucifixion for the world to have become altogether and irretrievably alien to the idyllic place of hospitality, beauty and rest that is shown in Rublev's icon. If this has happened once, it can happen again. And, of course, it has happened again and again. It is perhaps one of the bitterest legacies of the totalitarian era of the twentieth century that we know that evil is not just the work of monsters and sadists but of 'ordinary men'.[21] Who knows who is really to be trusted? What do we really know about that friendly waiter, that sad village schoolteacher, that smart lady on the train? Could not each of them, under a certain sort of pressure, have become one of the murderers, in the Third Reich, in Soviet Russia, in the Balkans? And what do we really know of ourselves? Would we have been any different? And even today can we be so sure of our judgements as to what is a war of liberation and what a war of aggression? Can we know that our cause, whatever it may be, is right? The questions pile up – but the worst of it is that however we answer them the killing and the cruelty go on.

Kierkegaard, then, was surely right to insist that if the God who is love is going to communicate to dwellers in such a world as this, then that communication will be paradoxical, fragmentary, 'a sign of contradiction'. What could be a greater contradiction that Christianity itself, in all its branches, could hold up a picture of a scene such as that painted by Grünewald and say 'In this event is the salvation of the world'? Yet paradox and contradiction are only possible when there are two incommensurable factors in play, and it would be a lie, albeit a tempting and even a persuasive lie, to look at Grünewald's painting and say to ourselves, Yes, that is the truth, that is what human life is like. It is sheer horror, but sheer horror is not all it is. It is also life, life in which, as in the story of Abraham and the three mysterious visitors, hospitality is given, communion is made or graced. The scope of Christian doctrine is, then, the parabola marked by these two extreme moments, the moment of abandonment and isolation, and the moment of perfect circumincession. The self-communicative being of God is what it is, not by enjoying its own inner plenitude in an endless circle of luminous bliss, but precisely by transforming the lie into truth, luring, drawing, mastering the victims of non-communication in such a way as to bring them into the dynamic of perichoretic love. But this is precisely the work of doctrine, the real and actual communication of the love to which the objective statements of the creeds bear witness.

Doctrine, then, is not the assertion of the truth of the statement that God is love but an actual communication of love to those who, in whatever situation of distress, need it. Similarly, defending the truth of Christian doctrine would not be primarily a matter of finding historical or reasonable arguments to defend the coherence or logic of what Christians say about God. These kinds of arguments have their place, but only if the concrete circumstances in which the doctrine is to be proclaimed are such that it will be an insuperable obstacle to the doctrine being heard as a word of love if they are not addressed. That is not an impossible scenario, least of all in a historical situation in which many – within and without the churches – believe the Christian word to be a word of judgement and condemnation, or to require the complete suspension or subordination of all our aspirations to freedom and creativity. Sometimes intellectual engagement and argument is indeed necessary if the word of love is to be heard as anything other than heteronomous or irrelevant. However, as a matter of fact, it is probably the case that a quite disproportionate amount of effort has been devoted to systematizing and defending what is regarded as orthodoxy rather than in taking the words and symbols of orthodoxy, delivered to us by the tradition, and making them live and sing as words and symbols of actual, liberating, personal address and love. In the course of its long history, doctrine has accumulated an almost immeasurable wealth of materials, and it is scarcely surprising if it has grown sclerotic, its arteries have hardened, and it has ceased to interact with the reality that, on its own account, it should be serving to redeem. There is nothing astonishing in the fact that it has become 'the sum of saving knowledge' and not the word of life. Even when the right thing is said, and even when it is said with the right motivations, the communicative word too often gets locked into a cycle of regressive self-referral, more and more taking on the features of an esoteric discourse. Some recent theology even affirms this situation as how things should be, since (it is argued) doctrine is something that only those who play the language game of theology can understand. But such a movement is the very opposite of genuine communicative action. If, as we have seen, the central matter of Christian doctrine is necessarily and in itself mysterious, it is nevertheless a mystery that exists to be proclaimed to the world, an open secret, a light to lighten the peoples.

Remember, that because the word that saves is a personal word, a word calling us to personal communion, it is ultimately determined in terms of content and character by the freedom of the speaker, a freedom that no system of words, symbols, rituals or holy orders can ever adequately or definitively embody. Or, rather, precisely because this loving freedom of the divine conversation is constantly embodying itself in a world of lies and non-communication, its words and other communicative forms will repeatedly be breaking the mould of any and every attempt to reduce it to the sub-personal, to make it something that can be managed and explained, the matter of know-ledge or technique. Doctrine is not defending a set of unchanging and timeless truths. Seeing it in those terms might inspire a certain sense of tragic grandeur, encouraging the faithful to think of themselves as a diminishing remnant bravely holding high the tattered flag of faith amidst the wrack and ruin of secularization and relativism (*Brideshead Revisited,* perhaps). This might encourage us to believe that we are engaged in something rather heroic. But, I suggest, it is a much harder task to attend to the complex, moving horizon of existential need that calls for the word of love to be spoken in such a way as to break open and transform just this unrepeatable situation of non-communication, to change the lie into truth by speaking the word in a way it's never been spoken before, making all things new.

Beginning in Chapter 1 with the contemporary concern to find forms of communication that might be capable of contextualizing the massively powerful discourses of science and technology in the life-world of human self-understanding, I argued that the task of Christian doctrine can to a large extent share this concern. In this chapter we have tried to look more closely into the ultimate sources of doctrine, finding them in the self-communicating *perichoresis* of the divine life, a spiralling conversational movement that reaches out into creation itself and into the distortion of our created possibilities encountered in the phenomena of evil. Whether we start from below or above, we find ourselves engaging a pattern of relation that involves a complex dynamic of affirmation, critique and transformation both from the side of doctrine and from the side of human experience and thought. This is how it has to be, if doctrine is understood not so much as a system of truths, but as a dynamic movement of communication. For the communicator of ethical and religious truths, Kierkegaard reminded us, can never abstract from the situation in which commu-nication occurs, and the form that the communication (in this case, the doctrine) takes, will be shaped by the need of that situation itself. As in Grünewald's painting of the crucifixion, the communication of doctrine may even go so far as to take the form of the lie itself, the most uncompromising depiction of a world in which communication fails and human beings refuse to be the partakers in the divine life that is ever and again on offer.

3

The Sacrament of Creation

The World as Divine Communication

Whether we start from above or below, it seems that, sooner or later, Christian doctrine finds itself facing an almost impossible task: how can it sing the Lord's song in such a strange land? how can it communicate the luminous mystery of God's divine life as manifested in Rublev's icon of the Old Testament Trinity if the world is capable of scenes such as that portrayed in Grünewald's Isenheim altarpiece? If we start from below, it seems we can never be really confident of overcoming the barrier constituted by our finitude and our collective and individual complicity in violence and injustice. If we start from above, it seems hard to imagine how the beauty of the divine being could become intelligible to inhabitants of a world such as this. Christian doctrine, however, claims that such communication is possible and that there is a middle ground where these two worlds meet. This middle ground is, in the first instance, what theology has spoken of as creation and what others simply call the world. Because the world exists, we are never confronted with God in some kind of vacuum. If we are to meet or be met by God, if we are to find ourselves being drawn into the illuminating exchanges of the divine conversation, it can only realistically be on the basis of our inhabiting a shaped and meaningful world.

Recall the idea floated in the last chapter, and developed in discussion with Hegel and Berdyaev. This was the idea that creation could be seen less in terms of something 'made' by God and more in terms of its being a moment in God's own self-expression. As a manifestation of God's dynamic self-expression, the world is not merely the 'product' of God's power and wisdom but, in its very existence, it communicates something of God to all who participate in it. To speak in this way of the world as an act of self-expression or self-communication from the side of God is both strangely familiar to yet also alien to popular Christian thinking. Something similar seems to be found already in Plato when, in the dialogue *Timaeus*, he described God's impulse to create as the generosity that wills not to withhold being from anything that could possibly come to possess it. The world, on this view, exists as the self-imparting of divine being to all possible beings. Yet, as this profound and beautiful idea was developed in later Platonic philosophy, it took a direction that Christian doctrine was to find uncomfortable (perhaps, one could say, uncomfortably close). It seemed to blur the distinction between Creator and creation that, in the early Christian centuries, came to be a hallmark of Christian thinking. Moreover, it seemed to limit God's freedom, since, on the Platonic account, it looked as if God couldn't not create – he simply *had to* pour himself out into all the myriad beings that collectively made up the world and all that therein is. Later, especially in response to Spinoza and Romanticism, this reserve would be crystallized into the objection that it was pantheistic, that it basically identified God with the universe and, effectively, made both of them subject to strict necessity. God became the totality of all that is and the highest form of the love of God was simply to consent to the world being as it is and to our own existence as a part of the whole. But, Christian theologians argued, this did justice neither to God's freedom nor to God's personality, nor, fatally, to the distinction between God and the world. For that matter, it also undermined human freedom and human personality. In fact, it was claimed, Spinoza's pantheism was simply a form of materialism.

What, then, is the Christian alternative? It is usually stated in terms of creation out of nothing: a sovereign, free, personal Creator bringing all that is into being solely by his all-powerful word of command or *fiat* (a Latin term meaning 'let it be done').This could easily be made to sound as if the relationship between God and the world was altogether external: God as the great designer, and the world as his handiwork. In the early modern period the analogy of the watch-maker and the watch became the most familiar formulation of this 'manufactory' view of the relationship between Creator and creation. The objection has been made that such a view actually degrades the world into being nothing more than a mere instrument, a tool for accomplishing the divine purpose that has no value in itself. And, even though some Christian philosophers have argued that seeing things this way allows us to infer the existence, the wisdom and the beneficence of God from a careful consideration of his handiwork, it could equally well be said that it doesn't really give us much ground for relating to God as a personal, saving presence in our lives. At its extreme, it led to the view known as Deism, according to which God had indeed wisely planned the whole thing and got it going but had subsequently retired, leaving it to run itself, as it had been designed to do. Such a God may answer certain intellectual needs, but says little to the spirit of living religion.

Although this 'handiwork' view of creation is widely found among proponents as well as critics of Christianity, it scarcely does justice to all that Christian witness, worship and devotion have wanted to say. Perhaps it does not even do justice to its own imagery. Handiwork, craftsmanship, artistry, creating, making – these and similar words cover a wide range of human activities. Since the nineteenth century we have become very familiar with the idea that a true work of art 'expresses' the inner feelings or insights of the artist, whether in painting, song or literature, whilst, in contrast to such expressive 'art', what is seen as mere 'craft' work is often said to focus exclusively on the work itself, its quality and craftsmanship. Handiwork or craft then become a purely technical kind of production. Such work doesn't – and doesn't even attempt to – give us anything of the individual personality of the craftsman. Now, if the pantheistic idea lends itself to seeing creation on analogy with an artist's self-expression (and Spinoza was very popular among the Romantics), the idea of God-the-designer seems to relate more naturally to a 'craft' idea of creating. This seems to make the world rather less expressive, rather more machine-like. But perhaps this is a false prejudice. For even a craftwork – a handmade chair, a knitted jumper or the repair of a stretch of motorway – cannot be undertaken and completed without some kind of personal investment on the part of the maker or makers. That the final work is as it is, that the worker can take some satisfaction in it and that it can be appreciated for its competence, its perfection according to its kind, is in some way, no matter how limited, 'expressive'. Only the most alienated forms of labour can really be said to sever all the links between the worker and the work, and we would scarcely want to envisage God's handiwork in those terms.

While continually registering a caution against what has become known as pantheism, both the Bible itself and Christian tradition have, in any case, used ideas and images that point to a far more inward relationship between Creator and creation than that which would reduce the world to a mere 'product'. In the Book of Proverbs the principle of divine Wisdom is personified as a female figure created as the first of all God's works – 'created', but, in a recent English translation also 'formed' or 'born' 'at the beginning, before earth itself . . . when there was yet no ocean, when there were no streams brimming with water . . . [b]efore the mountains were settled in their place, before the hills . . .' (Prov. 8.23–5). And, in what is the most vivid moment in this astonishing chapter, Wisdom goes on to say of herself that, in the entire process of creation, 'I was at his side each day, his darling and delight, playing in his presence continually, playing over his whole world, while my delight was in mankind' (vv. 30–1). Rather than the mighty but daunting image of the cosmic geometer planning and executing his great work with supreme and unstoppable might, this passage hints at a picture more like that of a dance, a love-affair even, in which the male creator creates not merely to give effect to his own mighty will but to delight and please his female beloved, allowing her to be a kind of co-creator. In such a picture, the creation is no mere 'work' but a kind of artistic play in which pleasure and delight are no less potent as aims and motives than are knowledge, justice and goodness. Such a view is also implicit in the (many) Hebrew Bible passages where God is depicted as caught up in an intensely personal relation to his people Israel, or to Jerusalem, his city, often personified in female terms. It is almost as if God feels his own identity, his own being, to be at stake in the defections and returns of the people variously described as his son, wife, or daughter. Of course, Christian theology itself, not to mention the Enlightenment, has taught us to interpret such passages as pictorial illustrations of a relationship that ultimately needs to be interpreted in the light of the great quasi-philosophical affirmations about God as omniscient, omnipotent and benevolent Creator *ex nihilo* – but why shouldn't the interpretative process run both ways, why shouldn't we perhaps allow such hints to alert us to something that might easily be missed in the more intellectually 'correct' versions of the creation story? And what is 'that something'? It is simply that the Christian tradition allows us not only to see creation in terms of God putting into effect some eternally premeditated plan but as something artistic, spontaneous, expressive and self-expressive on the part of God.

In the early Christian centuries Wisdom, understood as the co-worker in creation, became identified with Christ and, therefore, with the Logos, the Word, Christ in the aspect of the second divine person of the Holy Trinity. Although the Nicene Creed, one of the most frequently used and most authoritative of all the Church's various credal statements, specifically says of 'the Son' that he is the one 'by whom all things were made', I strongly suspect that, at least since the early Enlightenment period, most Christians have tended to think of creation as primarily the work of 'The Father' (i.e. 'God'!) alone. This has not always been the case. If we look back to medieval Christian art, we very frequently see illustrations of the creation that show Jesus Christ, dividers in hand, laying out the world. Such pictures do indeed refer us, once more, to a 'handiwork' model of creation, but the

identification of Wisdom with the Word suggests that, however sub-
liminally, Christian doctrine has also intuitively understood the act of
creation as something much more intimately communicative of the
mind of God than any act of mere manufacture. For the Word, understood from within the perspective of Trinitarian thinking, is itself the
full and complete shining-forth into comprehensibility of the divine
Being (Col. 1.15; Heb. 1.3). It is that Being as communicative event,
communicative action: a communication that is not about anything
other than that Being itself and thus a self-communication and a self-
imparting.

If, according to Genesis, it is only human beings who are made in
the image and likeness of God, this still does not exclude the possibility that the whole of creation is also, in some sense, stamped with
the character of that Word in which, by which and for which it was
made. Something like this was the idea of the highly idiosyncratic
Christian thinker, J. G. Hamann, who saw human language itself as
based on the fact that creatures themselves were, in their deepest
being, 'words' spoken by God in creation. In naming the creatures
with their proper names in our human language, then, we know them
as they were created. Something similar is rather genially suggested
in C. S. Lewis's Narnia novel *The Magician's Nephew*, in which Aslan
the Lion (essentially an allegorical representation of Christ, the Word)
creates by singing the creatures into existence. Such creative naming
and singing is by no means pantheistic, but it offers a very different
idea of creation from what we are accustomed to associate with ideas
of God the designer and maker. God is not identical with creation, but
neither is God outside it: God's very self is in it, with it, among it: it is
God's song.

The twentieth century saw a series of attempts to rethink the idea
of creation in such a way as to shift Christian thinking away from
denigrating the world as worthless in itself and towards seeing it
as, in some way, expressive of the very life of God. These attempts
were often very differently motivated and took a variety of forms,
philosophical, doctrinal and imaginative.

At the philosophical level, perhaps the most influential movement
in this direction was that known as process theology. With distant
roots in Hegel and other early nineteenth-century idealist thinkers and
under the more immediate influence of A. N. Whitehead, the process
theologians sought to develop what Charles Hartshorne called a 'di-
polar' God. On the one hand, this di-polar God retained many of the
attributes of classic Christian theism: infinite, eternal, etc. Yet, alongside
this, God was also involved in the changing, developing and evolving

world. Through the world-process – conceived in thoroughly historical and evolutionary terms – Godself was no longer merely 'being', as
in classical metaphysics, but 'becoming'. Time and history were not,
as in the past, construed as somehow eroding or depleting the fullness
of a Being that is sheer 'Isness': instead they served to enrich a divine
Being that would otherwise be merely abstract. Even the suffering of
this evolving universe is somehow to be taken into and reconciled
within the all-encompassing life of God. The world is not identical
with God, but it is, somehow, 'in' God. Whereas pantheism is generally taken to mean, simply, that all things *are* God, the process thinkers
argued for what has become known as *panentheism* – the view that all
things are within God.

If one line of process thought has an essentially philosophical cast,
being preoccupied with the intellectual coherence of the concepts of a
panentheistic world-view, an essentially analogous development can
be seen among a variety of modern theologians.

One of the most influential of these was the Jesuit Pierre Teilhard
de Chardin. I shall return to Teilhard shortly, and here mention only
that he offers an example of how the rise of an evolutionary world-
view played a crucial part in this movement. Teilhard was himself a
palaeontologist working on human origins and he was worried by
the way in which Christian theology had tied itself to a set of basic
concepts, chiefly inherited from Aristotelianism, that were simply
incompatible with what evolution was teaching us about human
beings, their origins, and the history of the cosmos that had made
human evolution possible. Rather than seeing creation as something
that happened 'in the beginning', once upon a time and long ago,
Teilhard wanted to see all the basic concepts of Christian theology –
creation, fall and redemption – recast in dynamic, evolutionary terms.
The history of the universe was not to be thought of as a once-off act
of creation, followed by a fall that was in turn followed by a divine
rescue operation (to be completed at some unspecified point in the
future). Rather, creation, fall and redemption were three aspects of
one unified and ongoing process. God was there in the beginning,
yes, but God was Alpha *and Omega*. In particular Teilhard identified
Christ as the *Omega-Point* of the creative process. Christ, the Word,
was not a divine person who merely happened to take a trip into
historical time 2,000 years ago: Christ, the Word, is a divine person
continually in the process of being brought into being by evolution,
history and the actions of human beings. Teilhard combined this
view with a thoroughly optimistic view of science and of technological progress. The development of modern technology, he believed,

was a key moment within the bringing to birth of a kind of cosmic Christ-consciousness. He foresaw the advent of a network of global communications which he called the 'noosphere', the sphere of mind, supervening upon the biosphere and marking the dawn of a new form of planetary consciousness. At this point, he hoped, we would be able to make a truly universal, truly human decision for Christ and that this decision itself would play a part in fully realizing Christ's advent as the Omega-Point.

Undoubtedly the desire to correlate Christian teaching with all that we are now learning about cosmic and human history has been and is one of the most important impulses behind the rethinking of the doctrine of creation. However, more recent contributions to such a rethinking have had a further motivation that can, very loosely, be labelled 'green' or 'ecological' and that is characterized by a much less optimistic view of science and technology. According to such ecological theologies, historical Christianity itself played an unfortunate part in preparing the way for the current exploitation and devastation of the biosphere, by demoting the world to the status of a mere tool or instrument, devoid of intrinsic worth. Not only did Christianity portray God as having an absolute power over creation, but its promotion of 'Man' as 'Master and Lord' of creation, having 'dominion' over the other creatures, to use them according to need and want, made a bad situation worse. The theoretical demythologizing and disempowering of the world by Christian theologians – the reduction of creation to mere worldliness – was given practical effect when Christian missionaries cut down the sacred groves of the pagans and taught that the spirits associated with animals, plants and places were either demons or simply delusions. The desacralization of the world consummated by modern industrial society had actually been set in motion by Christianity itself, even if, sometimes, popular Christian rituals and legends provided a medium in which fragments of the older view lived on. This analysis has led some to reject Christianity in favour of New Age invocations of the Gaia hypothesis, according to which the biosphere itself is to be conceived as a single, living organism of which we are members (not masters). But it has also influenced a number of Christian theologians and encouraged them to revisit the doctrine of creation in far more positive terms. Jürgen Moltmann, for example, has explicitly taken the 'ecological crisis' and the predominance of the 'objectifying, analyzing, particularizing and reductive' world-view institutionalized in the theory and practice of contemporary science and technology as a starting-point for a major revision of the doctrine of creation. This view serves the interests of those who see nature merely as a resource to be used for the fulfilment of human purposes, but it also opens the door to an abuse of nature that is potentially damaging to the future of planetary life, including human life itself. In sketching an alternative position Moltmann emphasizes that an 'ecological doctrine of creation' must be one in which knowledge is understood more in terms of participation, communication and integration. He argues that a genuinely Trinitarian view of creation would be one in which God's immanence in the world (through Christ and the Spirit) would need to be stressed alongside the more traditional Christian emphasis on divine transcendence, and that we should embrace an 'integrating vision of God and nature in togetherness'.[1] Such a Trinitarian view, he suggests, is the truest expression of the panentheist orientation of religious philosophy. To know the world as creation is to know oneself as a part of the community of creation, a community that Moltmann understands as eucharistic, that is, a worshipping, singing and praising community. Sallie McFague, an ecological and feminist theologian, well captures this new thinking when she describes the world as God's body, nicely quoting a four-year-old's prayer, which says 'Goodnight God. I hope you are having a nice time being the world.'[2]

Whatever else is to be said for or against these revisionary efforts by contemporary theologians (and we should, I think, give full weight to the meaning of 're-*vision*-ary' in this context), they certainly encourage believers to think of creation as an essentially communicative event. The world is no longer a mere stage on which the drama of 'Man' is tragically (or, more rarely, comically) enacted before the ever-observant eye of the divine spectator. The world is itself God's Word to all who have an ear to hear, a deepening and an extension of the divine conversation of which I spoke in the last chapter. To put it rather abstractly, creation is the maximalization of the communicative possibilities of this conversation. Or, recalling the imagery of Proverbs, it is the dance, play and delight in which this conversation unfolds all its fullest potential. In this perspective, creation is not merely there for the benefit of Godself, nor even for that of human beings (as a means of instructing or training them), but, in some way, essentially involves what Buddhists felicitously refer to as 'all sentient creatures' (though where the dividing-line between sentient and non-sentient should be drawn would be a task well beyond the scope of this short course: we already have much more than enough to be thinking about!).

Art and Sacrament

It is all too easy in discussing such things to find ourselves speaking as if we were able to be spectators of God's purposes in creation and to evaluate different ways of understanding this without too much difficulty. But, quite apart from the intellectual difficulty of following the conceptual analyses of those, like Hartshorne, who attempt to do full philosophical justice to rethinking creation in more dynamic, panentheistic terms, it has to be acknowledged that all that is being said here is and can only be very imprecise. It is not the matter of hard facts or explanations but of hints, guesses, analogies, models and metaphors. Consequently, it is by no means irrelevant to cite the testimonies of artists alongside those of philosophers and theologians, and, in this area at least, we may often have the impression that all the philosophers and theologians are doing is following up on and tidying up what the artists have given them by way of visionary inspiration. We have already mentioned C. S. Lewis's image of the Lion Aslan singing creation into being. Part of the beauty of such an image is that there is no way we could possibly mistake it for some kind of knowledge-claim. Of course, Lewis 'knew' that, objectively speaking, the world did not come into being by means of a singing lion, but his and our knowledge in this matter by no means takes away from the power of the image to move us and to make us think that it is actually saying something rather important to us about God, the world and ourselves. And learning what that something is, what it *means*, is, fairly obviously, going to be a very different kind of learning from that involved in cracking the genetic code. So too for other 'visions' of the world as God's self-expressive Word, as God's body, or as God's own self-creating, self-discovering life.

Such visions were central to many of the key texts of that great literary, artistic and cultural movement known as Romanticism. In England it was pre-eminently William Wordsworth who popularized this vision in poems such as 'Lines composed above Tintern Abbey', in which the experience of nature acquires an unmistakably religious depth, as if nature is God's way of becoming present to us:

> And I have felt
> A presence that disturbs me with the joy
> Of elevated thoughts; a sense sublime
> Of something far more deeply interfused,
> Whose dwelling is the light of setting suns,

And the round ocean and the living air,
And the blue sky, and in the mind of man:
A motion and a spirit, that impels
All thinking things, all objects of all thought,
And rolls through all things.

It is no coincidence that Wordsworth is one of the most-quoted authors in John Ruskin's great work, *Modern Painters*. This multi-volume work, which began as a defence of J. M. W. Turner against his critics, developed into something very like a theology of art, as Ruskin showed how the natural creation offers something like a language of communicative forms that the great painters are able to interpret. In developing this idea, he does not hesitate to see the materials of painting – tone, colour and space, for example – as forms of *truth*, and he can also devote astonishing pages to the truth of clouds, mountains, water and vegetation. The artist, he maintains, has not merely to imitate these forms, but to show us their truth. That they can thus be counted as forms of truth is because, according to Ruskin, they are ultimately the way in which the divine ideas of Beauty are communicated to us. Ultimately, painting can rise to the level where it reveals such divine ideas as infinity, comprehensiveness, permanence, justice and energy. Painting even has a moral dimension, he argues. But in all of this, the painter is, naturally, entirely dependent on his faithfulness to the primary revelation of these ideas in our common experience of the material world and its God-given forms.[3]

In a very different register from that of the Pre-Raphaelite artists later championed by Ruskin, Van Gogh provides another outstanding example of how nature can reveal an almost divine depth. In the dynamic dramas of his great whorled skies, whose overbearing darkness is mastered by the brilliant radiance of the stars, or which, heavy with impending storms, weigh down upon the trembling cornfields; in the sheer effulgent waste of golden light spilling out from his suns, sunflowers and piles of fruit, Van Gogh created a visual language of nature in which to articulate his own spiritual passions and crises: the world itself became for him 'a kind of Bible' in which the great struggle of despair and hope was fought out and given expression.[4] D. H. Lawrence could have been thinking of such epiphanies when he wrote that 'It is art which opens to us the silences, the primordial silences which hold the secrets of things, the great purposes, which are themselves silent; there are no words to speak of them with, and no thoughts to think them in, so we struggle to touch them through art . . .'[5]

More recently, it is true, art seems to have become more self-consciously urban, ironic, and conceptual, and we have been instructed by postmodern philosophers that there is no world outside language and textuality. Yet there remains a continuing strand of contemporary art that finds something like a spiritual inspiration in the natural world, and some of the best-known figures of contemporary British art (I think of Antony Gormley, Anish Kapoor, Andy Goldsworthy and Richard Long) could well be cited here.[6] These are, of course, only a few, more or less random, examples out of a vast range of possibilities. And, whatever academic theorists say, the Romantic vision of nature as the medium in which the ultimate truth of our being – divine or otherwise – is revealed remains powerful at the popular level.

In fact, theologians have had and have good cause to worry that those influenced by Romanticism have turned to nature and to art as a kind of substitute for ecclesiastical religion. Since the late eighteenth century, art has been at least as likely as religion to be the source of the great visions that synthesize and give shape to our attempts to make sense of 'it all'. But leaving aside all the possible counter-arguments that believers might want to put to the advocates of such a religion of art, the kinds of representations of nature in art that I have all too briefly indicated give us fresh insight into a very traditional and very central Christian idea: the idea of the sacramental. The Catechism printed in the Book of Common Prayer (which, in the olden days, all those coming to confirmation were presumed to have learned!) begins its definition of a sacrament as 'an outward and visible sign of an inward and spiritual grace'. Curiously (or not!), this is almost identical with the definition of art found over and over again in Romantic thought: that a work of art is 'an outward and visible expression of an inward and spiritual idea'. In the first instance, the 'idea' that was to find expression in the work of art was the genial idea of the artist himself. But for artists such as Wordsworth, Coleridge, Hopkins and many others, this creative human idea was itself essentially an echo in the finite mind of the infinite creative idea of God.

Returning to the question of creation – that is, 'creation' in the sense of the world, the universe, all that is – we thus have the possibility of seeing it as itself deeply and fundamentally sacramental, as an outward and visible sign of the creative grace of God. Or, to put it more succinctly, creation is itself outward and visible grace. The most fundamental sacrament of all is what as the Russian Orthodox thinker, Alexander Schmemann called 'the world as sacrament'.[7]

In helping us to see creation as sacramental, art also helps us to relativize the rather artificial distinction between theologies from above and from below. Once we start to think of creation in these terms, we find ourselves thinking both from above and from below: from above, in that we are seeing creation as the self-communication of God; from below, in that it shows how we can experience creation – our world – as a word, a communication from God. The further thought suggests itself that, of course, we never really do start from above or below, but from somewhere in the middle, in a relationship in which we are seeking, finding, fleeing or losing God, and sought by, found by and transformed by God. All this, in fact, is what the world gives us to experience. The world, life, is the one, unique, all-encompassing environment of our God-relationship. Every thought, every doubt, every experience, every taste we have of God is, necessarily, an event within the world, an event mappable in terms of the electrical and chemical processes of the brain. Outside the world we have no God-relationship. The way in which we experience and exist in the world is, by the same token, the measure of that relationship. Our being in the world is the way in which the divine conversation takes shape as creation.

I have already mentioned Teilhard de Chardin as one Christian thinker who did much to further a re-envisioning of the threefold relationship between God, creation and humanity. Particularly helpful at this point is Teilhard's notion of the cosmos as *le milieu divin*, the milieu or medium in which the divine is itself, through human action and suffering, coming to birth. On this view the incarnation is not going to be understood simply be referring to what happened between the years 1 and 33 of the Christian era: what happened then was crucial but, essentially, it focused and brought to expression a process that was fundamentally identical with the process of creation itself. The whole life of the universe was, for Teilhard, a single complex process of what he – admittedly inelegantly – called Christification: 'it is *Christ whom we make or whom we undergo in all things*', he wrote.[8] As the Omega-Point yet to come, Christ will be the one in whom the fullness of all that is, matter and spirit, will be gathered into one and harmonized. However, this Omega-Point is not just something waiting in the future: it is itself the creative centre of the universe, creating from the future, as it were, drawing all things into being and giving them the opportunity of finding their fulfilment in Christ. Teilhard's style is a heady concoction of Catholic devotional writing, science fiction and vitalistic poetry, but his central vision is clear enough:

> . . . *the divine omnipresence* translates itself within our universe by the network of the organising forces of the total Christ. God exerts

pressure, in us and upon us – through the intermediary of all the powers of heaven, earth and hell – only in the act of forming and consummating Christ who saves and sur-animates the world. And since, in the course of this operation, Christ himself does not act as a dead or passive point of convergence, but as a centre of radiation for the energies which lead the universe back to God through his humanity, the layers of divine action finally comes to us impregnated with his organic energies.

The divine *milieu* henceforward assumes for us the savour and the specific features which we desire. In it we recognise an omnipresence which acts upon us by assimilating us in it . . . As a consequence of the Incarnation, the divine immensity has transformed itself for us into *the omnipresence of christification*.[9]

That this is an essentially *sacramental* vision is revealed in one of Teilhard's best-known works, *The Mass on the World*. The occasion was a scientific field-trip in the steppes of Asia where Teilhard found himself without the conventional materials for celebrating Mass (which, as a Catholic priest, he was obliged to say daily). Instead, he composed a prayer in which, in intention, he took the materials of the world itself as the matter of his offering:

All the things in the world to which this day will bring increase; all those that will diminish; all those too that will die: all of them, Lord, I try to gather into my arms, so as to hold them out to you in offering. This is the material of my sacrifice; the only material you desire.

Once upon a time men took into your temple the first fruits of their harvests, the flower of their flocks. But the offering you really want, the offering you mysteriously need every day to appease your hunger, to slake your thirst is nothing less than the growth of the world borne ever onwards in the stream of universal becoming.

Receive, O Lord, this all-embracing host which your whole creation, moved by your magnetism, offers you at the dawn of a new day.[10]

The 'materials' of religious worship are not to be limited to the 'sacred' objects of church ritual – whether these are sanitized white wafers printed with crucifixes or chunks of mealy brown bread, carefully wrought silver vessels or folksy pottery, brocaded Gothic or minimalist modern vestments – but *all* that the world offers us: *that* is the material in which God supremely takes shape as sacrament, because that is the material in which God takes shape as incarnate, and that, in turn, is the most intense focusing of the whole movement of creation itself.

Importantly, the subtitle of the essay *Le Milieu Divin* is 'An Essay on the Interior Life' and it can be read as Teilhard's attempt to transform the basic understanding of the spiritual life. As it had been developed in the Church (and one has to say that this was more or less the same in both Catholicism and Protestantism), the shape of Christian life and devotion was determined by a profoundly dualistic view of human nature. The 'aim' of the Christian life was generally taken to be the cultivation of the soul and the suppression of the 'animal' instincts. Teilhard's model, however, aimed at integration, a seeing the life of the body as the way in which the soul is or becomes real. This, he said, involved the sanctification of the soul's activities and of its passivities. 'It is the whole of human life, down to its most natural zones, which, the Church teaches, can be sanctified. "Whether you eat or whether you drink", St. Paul says.'[11] Perhaps especially important here is what Teilhard says about our passivities, those depths or reaches of our lives in which, basically, we exist as biological entities, subject to external physical pressures and, internally, from biologically determined instincts. And our passivities reveal the presence of our environment within our own being, as when we are subject to processes of transformation over which we have no control (e.g. the onset of adolescence), very often in the direction of diminishment (ageing, sickness) and, finally, death. I shall return to the point shortly, but here point out that the domain of such passivities is precisely that where anthropologists are most likely to encounter the role of religious rituals – around birth, puberty, mating, sickness and death. It is precisely where nature makes its presence unavoidable within human life that ritual – the sacramental in a specifically religious sense – stakes its claim.

Here too we might add such basic human realities as eating and drinking, as did the Orthodox theologian Alexander Schmemann, who, in drawing attention to the sacramental possibilities of eating and drinking, brilliantly turned on its head Ludwig Feuerbach's dictum 'you are what you eat'. Feuerbach had meant by this that human beings were nothing but material beings, totally dependent on the material nourishment of food and drink, without which we would cease to be. Schmemann was not fazed by Feuerbach's claim, pointing out that, in the Bible, the instruction 'to eat of the earth' is one of the first words God speaks to Adam. Schmemann comments: 'Man must eat in order to live, he must take the world into his body and transform it into himself, into flesh and blood. He is indeed that which he eats, and the whole world is presented as one all-embracing banqueting table for man.'[12] But, he argues, it is wrong to conclude from this that man is a merely material being. Rather 'All that exists is God's gift to man, and it all exists to make God known to man, to make man's life communion with God. It is divine love made food, made life for man.'[13] Our natural hunger for food is a kind of preparation for something more: 'Man is a hungry being. But he is hungry for God. Behind all the hunger of our life is God.'[14]

Protestantism is generally regarded as less sacramentally orientated than either Catholicism or Orthodoxy, but one important modern Protestant theologian who had both a keen sense for the sacramental and acknowledged a profound kinship between his own thought and that of Teilhard was Paul Tillich.[15] Addressing the relationship between the two basic categories of Christian communication, word and sacrament, Tillich commented that this duality 'represent[s] the primordial phenomenon that reality is communicated either by the silent presence of the object as object or by the vocal self-expression of a subject to a subject'.[16] In this perspective 'the sacrament is older than the word',[17] Tillich says. At the same time, he insists that this is not to be understood in such a way as to imply that sacramentality is somehow a more 'primitive' communicative form, addressing only that part of us that is incapable of speech or free response. On the contrary, he says, sacraments, no less than words, also address the human being as spirit, that is, as a being endowed with thought and the power of decision. The word, he remarks, 'is implicit in the completely silent sacramental material . . . It cannot be without the word even if it remains voiceless.'[18] Sacramentality does not mean a form of communication that, as it were, seeps into our unconscious being. Sacramentality is a quality of well-formed, meaningful communication.

Tillich could not avoid being aware of a long-standing debate in and between the churches about the scope and definition of the sacraments. Conventionally, Catholicism has been regarded as the church of the sacraments and Protestantism as the church of the word. Whereas Catholicism allowed seven sacraments – baptism, confirmation, communion, penance, marriage, holy orders (i.e. the ordaining of bishops, priests and deacons) and extreme unction (the anointing of those preparing for death), Protestantism limited this to two, baptism and communion, since, it was claimed, these were the only rituals for which there existed an explicit instruction from Christ. While the two Protestant sacraments are thus defined in terms of what can be justified on the basis of the biblical word, the Catholic system seems to approach a more universal human pattern in which, as previously indicated, religious rituals come into play at just those moments in life where our conscious, rational existence finds itself invaded by natural processes that we are powerless to ward off. In such moments our freedom and rationality and, therefore, our humanity itself are, as it were, suspended, as, consequently, is our capacity for spiritual community. Tillich – addressing a chiefly Protestant readership – insists on what he calls 'the largest sense' of the sacramental, adding that, without this, 'sacramental activities in the narrower sense . . . lose their religious significance'.[19] There is no doubt that Tillich, rational Protestant that he was, saw the Reformation's repudiation of Catholic sacramentalism as involving a not inconsiderable religious loss. At the same time he is no less critical of a certain Catholic understanding of sacramentality summed up in the phrase *ex opere operato*, 'by the work the work is done' – the effectiveness of the ritual is guaranteed merely by the fact of its being performed by a duly authorized person. 'It is', Tillich states, 'important to draw the boundary line between the impact of a sacrament on the conscious through the unconscious self and magical techniques which influence the unconscious without the consent of the will.' If a sacramental act bypasses or attempts to bypass the centred personal being of the one to whom it communicates, then, Tillich says, it is 'a demonic distortion' and, he adds, 'every sacrament is in danger of becoming demonic'.[20] Which implies that sacramental, ritual or symbolic acts are immensely powerful, probably much more so than our conscious mind is at any one time aware of. Tillich, of course, wrote these words in the aftermath of the German experience of the 1930s and, as an active anti-Nazi, was painfully aware of the ways in which 'sacramental' ritual could be abused to bind a people together in a covenant with the kind of demonic powers that were at work in the Nazi phenomenon, as in the great Nuremberg rallies. However, a healthy awareness of the possible excesses of a sacramental orientation should not lead us to confound all forms of sacramentalism with their perversions. Unfortunately, Tillich thinks, this confusion is what happened historically in Protestantism, especially in those sectarian groups that reduced the sacramental mediation of the divine spirit to an absolute minimum, so that it became either a pure intellectualization or a pure moralization of the divine–human relationship.

In contrast to such a narrowing of the religious consciousness, Tillich advocated a rediscovery of the 'multidimensional unity of life',[21] which, in turn, meant that Protestants needed once more to become open to the power of the great symbols operative in humanity's own natural being and to allow these symbols to play an acknowledged part in their common religious life. It is therefore no coincidence that Tillich is also remembered today as the Protestant theologian who, more than any other, brought the arts back into mainstream Protestant theology. Equally significantly, he was also involved over a long period of time with the meaning of depth psychology (Freudian and Jungian psychoanalysis) for theology. Both in the arts and in the materials revealed by depth psychology, religion found itself once more faced with powerful symbols that had much to communicate, if only Christians did not insist on limiting this communication to what could be 'said'.

From this point of view, a certain 'Catholic' way of defining the sacraments, though obviously broader than conventional Protestantism, may, in fact, be no less limited and limiting, tying the idea of sacramentality to particular forms of church practice. What is important is not to be able to count how many sacraments there are but to become aware of the sacramental dimension of life as such, to experience the world and all that therein is as a divine communication. This is something much greater than both scriptural correctness and ecclesiastical definition. That such an approach is more than a sign of much twentieth-century theology's impatience with ecclesiastical discipline is indicated by David Brown, an Anglican theologian, who, in his recent book *God and Enchantment of Place*, shows that in the first thousand years of Christianity the term 'sacramental' did in fact have something like the much wider sense for which Tillich is appealing. It was only in the Middle Ages, he suggests, that the question as to the number of sacraments really forced its way onto the theological agenda, narrowing the meaning of the term 'sacrament' itself and setting the stage for the bitter Catholic/Protestant disputes of the Reformation era. Brown urges that we need to recapture something of the earlier breadth if we are to reanimate what is all too often the rather deathly state of Western Christendom. In his book he draws attention to such overlooked forms as landscape painting, architecture, dance and sport as providing opportunities to experience the sacramentality of the world – all media in which the spatial and bodily dimensions of being are very much to the fore and which much traditional Christian spirituality, with its emphasis on the culture of the soul at the expense of the body, would have regarded as 'merely' external or physical.[22]

It is striking that most of Brown's examples are, in fact, drawn from human culture. If nature speaks sacramentally to us, the condition of our bond with nature is such that we rarely, if ever, experience it 'in the raw'. Even a Shackleton, finding the face of God in only the most humanly uninhabitable landscapes of the planet, was also, at the same time, responding to a very culturally specific modelling of the relationship God–man–nature. Nature *can* become sacramental, but we must learn to see it that way. Or – which is to say the same thing differently – if in our experience of nature we believe that we encounter God, that experience and that encounter only become meaningful as a cultural act, as a word, a poem, an image, a symbolic act. This sounds more sophisticated than, perhaps, it should. All that is necessary is that I pick up the pine cone or the leaf and, for a moment, let it be the focus of my attention or, looking out at the stars, turn to my friend and, in a hushed voice, gasp 'Amazing!' With such actions and such words, nature becomes a part of culture, and culture itself is opened up to the currents and movements of nature.

This chiasm of nature and culture is beautifully illustrated in Andrei Tarkovsky's film *Solaris.* The central motif of the film, based very loosely on the novel of the same name by Stanisław Lem, is that the planet Solaris has the power to bring to life the dreams of those who come into its vicinity. This drives most of them mad or to suicide. For Kris Kelvin it provides an opportunity to relive his love for his wife Hari, who committed suicide after they had broken up. The new Hari is, in the expression familiar from Ridley Scott's *Bladerunner*, a replicant. Although she looks and, to some extent, acts like a human being, all she is 'really' is an externalized image of Kelvin's memory. However, the longer she is around, the more 'real' she becomes. In a pivotal scene she is left alone in the space station's library, and we follow her gaze as it falls on a painting of a winter scene by Breughel. The camera moves slowly backwards and forwards over the figures of the hunters and their dogs, the trees, birds and snows of the winter landscape, and the town with its huddled houses and busy streets. It is a picture of a world that Hari has never seen – yet, as she looks at it she (and, through her, we the viewers) seem to hear distant noises such as the barking of dogs, the cries of children and bells. Somehow the painting gives her a way into what she has never known. This empowers her to turn to the audience and declare that though she is not a human being, she is *like* a human being, for she too has entered into the dialogue between man and nature that we call culture and that is, for us, the concrete reality of 'the world'. Nature gives itself to us as culture: culture explains to us the meaning of nature.

Sacramental Revelation in an Age of Technology

This, however, hints at what is a very particular problem for us, inhabitants of a particular era that can, loosely, be referred to as that of globalized technology. For, despite the optimism of a Teilhard de Chardin, the social and technical complexity of contemporary life seem to have brought about a situation in which, far from culture revealing nature or nature giving itself in and as culture, nature has been pushed away to an almost impossible distance. We have experienced what many commentators refer to as 'the disenchantment of the world' and many of the great works of twentieth-century culture are predicated on just this loss. As one of many examples, and which has the merit of speaking both to high and to popular culture, think of the conclusion of Tolkien's *Lord of the Rings* trilogy, where (in the book – not, alas, in the film) the adventurers return to a land that has been disfigured by industry while the immortal elves merely pass through the Shire on their way to the islands in the west, where alone their songs of a beautiful and harmonious relationship between free, conscious beings and nature can be preserved. Already, at the threshold of the nineteenth century, Schiller touched a similar chord in lamenting the gods of Greece: 'What lives undyingly in song, in life must pass away,' he wrote. Culture, it seems, is permeated by nostalgia for a lost immediacy or plenitude.[23]

The idea of communication has been a guiding thread of this short course and it would be hard to deny that this technological world is, very much, a world of communication, a world in which the media of communication surpass those of any previous age with regard to complexity, rapidity and efficiency. The question – which should not be prejudged by calling it a problem – is whether communication of the kind that has become normative for us is or can be 'sacramental'. Can it still be communication that communicates the Word in and to world and, in doing so, communicates God? Or is it simply the play of layer upon layer of simulacra, media without a message?

In the face of such questions the works of high culture, of the cultural heritage from the Renaissance to the modern, are only ambiguously helpful. I have cited several works from this great tradition, from the poetry of Wordsworth through Van Gogh and on to Antony Gormley and other contemporaries. The problem, from our historically aware point of view, is that such works and the tradition they bear – whatever the authenticity of their origin in the creative passions of great artists – seem to be fatally compromised in the historical development that has brought us to just this point. 'Art' and 'culture' have themselves become domains of objectified value, 'resources' for a technically smart negotiation of successful living in the first decade of the twenty-first century. As an earlier, more humanist philosophy already saw, culture may simply be a repertoire of symbolic forms in which human consciousness explains itself to itself, and nothing more. If culture speaks of 'eternal values', then this is only a rhetorical inflation of what is really meant, namely, the universally human. But whatever the Christian doctrine of creation means, it means at least this: that there is something more; that in the creation and reception of culture we are not just talking to ourselves, but attending to and interpreting an act of communication, a self-communication delivered to us and bestowed upon us by one who communicates from beyond the relativities of culture.

It is, maybe, an exaggeration to say that the disenchantment of nature and the technologization of the human world have reached the point at which there is *no* possibility of culture serving as sacramental communication. There are contemporary works that aim at just such a kind of communication (and I have already cited Antony Gormley as one example of this) and there are, still, ways of experiencing the great works of the tradition that can break open the seals of the culture industry or of an exclusive academic discourse and allow them, once again, to say that 'more' that gives great works their greatness. When and where this happens, however, we seem to find ourselves swimming against a stream whose tide runs ever more powerfully in the direction of integrating culture into the market forces of a globalized technological society. In this situation it may be tactically appropriate to step back from the temptation of 'experiencing' a Van Gogh painting in the way in which we all know we are meant to, even though that experience may be genuine enough for the individual concerned. Instead, perhaps, we should linger with objects or events that lack the overdetermined cultural meanings of 'the great artists'.

What might that mean? One answer to this question is offered in a renowned meditation on a simple earthenware jug by the philosopher Martin Heidegger. The meditation is found in Heidegger's essay 'The Thing', and Heidegger begins by drawing attention to some of the problems generated by the technological character of contemporary reality. Among these problems is that of distance and nearness. The world is shrinking, Heidegger comments, yet this doesn't really seem to mean that we are getting any closer to each other. On the contrary, in a strange way, genuine nearness and real intimacy elude us as never before. Where television creates an illusion of intimate 'chat' in every living room, it actually disrupts the real conversations that we might otherwise have been having, offering only the staged 'spontaneity' of the studio instead. We feel we 'know' the host, he is as familiar to us as our friends and family, but, of course, all we really know is the image the host represents. As the title of Heidegger's essay indicates, all of this is tied up with the situation that, in a technological society, everything that exists exists only as a 'thing', something that we can know and manipulate or even replace in terms of a set of universal, calculable laws. As was mentioned in the first chapter, the modern hospital doctor no longer sees patients as personalities, whose illnesses have complex implications for the network of relationships that constitutes their life, but as mere 'things', bodies determined by the same processes that determine animals and even sub-organic entities. Such abstraction from the patient's life-world is, of course, necessary for the doctors' own mental survival and for the success of the medical science they practise. It is a necessary and, most people would say, a justified suspension of a more holistic way of looking at the human being. Nor does Heidegger want to say that we should just get rid of modern medicine, televisions or defence systems. The question is whether we are not in danger of losing the capacity for experiencing the world in any other way.

So, as a kind of experiment, Heidegger tries to think in a different way about the things with which we are surrounded, taking as an example a simple, empty, earthenware jug. Science, he suggests, cannot tell us what the jug 'really' is. From the point of view of science, it is entirely indifferent whether the jug is filled with water or with wine, whether it is to be used for slaking thirst, or to serve the guests at a banquet. What the jug means in being used is quite irrelevant to the scientific view of the thing. Heidegger's alternative is to take the opposite tack and to see the jug not in terms of its materials, dimensions or cubic capacity but as a vessel shaped and intended for what he calls 'the poured gift'.[24] Even the empty jug, he remarks, is what it is by virtue of its capacity to pour out its contents as a gift. But what is this gift and for what purpose and to whom is it to be given? It may, he says, be water or wine. Christians, familiar with the offering of the eucharistic gifts of bread and wine as 'the fruit of the earth and work of human hands', may find resonances of just this sacramental understanding of matter in Heidegger's developing line of thought:

> The spring stays on in the water of the gift. In the spring the rock dwells, and in the rock dwells the dark slumber of the earth, which receives the rain and dew of the sky. In the water of the spring

dwells the marriage of sky and earth. It stays in the wine given by the fruit of the vine, the fruit in which the earth's nourishment and the sky's sun are betrothed to one another. In the gift of water, in the gift of wine, sky and earth dwell. But the gift of the outpouring is what makes the jug a jug. In the jugness of the jug, sky and earth dwell.[25]

In other words, water is never 'just' a liquid to slake our thirst and wine is never 'just' a liquid used for intoxication: both, if we stop to think about it, presuppose that our own lives are, in a very deep sense, bound up with what one might call the planetary rhythms that take shape in rocks, earth, rain, growth, etc. – summed up by Heidegger in the two words, 'earth' and 'sky'. But this is not all. For we might also think about those to whom the gift of the pouring is to be given. Heidegger suggests two possibilities. The first is that they are 'mortals', human beings, for whom the gift might mean refreshment or conviviality. The second possibility is that the gift is to be poured out as a sacrificial offering for the gods or immortals. Naturally, Heidegger is aware that most modern people do not pour libations to the gods, but even for secular modern people the possibility of pouring the drink, the water or the wine, in a way that does not immediately serve some 'useful' function, remains. I can pour water from the jug just to see it run, 'wasting' it, if you like, but thereby also setting it apart from the profane everydayness of usefulness.

Heidegger now has four contexts of relationship in which to see the jugness of the jug: earth, sky, mortals and gods. In many of his later essays this 'fourfold' (the German term also means an agricultural enclosure, like the English 'fold') appears as offering a new framework in which to understand ourselves and our relation to the world. For seeing ourselves as the 'mortals' of this fourfold means seeing ourselves very differently from our more usual self-image as either the rational or the emotional subjects of knowledge or experience, standing over against the world and alternately acting upon it or being acted upon by it. It is no longer a question of 'Man' having to find his place in the cosmos and, still less, of 'Man' having dominion over the earth. For the mortals of this fourfold never exist at all apart from their relatedness to the earth and sky that sustain them, to the gods that inspire and limit them and to the mortality that permeates their own identity. 'I' am inseparable from the whole complex body of meanings and relations in which I live and move and have my being. 'The thing', as Heidegger sees it, is not to be seen simply as an object, out there 'in space', over against me, something to be used or known or something getting in my way. It is, rather, a potential focus of all those meanings and relations: everything I touch, everything with which I have to do, everything I allow really to come close to me can be such a focus, for in all the 'things' that make up my world, the basic relations of life take shape. In a way that technologically determined products cannot, these things give me a sense of being present in my world or of the world being a real presence to me.

'Real presence' is, of course, a word with powerful resonances in Christian history, and the question as to the real presence of Christ in the Eucharist has been one of the points of perennial conflict between different church traditions. John Macquarrie is one theologian who has taken Heidegger's meditations as inspiration for revisiting the idea of Christ's presence in the sacraments. The bread and wine of the Eucharist, he says, gather to themselves 'a considerable aura of meaning',[26] drawing the whole world of my life-experience into their light and, in doing so, also illuminating the 'human and personal' dimensions of that world.[27] Just as 'things' can communicate the presence of the whole body of 'the fourfold' without ceasing to be the simple things they are, so the particular 'things', the bread and wine, of the sacramental action do not need to cease being just things in order to communicate Christ to those who receive them.

However, I am not suggesting that we use Heidegger's meditation as a starting-point for rethinking the sacraments in a narrower sense but, rather, as a way of helping us see how the sacramentality of the world can come alive even under the conditions of an age of technology. And that larger sense of sacramentality, to repeat, is something essentially prior to sacraments in a narrower, churchy sense. If the world is incapable of being a sacrament of the divine presence, then it becomes extraordinarily hard to see how any particular ritual or liturgical actions could be sacramental. Nor is this a matter of thinking of the world as sacramental in relation to God the Creator, 'the Father' (as, I think, the popular imagination sees it), while the Church's sacraments communicate the presence of 'the Son'. Rather, if the world is sacramental, it is as the sacrament of the presence of the threefold life of God as Source, Word and Spirit to all those myriad creatures whose complex interconnection is, simply, the world.

These reflections on the idea of creation as a sacrament of the divine presence are no more than a sketch, and many questions are left unresolved. In each of the previous two chapters I drew attention to the fact that whether we are thinking of a purely human communication or of a divine–human communication we cannot escape the recognition that all our communicative practices and experiences are prone to distortion or subversion by our potential lack of good will, a lack made manifest in the kind of violence represented in Grünewald's 'Crucifixion'. Whatever else there is to be said about the world as we actually experience it, it would seem hard to claim that it is simply a transparent medium of divine self-communication. Everywhere we look, in nature as well as in human society, we seem to see violence, imperfection, suffering and futility. Tennyson's vision of 'nature red in tooth and claw' was already anticipated in Paul's allusion to a creation 'subject to frustration' and 'shackled to mortality' (Rom. 8.20), while even earlier the religion of the Vedas had portrayed the universe as an infinite chain of beings endlessly devouring each other in an unmitigated cycle of bloody sacrifice. Such questions apart – though we can scarcely shut them out for long – it could also be objected that, enticing as the idea of a sacramental cosmos might be, it is all rather abstract. Yes, we can wander off into the hills with Wordsworth and contemplate the beauties of nature in a quasi-religious way, and, yes, we can take time out from our science to ponder the mysteries of an everyday earthenware jug under the guidance of Heidegger. But what does any of this say to the real life of human beings, that is, the real life of history, society and work? How can the sacramental sense of the presence of God that we might find in the outward and visible grace of creation become a liberating, effectual and quite definite reality in the world?

These two questions – the question of evil as the failure of divine self-communication and the question of the social reality of what we might nevertheless still experience of God – come together in the question of time. For it is time that has provided human beings with their most powerful and most unconquerable argument for the irredeemable subjection of creation to change, decay and death and it is time that, as history, is itself the concrete shape of our common social reality.

4

The God in Time

The Fall

We have now several times been confronted with the clash between the beauty and splendour of the divine life as portrayed by Rublev, and the reality of the human condition laid bare in Grünewald's vision of the crucifixion. Again and again life makes us realize that no matter how passionately we might want the world to be a glorious God-revealing sacrament, it isn't. Even if we feel that we are hovering on the brink of realizing the dream, it never quite happens, or happens only in isolated moments of personal encounter or radiant beauty, which are fated to be reabsorbed into the ongoing chaos, confusion and ugliness of a world that is palpably not the kingdom of heaven and, all too often, scarcely recognizable as God's good creation.

Grünewald shows even the redeeming Word as despised and rejected of men, and where later, more sentimental ages, could speak of Jesus as the most beautiful of men, there is nothing beautiful about this Saviour. Such a work – or, simply, today's (any day's!) world news – suggests very strongly that if the divine is really to communicate itself to us, if we are really to have our lives transformed into a moving image of the divine conversation, then something more is needed than the kinds of revelations of 'something far more deeply interfused' that are offered in the epiphanies of God in nature or in the sacramental moments of reproduction and death. There seems not only to have been a catastrophic breakdown in communication between God and human beings and between human beings themselves, but serious reflection on the extent and implications of this breakdown suggests that it is not simply a matter of dealing with external obstacles: it is we ourselves who need to be changed. All of us. And we need something more than a simple conversion of the will that would transform our present bag of mixed motives into the constancy of a pure heart. The change needs to go deeper, to embrace the sensibilities, fears and desires that precede and shape both consciousness and will. *We* need to be changed: not just our ideas or our volitions but *we ourselves and what we want.* But if this is to happen there needs to be a closer, more direct, more urgent and more powerful communicative act than we have yet considered. Something that tells us not just that God exists or that God is the wise and benevolent orderer of the universe, nor even what it is we might become, but, more precisely, *how* we might actually become the beings we were created to be. The self-communication of God in the divine bliss of God's own life and in the beautiful and fearful geometry of creation needs to take a form that can make it humanly effective. There needs to be something that speaks in and to the dark regions of our fate and of our spirit, something that communicates through, or even *despite* our sometimes overwhelming experiences of futility, suffering and defeat, something that grips and breaks open such experiences from the inside out, restoring us – or even bringing us for the first time – to that place where we can receive the Word that calls us to be who we are as participants in the divine conversation.

It is questions such as these that are addressed in Christian teaching in the doctrines of the fall and redemption. It should immediately be said that these are, or should be, complementary, and it is especially important that the fall is never presented as an isolated theme, something that could hold the rest of the teaching hostage. For the very fact that it belongs to Christian doctrine means that we always encounter the fall in a context that is fundamentally determined as and by the communication of the Word that redeems. To see the human being as fallen is, in a sense, only really possible once we have entered the orbit of redemption. To speak of the phenomena of the human condition as fallen is already to have ventured that great act of hope that sees humanity as redeemable. These phenomena are not simply brute facts with which we have realistically to reckon but marks of a situation that not only should but can be transformed. If, as in some forms of secular humanism, we cling on to the language and metaphors of the fall but without setting these in the context of redemptive hope, then, as Jean-Paul Sartre candidly stated, our philosophy would indeed be a philosophy of despair.

With this proviso in mind, let it then be said: we are fallen, we are not as we were created to be, we have stepped out of the garden of nature into the open and boundless plain of history. Leaving behind a world and a life at one with itself, a life lived just as it came, in and for the moment and with no care for the morrow, human beings found themselves exposed to all the contingency and uncertainty of life in time, where survival meant struggle, labour and a collective organization that involved thinking, planning and – over millennia – the development of all the vast social, cultural and technical apparatus that is modern society. Even where life under such conditions is lucky enough to escape war, violence or the anomic rootlessness of urban living, it is inevitably subjected to the relentless pressure of constraints and demands that culminate in the more or less vocal sense that 'there must be more to life than this'.

Mircea Eliade, one of the twentieth century's most eminent theorists of religion, made extensive use of the distinction between sacred and profane ways of experiencing the world. In societies not yet touched by modernity it was or is the sacred that predominates. In these societies myth and ritual integrate the human experience of time into a cycle of growth and decay that ensures an ultimate sense of stability. Human beings who live within such societies are able to feel that they belong within the cosmic cycles of nature, whether these were understood simply in terms of the annual cycle of seasons or, on a larger scale, in terms of great sequences of cosmic time running across thousands of years, in which worlds and eons were born, decayed and reborn. Even within Christianity, in its pre-modern forms, history is, as it were, *contained* within the cycle of the liturgical year. In the modern world, however, human beings are exposed to the terror of history. Modern society is a society that has been stripped or that has stripped itself of what it believes is the illusion of a stable cosmic order, in which creation and dissolution follow one another with the same reliability as summer follows winter. Time has become historical and, therefore, uncertain. Life has been severed from the realm of sacred origins and now progresses into ever bleaker landscapes in which there is no promise of return to the plenitude of ancient times.[1]

Eliade is today largely regarded more as an inspirational than as a strictly social scientific thinker. Nevertheless, his ideas highlight what, for modern Christian thought, has been a crucial conjunction of themes: that the fall, however else we understand it, is tied up with our experience of time and history and that the question as to how we can overcome the evil unleashed by the fall is in some way inseparable from the challenge to find meaning in time, whether the time of history or, more modestly, the time of our own individual lives. For time, experienced without the cushion of belief in some eternally recurring renewal or restoration of the things that have grown old and decayed, seems to resemble nothing so much as a free fall into the utter, bottomless abyss of the future, a headlong tumble into annihilation in which whatever good we might achieve will be as surely obliterated as the harm we have done. 'Like water hurled from rock to rock, we plunge continually down into uncertainty!'[2] Can God's divine discourse still reach us in the rush of this endless collapse? Can God in any way be or be heard in time?

For modern Christian doctrine, taking its bearings from the historical cast of mind that is the inheritance of the nineteenth century, this question has to a large extent displaced the questions that lie behind many of the classical debates in doctrine, questions such as whether a divine nature can be conjoined with a human nature in some way that allows both to exist in a single person, or, in the language of popular devotion, whether God can come 'down' from heaven 'into' such a world as this. Instead of such questions, ultimately reflecting a spatialized view of the cosmos, modern theologians have asked more about what the revelation of God in time could mean, how such a revelation could be known and how it could serve to mediate God's presence to those who were not present at the actual historical moment of the saving events. Even when we accept that the divine presence has been communicated in Jesus Christ, the question could still be raised as to how that communication remains valid for us, 2,000 historical years and 2,000 cultural light-years away from his lifetime. The question seems challenging, but many modern theologians have been quick to point out that such a reformulation of the question of redemption in terms of history is itself close to the Bible's own way of picturing things.

As the Bible tells the tale, the expulsion of Adam and Eve from the Garden of Eden is followed by the beginning of a narrative, a history. In the first instance this is the history of the family of Adam and Eve themselves, and, later, of such more historical families as that of Abraham. In this history the Bible not only tracks the founding legends of one particular Semitic people – it also offers a wide-ranging commentary on historical existence as such. For where the life of paradise was a life without time, a dream-life not subjected to the logic of cause and effect, life outside the garden is a life lived under the conditions of time and historical causality. Such a life seems to be intrinsically prone to misunderstanding, conflict and injustice. As the human family fans out, developing into different tribes with mutually incomprehensible languages, customs and even gods, so competition over land, goods and women proliferates. Even within the families of this 'patriarchal era' of the biblical narrative, murderous disputes arise over inheritance and favours. History thus emerges as a process of endless dispersals and fragmentations that are followed by an equally endless series of attempts to reimpose unity within the tribe or between tribes. Let us note some of the main points of the story the Bible tells.

From Abraham's sometimes apparently aimless wanderings between Mesopotamia and Egypt, a coherent and continuous history gradually

takes shape until it becomes the history of a nation and a land. Charismatic leaders, warlords, prophets and kings rise and fall in constant
succession. Their attempts to found a unified and peaceful society
repeatedly founder, however. Sometimes the failure is ascribed to the
anarchic nature of a society in which each man does what is right in
his own eyes, an anarchy so extreme that not even the best of rulers
could succeed. This would seem to have been the situation in the
period of the so-called 'judges'. At other times, the blame is laid on
the violence of the rulers themselves, when they seek to secure unity
at the cost of grinding all opposition under heel and expropriating
the poor (as did Ahab and Jezebel) or uniting around idolatrous cults.
Those periods in which some kind of stability appeared – as in the
rule of David – seem like islands of calm in a turbulent ocean. But,
if we look closer, even these periods are soured by faction, rebellion
and injustice. On his death-bed, even King David enunciates a list of
scores he wants his successor to settle. The atmosphere is more that
of a Mafia movie than the last words of a King who was to be remembered as the supreme example of a ruler well-pleasing to God. The
problem of violence, far from being diminished by the people acquiring its own land, a royal dynasty and a dominant religious tradition,
resurfaces again and again with fearful consequences.

Indeed, the history depicted in the biblical narrative, from the time
of Cain and Abel through to the period of the Kings, offers plenti-
ful illustrations to René Girard's challenging thesis that the genesis
of human society is inextricably tied up with the phenomenon of
violence.[3] Though controversial, Girard's insights are so useful in
helping us see important connections between the world of the Bible
and our own time, that it is worth pausing to outline the main features
of his thought.

Girard's theory, which embraces social scientific, literary and theological perspectives, hinges on the recognition that what is distinctive about human beings is that, in comparison with other animals,
we are seriously underdetermined by our instincts. Our desires and
our behaviour are not so much instinctive as learned. The primary
means of such learning is not through planned instruction but, simply,
imitation. The child learns what is desirable, what is good to eat, to do
or to possess, etc. through internalizing what it sees in those who are
its most significant role models. But, Girard points out, this inevitably
leads in pretty short order to some intractable conflicts, as the child
and (in the first instance) parent each end up wanting the same thing.
Thus, whereas Freud's renowned Oedipus theory traces conflict
between father and son back to what Freud regards as the son's

instinctive sexual desire for the mother, Girard sees the same conflict but explains it not in terms of instinct but of learned desire. Thus, Girard is not tied – as Freud was – to a *sexual* theory of conflict and repression. Although sexuality remains an area of especially powerful desires and conflicts, the mechanism by which the role model through whom I learn my desires becomes the obstacle through which my fulfilling them is blocked is, in effect, universal.

All social relations are therefore potentially conflict laden, and it is all too easy for these conflicts to break out into the open. When they do so, society can very rapidly find itself plunging out of control towards an anarchic condition, the war of all against all. If this process was unhindered, social life would soon become impossible and humanity would regress to a sub-human condition of wretched and insurmountable strife. How, then, did stable societies emerge or re-establish themselves in the face of these chaotic forces? Girard's answer is disarmingly simple. They united behind the identification of one individual or subgroup as solely culpable for the general disorder. In a word, they chose a scapegoat. In identifying and destroying the scapegoat, a fractured society is able to reunify and, for a while at least, to find a certain peace. Girard thus sees the scapegoat sacrifice described in the Hebrew Bible as an especially clear ritualization of what is in fact a universal phenomenon of society. Only, as he argues, behind the merely ritual act of sending the scapegoat out into the wilderness lies a history of very real acts of scapegoating in which human beings, not animals, were expelled or collectively murdered.

This, Girard claims, is the original form of all sacrificial religion, which, by providing a ritualization of the collective murder, anticipates and satisfies the need that a real act of murderous scapegoating expresses. Ritual sacrifice thus becomes a focus of social unity. And yet, as he points out, neither the basic pattern of excessive mimetic desire, nor the tendency to respond by choosing a scapegoat, is thereby overcome. On the contrary, society itself learns through the sacrificial ritual that the way to deal with evil is, precisely, by sacrifice. The peace won by the ritualization of the founding act of violence is necessarily fragile, and a violent society is always at risk of reverting to type. And if, in the first instance, all of this is said of societies at a relatively early stage of historical development, the pattern is far from conquered in medieval and modern Western society, as the repeated murderous scapegoating of Jews and others only too tragically demonstrates. The basic attitude of looking for scapegoats needs to be overcome at a much deeper level than that accomplished by sublimating it into the form of religious ritual. Such sublimation can only ever be a palliative and, in its own way, perpetuates and even inculcates the mind-set of scapegoating.

Hope

Girard's theories have some interesting applications to the death of Jesus Christ, to which I shall return later. In the context of the prophetic history they illuminate some of the complex forces underlying the failure of Israelite society to overcome its own internal anarchic tendencies through sacrificial cultic worship. In any case, whether we agree with Girard or not, the story as told by the Bible testifies to a society prone to chronic fragmentation and internal violence. At the same time, within the larger order of ancient Near Eastern society, Israel itself seems often to have played the role of scapegoat among the nations, a people to be enslaved, expelled, conquered, exiled and humiliated. No wonder, then, that deeply aware of the impossibility of a return to the lost paradise of a pre-historical life, the prophets of Israel turned to the future, to the hope of a divine redemptive act that would not be a simple restoration of the past but a lifting-up of the people, with all its historical experience and in all its human reality, into a new order of things where the lion would lie down with the lamb and swords be beaten into ploughshares. Only a divine act could put an end to what would otherwise be an interminable history of failure and disappointment. In the development of prophecy there thus occurred a dramatic shift away from nostalgia for a lost paradise to hope for a new and better Jerusalem. Via the experience of the desert and the generations of wandering and exile, the dream of the garden became the vision of God's city. From the archetypal lament of the ancient world that 'we have seen the best of our times', a new sense arose that 'the best is yet to come'.

Yet even for the prophets themselves, the constant disappointment of these hopes, whether as a result of the people failing to heed their message and repent or because renewal movements begun in hope soon ended in disappointment and new injustices, meant an ever more risk-laden escalation of the stakes. Everything, it seemed, came to hang on a promise whose realization defied all experience. For wise men such as the author of Ecclesiastes, life in time could seem simply meaningless, while the great poet of the Book of Job gave unsurpassable voice to the sense that human purposes are doomed to frustration in the face of the inexplicable powers of overwhelming nature and violent humanity. In the period leading up to the emergence of the Christian movement, many were led to speculate that, given the lack of any clear message concerning the future to be gleaned from experience or even from Scripture, there must be a secret, hidden plan, accessible only to those few to whom God chose to reveal it.

This situation reaches its climax in texts such as that known as the Second Book of Esdras, in passages such as the dialogue between Esdras (supposedly a member of the exiled Israelite community in Babylon during the sixth century BC, although the text dates from much later) and the angel Uriel. In Chapter 3, Esdras summarizes the familiar biblical story from creation, through the patriarchs, the Exodus, the monarchy and down to the exile itself. But where in this history can one see any decisive sign that God will ensure the triumph of goodness? In the face of his own experience in Babylon, he says, 'my heart sank because I observed how you tolerate sinners and spare the godless, how you have destroyed your own people but preserved your enemies. You have given no indication to anyone how your ways are to be understood' (2 Esd. 3.29b-31a). Uriel replies by asserting the inappropriateness of mere mortals, such as Esdras, being able to measure God's purposes. He challenges Esdras to weigh a pound of fire, to measure a bushel of wind or – perhaps most significantly in terms of what I have been arguing about the interrelationship between the fall and time – to call back a day that has passed. If you cannot understand these 'things you have grown up with' (fire, wind and time), Uriel chides him, 'how can you with your limited mind grasp the way of the Most High?' (2 Esd. 4.11). Esdras, though incapable of answering, is not finished. 'Better never to have come into existence than be born into a world of evil and suffering we cannot explain!' he cries out despairingly (2 Esd. 4.12). Uriel comes back at him with a further parable illustrating the idea that some knowledge is necessarily reserved to God alone. But Esdras, like Jacob and Job, does not give up without a fight. '"But, my Lord, please tell me," I asked, " why have I been given the faculty of understanding? My question is not about the distant heavens, but about what happens every day before my eyes"' (2 Esd. 4.22–3). This time, Uriel does promise a better future, a future at which Esdras, if he lives long enough, will marvel. To which the tenacious Esdras replies 'But when ? How long have we to wait? Why are our lives short and miserable?' Assured that this better time is nearer than the past, Esdras still wants to know if he will live to see these days. 'If you ask me what signs will herald them,' Uriel replies, 'I can tell you in part. But the length of your own life I am not commissioned to tell you; of that I know nothing' (2 Esd. 4.52).

Uriel then proceeds to run through the signs that herald the end-times, so that Esdras can be assured that no matter how bad things get, God's purposes will yet be fulfilled. For the author, as for the book's first readers, these signs were not so much features of a distant future, as signs that could be discerned in the events of contemporary history. As in the Christian Book of Revelation, the visionary details provide a coded commentary on current affairs. Both works belong to a genre that is often referred to as 'apocalyptic' literature, a term that points to the motif of revealing or disclosing something that is otherwise hidden or concealed. An apocalyptic book is thus a book that reveals the divine secret behind the contrary appearance of a dark, violent and incipiently meaningless reality. It is important to hold on to this since in our times the term 'apocalyptic' (as in the movie *Apocalypse Now*) has come to mean something more like 'disastrous' or 'catastrophic'. Of course, the events described in apocalyptic literature are often extremely violent and catastrophic, since they deal with the decisive defeat of large and dark forces given over to the violent persecution of God's people. The idea of an apocalypse, however, is not primarily or, at least, not exclusively to do with the violence of the events of which it treats, but the revelation within these events of a divine purpose or presence and thus the assurance that God is with us *despite* everything that seems to speak to the contrary. Nor, while there is undoubtedly a predictive element in apocalyptic literature, is it exclusively about prediction in the sense in which this is understood by those readers who scan the pages of the Book of Revelation in order to find out the date when the world is going to end. Alongside the predictive element there is also an arguably more pressing concern for the present, for communicating the abiding presence of God in a situation that seems, to all appearance, godless. In the mirror of the apocalyptic imagination, peopled by angels and monsters and alive with events that defy easy conceptualization, the sufferings of the present are in this spirit reinterpreted as signs that God is nearer at hand than ever before. The world is no longer to be experienced as an overwhelming, undifferentiated reality, indifferent to human purposes, but shows itself to be a kind of dynamic, moving text that urgently and insistently communicates God's purpose and presence to those who know how to read it.

It is, inevitably, a matter of scholarly debate as to how far such apocalyptic speculation influenced Jesus and the early Christian movement. In the last hundred years or so there have been scholars who have made it pivotal to their understanding of Jesus' teaching and self-understanding, while others have effectively airbrushed it out of the picture. If, however, we suspend the question of its predictive function, there are aspects of apocalyptic thought that can usefully be used to highlight certain key elements in the Christian gospel.

I have emphasized the sign-character of these writings, and it is clear that the question of signs is of great concern to the gospel writers and, as they describe him, Jesus himself.

The Sign

Already in one of the most familiar stories of Jesus' birth, when the shepherds are told by the angel that the Messiah has been born in the city of David, they are also told 'This will be the sign for you: you will find a babe wrapped in swaddling clothes and lying in a manger' (Luke 2.12). The sheer familiarity of this text probably lures us into overlooking just what an odd formulation this is. Why didn't the angel just say that the Messiah who has been born *is* the baby wrapped in swaddling clothes, etc.? There's no doubt that the shepherds are meant to know that this is so, since Luke's Gospel clearly identifies Jesus as 'the Messiah, the Lord'. Why, then, say that the baby is simply a 'sign' of the truth of the message that the Messiah has been born? A strange sort of duplication seems to be taking place, in which the baby is both *the Messiah* and *a sign of* the Messiah's coming. But the picture is complicated further if we add in the angelic words spoken to Joseph, as recorded in Matthew's Gospel: that Mary's pregnancy is the fulfilment of the prophetic word: 'A virgin will conceive and bear a son and he shall be called Emmanuel' (Mt. 1.23). This, in turn, is a reference back to Isaiah 7.14, where the birth of the child to the virgin (or, as the translation of Isaiah sometimes has it, young woman) is also called 'a sign' that God will turn back the enemies of King Ahaz.

From these simple narratives we thus have a structure in which the simple event of the birth – the baby wrapped in swaddling clothes and lying in a manger – becomes, in Luke, a sign and, in Matthew, is explained in terms of another 'sign', the sign of the young woman who was a contemporary of Isaiah, and who gave birth to her child 700 years previously. The transformation of this past event into a sign of the birth of the Messiah who is Jesus is underlined when, as the dialogue with Joseph suggests (and as Christian piety too has often implied), the 'Emmanuel' (literally God-with-us) of Isaiah's prophecy is used as if it were an actual name for Jesus. Whether in Luke or in Matthew, there seems to be a certain kind of circularity in play, as if (in the case of Luke) the Christ was a sign of himself or (in Matthew) he is understood as a kind of higher-level repetition of the sign-event of the birth of Emmanuel. But such duplications are not the result of a failure in logic. Rather, they are the manifestation of a communicative situation in which words and events function at a variety of interacting levels and in a variety of ways as 'signs', taking the term to mean simply the form in which the act of communication finds expression. The signs speak, and speak only, to those who are already in the orbit of the communicative event that the signs articulate. What one theorist has called the 'semiosphere', a system of mutually defining signs, is open only to those who have an existential interest in what is at issue in the act of communication. Putting it more simply, the 'meaning' of the babe wrapped in swaddling clothes, embedded as it is in a system of cross-referring signs, is 'meaningful' only for those who are open to the whole discourse concerning Messianic hope that links the texts of Luke, Matthew and Isaiah, in other words, those who are looking for salvation from God. What is at issue is not that such and such a baby has been born in such and such a place and that this baby is the Messiah, as if this were an assertion of the kind that 'There is a man called Tony Blair residing at Number 10, Downing Street, and he is the Prime Minister of the United Kingdom.' This would make the announcement of the birth into a string of propositions along the lines of 'There is a child called Jesus who has been born at Bethlehem and he is the Messiah' and suggest that each of the 'facts' thus presented could be checked out and validated. But this would be to read the angel's message merely as a matter of information, and, whether the facts were provable or not, would obscure the more important point that God is here and now offering a sign of God's sovereign presence with and in the midst of the expectant people, a message confirming the need and legitimacy of the absolute hope that, in Israel, finds its focus in the Messiah. For 'being the Messiah' is not something that could be proved or disproved in the way that a pretender to the Russian throne might, in principle, be able to prove that he or she was descended from the Princess Anastasia who somehow escaped the massacre of her family. Neither the Gospels nor the prophetic words on which they draw 'prove' anything about the baby in these terms. Rather, the question is how to interpret the sign, the communicative event or word that the baby *is*.

This theme of the sign-character of the one born at Bethlehem does not end with the closing of the infancy narratives, and the way in which Jesus is to be regarded as a sign is indicated in a variety of ways in the Gospels. One of the most instructive is the way in which he responds to the various people who ask him for 'a sign', whether they are those who are, perhaps, inclined to accept him but, in the absence of an unambiguous sign, hesitate to do so, or whether they are those who do not believe that he can, in fact, give them the sign they demand. A variety of responses are recorded, the bluntest being that found in Mark – 'Why does this generation ask for a sign? Truly I tell you: no sign shall be given to this generation' (Mark 8.12). Elsewhere, the responses are more indirect, yet they converge on a single, simple, yet mysterious answer: that Jesus himself is the sign, the message that God is with them in their affliction. In Matthew (twice) and in Luke (once), he declares that the only sign that will be given to such an 'evil generation' is the 'sign of Jonah', a sign that Jesus himself interprets in terms of Jonah's three-day sojourn in the whale prefiguring his own ('the Son of Man's') burial and resurrection. The meaning of this sign, then, is, simply, himself, or, more precisely, what God will work in him. Such a 'sign of Jonah' might, as many Christians have argued, seem pretty conclusive. What could be more persuasive than a death followed by a resurrection? But such a sign, since it can only be proclaimed as the matter of human testimony, is not, finally, a 'proof', if we understand it in the light of the conclusion of the parable of the rich man and Lazarus, where Jesus himself remarks, that if people will not believe on the basis of the Scriptures, 'they will pay no heed even if someone should rise from the dead' (Luke 16.31).

In the following chapter of Luke, Jesus denies that the kingdom of God is coming with signs such as those explained to Esdras by Uriel: 'You cannot say "Look, here it is," or "There it is!"' he says, 'For the kingdom of God is among you.' Although these last words have given rise to widely differing interpretations in Christian history (especially in the form 'the kingdom of God is within you'), they seem to be pointing to the way in which the kingdom of God is even now being made present in Jesus' own ministry. Signs are not to be taken as mere pointers to things that can be evaluated independently of our readiness to relate to what they are communicating.

John's Gospel gives particular weight to the category of signs, especially with reference to Jesus' miracles. But to treat the miracles as signs is something different again from seeing them as 'proofs', as when Christians argue that the miracles 'prove' Jesus to have been the Messiah or the Son of God. A sign is not a proof. It points beyond itself to an offered relationship and suggests an interpretation of what is happening that the viewer or reader is free to accept or reject. Here in John's Gospel the miracles are indeed external signs of a quite powerful kind but they are only meaningful when brought into connection with Jesus himself. This is the connection that makes sense of the otherwise rather weirdly disjointed sequence of events and dialogues in John 6. Following on the miraculous feeding of the multitude, the crowds follow Jesus and ask him for a sign (though surely, readers find themselves asking, they have just been given one in the miraculous feeding itself). They remind Jesus of the bread that Moses gave the Israelites in the desert, a 'sign' that God was with him. But, again, Jesus turns the question into a question about himself. '"I am the bread of life,"' he tells them. The miraculous sign is, as it were, only the outer husk of the true sign, the Christ himself, in whom all that the Father has to give is already being offered to those who believe. It is not that the miracles are the signs that prove or explain who Jesus is: he is the sign without which the miracles remain unintelligible. To follow the way pointed to by the sign is, as Jesus will expound at length in the farewell address recorded by John, to enter into the love in which the Father and the Son are themselves united, to find oneself opened up to the present reality of the divine love. There is, in other words, nothing coercive, no 'proof', but simply and solely an invitation, an offer, that opens up a possibility for believing in the presence, the claim, the empowerment and the consolation of God's being here and being now.

In focusing on the idea of 'sign' as a key with which to interpret what happened in the coming of Jesus Christ I am, of course, taking my cue from the guiding thread of this short course, namely, that doctrine is to be understood as teaching, as a dynamic communicative event or practice. And the idea of a 'sign' belongs naturally in such a horizon. At the same time it has clear connections with other terms that have recently played a significant role in thinking about the doctrine of Christ. The word itself, for those who remember the definition of sacrament given in the old catechism as 'an outward and visible sign of an inward and spiritual grace', dovetails into the idea of sacrament and sacramentality we have already explored at some length. The idea of Christ as the 'sacrament of the encounter with God' was central to the early Christological thought of the Catholic theologian Edward Schillebeeckx.[4] Schillebeeckx also allows that one can justly speak of a pre-Christian sacramentality, which, he argues, is brought to focus and fulfilment in Christ. And, certainly, I would wish to affirm that everything said in the previous chapter about the sacrament of creation could be re-said more intensely, more inwardly and more historically about the way in which Christ as 'sign' sacramentally makes present the saving divine love.

Another term, overlapping both 'sign' and 'sacrament' in theological usage is 'symbol'. This has recently been the central theme of a major study in Christology by another Catholic theologian, Roger Haight. The core of Haight's argument is to see Jesus, precisely, as the symbol of God. In terms similar to those in which I have just written about signs, Haight says of symbols that 'The idea of a symbol is essentially tensive, dynamic, and dialectical; a symbol mediates something other than itself by drawing or leading beyond itself to a deeper or higher truth.' And, he adds, 'Symbols do not provide objective information about God; but symbols draw human consciousness and life into a deeper world of encounter with transcendent reality.'[5] Haight also acknowledges the proximity of the ideas of symbol and sacrament. However, as he sees it, the idea of sacrament fits better with a theology from above and that of symbol with a theology from below, since 'sacrament' presupposes that we are thinking of how God communicates Godself to human beings more than of how human experience can become open to God. Yet if, as I have argued, sacramental experience is integral to our very experience of the world, this distinction is really only one of definition and Haight's downplaying of the idea of sacrament assumes a very particular view of sacramentality.

Tillich too made symbol central to his theology. All religious language, he insisted, was essentially symbolic. But what particularly engages Tillich is (again) the idea that symbols are not primarily about the communication of information. Symbols, he wrote, communicate the power of that which they are symbols of and, in doing so, enable us to participate in that power. Signs, according to Tillich, stand in a merely external relation to that which they signify. 'The sign can be changed arbitrarily according to the demands of expediency,' he writes, 'but the symbol grows and dies according to the correlation between that which is symbolised and the persons who receive it as a symbol.'[6] However, if we take seriously the idea of the semiosphere, that signs mean what they mean only as parts of a whole system of cross-referring signs (as in Matthew's reference to Isaiah's prophecy of the birth of Emmanuel), then Tillich overstates his case and the 'sign' too can be used to articulate the relationship between what is signified 'and the persons who receive it'. Usage partially supports Tillich, it might be said, in that when we speak of a sign and a thing signified we spontaneously picture two quite distinct kinds of things, a mental event on the one hand and a reality on the other. Yet if the term 'sign' does imply an element of distance, that may not be inappropriate where what is being communicated is not a relationship between a person and, say, 'Being', but a relationship between persons, each of whom stands within the circle of their own freedom. The term 'sign' allows both for relationship, but also, within that, for the mutual freedom of those to be related. A sign does not compel but calls for interpretation and, in the act of interpretation, for decision. In these terms, the very indeterminacy of the sign and the fact that it does not, as the symbol does, 'contain' its own meaning makes it more appropriate for the communication of personal reality.

The Sign of Contradiction

Yet there is something unsatisfying or, at best, ambiguous about this idea of 'signs'. To start with, it seems to leave it to the reader to interpret it as best he or she may. Even in John's Gospel, the apparently invincible evidence of the signs is presented as having been ultimately inadequate. Only those who know how to read the signs understand them. To the rest they say nothing. But, to compound matters, some of the signs offered by the Gospels are downright contradictory. Jesus speaks repeatedly in John's Gospel of 'glory', yet what he calls the hour of his own glorification is nothing other than the crucifixion itself. A strange kind of glorification in any theology! In the face of such signs, it seems to be very much a matter of 'If you have ears to hear, then hear' (Mark 4.23). Are we not being invited simply to take a leap into the dark? And, no matter how beautifully we depict the glories of the divine dance that opens up for us on the far side of such a leap, and no matter how far those glories are corroborated by the ethical glories of Christian living, does not such an either/or inevitably carry with it the possibility of offence?

That, as we have seen, was Kierkegaard's conclusion in reflecting on the category 'the sign of contradiction' and it will perhaps be helpful at this point to return to the New Testament source of this expression. This is found in Luke 2, where the evangelist tells the story of how, when taking the infant Jesus to the Temple to offer the accustomed thank-offering for the birth of a boy-child, Mary and Joseph were greeted by the old man Simeon. Having spoken his own word of thanks to God for allowing him to live to see the long-awaited Messiah, Simeon next turns to Mary '"This child is destined to be a sign that is rejected; and you too will be pierced to the heart. Many in Israel will stand or fall because of him: and so the secret thoughts of many will be laid bare"' (Luke 2.34–5). It is the words translated here as 'a sign that is rejected' that lie behind the Kierkegaardian expression 'a sign of contradiction'. Whatever liberties Kierkegaard may have taken with the text in the development of his own ideas of a 'sign of contradiction', he shares three insights with Luke: (1) that the sign-character of the child is tied up with his rejection and thus with his death, the ultimate consequence of his being rejected; (2) that, qua sign, this child is not some kind of lapel-badge that speaks a simple, direct language that all can understand, otherwise it would not have been possible for anyone to have mistaken who he was and to have spoken against him as they did; and (3) that the interpretation of the sign is interdependent with the self-knowledge, the revelation of the secrets of the hearts, of the interpreters. Even considered as a sign, the Christ-child is not the simple revelation of divine truth, but the communication of God's mysterious presence in a form that is essentially ambiguous and that can only be truly understood when we really, really want the self-knowledge that the God-relationship bestows.

As we have seen, it was not only the teasing indirectness of his parables, but the ambiguity of the sign that he was in himself that confronted Jesus' hearers with the challenging 'If you have ears to hear, then hear.' The clear implication of this is that our ability to read the sign that Jesus is, will not just depend on some kind of skill in decoding the words of religious teachers and prophets, but will much more depend on our readiness to allow our own presuppositions, the secrets of our own hearts, to be brought to light. The possibility of an affirmative response will itself be dependent on the openness of the recipient of the message to believe, for example, that God *can* be with us despite and in the midst of everything that darkens the outer and inner worlds. The cynic, the sceptic, the one in despair, the advocate of *Realpolitik*, the apostles of unrestricted self-assertion and the addicts of self-gratification will find their refusal to believe fully justified by the sheer inanity of the claim that this world *could* be lived in as if it were an outpost of heaven, never mind the effrontery of the claim that it could become so through accepting this one, particular man as the 'Sign' of God-with-us. At this point, in the face of this claim, believing would, minimally, require confronting not only 'the evidence' but whatever it is in ourselves that would hold us back from such an offer, whoever offered it, and, therefore, confronting that in ourselves which we are not yet ready to renounce, to conquer or to transform for the sake of any possible heaven. What Simeon called 'the light that gives light to the gentiles' is also a light of self-knowledge. Not, as we might be tempted to think, because it penetrates the dark field of our subconscious motivations like the harsh light of an interrogation room. Not because it forces us to see the things we'd rather not see. That, in New Testament terms, would be to think of it as 'Law', as the merciless exposure of weakness, obstinacy or defiance. Rather, it is its very lack of definition, its mysterious indeterminacy, which results in our being able to make of it what we will and, as with an ink-blot test, our response reveals much, perhaps too much, about the real nature of our desires. Human hearts being what they are, many, understandably enough, prefer the darkness. As a sign communicating the possibility of knowing God in our lives, this sign, the sign of Jonah, the sign of contradiction, is not simply a proclamation, nor even an invitation or offer, as it is often described (and as I have been describing it here). It is also a question, a question we must, in the first instance, ask ourselves.

But this is not to make the gospel merely academic, merely the posing of a question to be reflected on at philosophical leisure. In his poem 'Well?' the First World War padre and poet, Geoffrey Studdert-Kennedy, portrays a soldier musing on the mysteries of the Last Judgement.[7] The soldier finds the blustering of his padre incredible. The padre's God seems to be overly preoccupied with such trivia as swearing, for which, it seems, a man may be sent to everlasting damnation. The soldier falls asleep and dreams. In his dream he has died, but, as opposed to what the padre taught, there is no Great White Throne, no judge. There is only the memory of his life, the good, the bad and the ugly all passing before him in succession. But, as he watches, he becomes aware that he too is being watched by a face he cannot describe, ' 'Twere all men's face yet no man's face'. And, silently, the soldier becomes aware that the true face of each person he had hurt or mistreated in his life, including a prostitute he had used, is 'his' face. Even so, there is no word of condemnation, only the question, 'Well?' But such an invitation to self-knowledge is almost more than the soldier can bear. 'And boys,' he concludes,

I'd sooner frizzle up,
I' the flames of a burnin' 'Ell,
Than stand and look into 'Is face,
And 'ear 'Is voice say – *'Well?'*

In the face of this silent, questioning look, the only possible response is transformation of life. Conversely, it is only a short step from not being ready for the possibility of self-knowledge to which the question points to the rejection of the one – anyone – who poses it. The passion of the Christ is already implicit in the sign to which the angel directed the shepherds' steps, the sign that Simeon recognizes in the infant brought like any other for the customary thanksgiving.

We have several times now seen that rejection figured, perhaps definitively for the Western Christian tradition, in Grünewald's painting of the crucifixion. For Christians, the crucifixion remains, and always will remain, the unequalled expression of what it means to refuse God's constant self-communication as faith and hope and love to the creature. It was, as the Muslim novelist M. Khamel Hussein has described it, 'a decision to crucify the human conscience and extinguish its light', a decision which, as he also comments, was not the particular crime of those then living, but an event that makes all of us potentially 'contemporaries of that memorable day'.[8] Yet, no less importantly, the crucifixion is not simply the outcome of human beings' refusal of the offered communication of self-knowledge and the possibilities for creative living flowing from that self-knowledge. For those who see in it the sign of faith, it is also a further and decisive communication of such self-knowledge and such possibilities. Even as we gaze upon the desolation of the cross it is not, for faith, too late. It may be the last moment, but, nevertheless, in the face of the cross, there is still time. The offer is still being made. The world is not yet closed to hope.

Here the logic of the 'sign of contradiction' reaches its most intense. If a leap of faith motivated solely by readiness to trust an offered word about a kingdom in which forgiveness and reconciliation count for more than the experienced harshness of the world is already likely to seem absurd, what can be made of a 'sign' of God's being with us that looks more like a sign of the utter and endless absence or simple non-existence of any good Creator? No wonder that Paul predicted that his message would be received as if it were foolish or scandalous, making sense neither to the demands of rationality nor the high standards of a purely ethical religion. Such a sign does not in any obvious way 'explain' the how or why of evil and salvation, but to those who have ears to hear what lies concealed in ambiguity and mystery it can still speak the word that redeems and inspire them to seek the overcoming of sin's work in their lives.

Of course, sin too is often no less ambiguous than the divine Word. If sin always and everywhere showed its true face, there'd surely be no problem with it. But as Jewish and Christian tradition have long maintained, deception and lies are the devil's primary character traits! If we were to see a crucifixion, we'd know, wouldn't we, that something had gone wrong, that there had to be another way. But, as history shows, we don't even see crucifixions for what they are. We see them as something else, as collateral damage, rough justice, the price of progress, or simply tragic events we can neither comprehend nor control. Albert Speer, one of Hitler's inner circle and one of the few Nazi leaders subsequently to express remorse for his involvement in the crimes of the Third Reich, perceptively remarked that the German electorate did not vote for Adolf Hitler because they regarded him as evil, but because they regarded him as supremely good. We might also understand Hannah Arendt's thesis concerning 'the banality of evil' in similar terms – that people such as the war criminal Adolf Eichmann were not 'monsters' set upon a course of coolly chosen murderous evil. Rather, they were fairly average middle managers

who slipped into doing what they did for the same sorts of motivations and opportunistic career decisions that are in play in most people's lives. The moment when the good makes its claim on our hearts
and consciences is thus subtly obscured in the complex chiaroscuro
that allows even a Hitler to appear as a redeeming saviour and an
Eichmann to think of himself as merely a civil servant doing his duty.
And, of course, when, as it usually is, crime is less extreme than the
crimes for which the Third Reich will for ever be remembered, the
shading and the nuances are still harder to read.

If we were, truly, to be faced by one who, in himself, had become free
of the resentments and furies – Girard's mimetic rivalry! – that hold us
back from real goodness, would we be able even to recognize such a
one? The disturbing possibility that we might not has been unforgetta-
bly worked out for modern times in Dostoevsky's novel *The Idiot*. Here,
in the central character of the novel, one Prince Myshkin, Dostoevsky
attempted to portray a perfectly good man. The Prince arrives in St
Petersburg from abroad, where he has been recovering from a con-
genital 'idiocy' (the exact nature of the ailment is not specified, though
it is associated with epilepsy). He is a man without malice or guile, a
man who sees the good in the contemporary equivalents of the tax-
gatherers, harlots and sinners that people the pages of the Gospels. He
judges no one, but is ready to offer help even to those who slander and
abuse him. Yet, far from converting those around him to his view of
life, his presence only catalyzes the complex set of destructive relationships in which the other main characters are entangled. Even when
they acknowledge his innocence, they take no steps to make it their
own. The result is that he is not only powerless to prevent a tragic
denouement, but his presence itself plays a part in the unhappy chain
of events leading to the devastating final murder scene. The Prince's
goodness counts for nothing in a world given over to sexual power
play, social ambition, the ruthless pursuit of wealth and with the
constant chorus of argumentative drunks in the background.

Yet, for those who have ears to hear, the Word is, nevertheless,
spoken; and even if men love darkness before the light, the light
shines still in the darkness. Here is the paradox, the absurdity of
Jesus, a crucified first-century prophet, healer or wise man, whose
earthly life is so fragmentarily recorded that scholars can interpret
it in innumerable and even incompatible ways, being believed on as
the Word who can assure us of God-with-us in all extremities of the
human condition. Strangely, it had to be as ambiguous as this if it was
to be in freedom that we became hearers of the Word. For only as free
hearers of the Word could we be free respondents, free participants in

the dance-like discourse of the divine life that spirals infinitely from glory to glory.

To construe the redemptive activity of Jesus in this way is in accord with many strong lines of Christian tradition. Yet it also seems to leave out or merely to brush against several points that many would regard as absolutely central in any exposition of Christian doctrine. For speaking of Jesus as the 'sign' by, in and through which we can experience the communication of God's presence in a world of suffering and sin would seem to fall far short of 'classical' Christian definitions of him as the incarnation of the second person of the Trinity, the divine Word or Logos 'by whom all things were made'. Nor have I said anything about the atonement, the way in which his death came to be regarded as a 'sacrifice for sin', the blood that washes away our transgressions. And, similarly, I have not discussed, though I have alluded to, the resurrection. Yet these points – the doctrines of Christ's transcendent identity as the only-begotten Son of God, his incarnation, the atonement and the resurrection – would generally be taken as pivotal in an account of Christian doctrine. In turning now to address them, we shall see that, in fact, we have already established a framework that allows us to see both why they became important foci of teaching and how they can inform Christian communication today. If my argument is not uncontroversial, I am sure that even those who might disagree with my interpretation would also wish to emphasize that we are moving into a territory where words, images and concepts crumble in our hands, where our desire to express only what is helpful to those of good will is constantly undermined by our own participation in the 'structures of destruction', and where the decisive move 'passes all understanding'.

Debated Points

I have spoken of what happened in Jesus as being the occurrence of a human life that both its contemporaries and we who come after experience as a 'sign', draws us into understanding our lives as participating in the divine life and that, as the sole condition of this transformation, requires of us the readiness to accept the self-knowledge it also discloses. Yet it could seem that in all of this Jesus Christ was being treated as no more than the prophet or apostle of the divine Word, not himself divine. But how meaningful is this distinction? If we take seriously the dynamic model of the divine life sketched in Chapter 2, then the clear-cut distinctions between divine transcendence, the ongoing process of creation and the promise of a completed redemption in which God will be all in all, then it is no long a matter of 'here God – there humanity'. Rather, there is no point at which we can look at ourselves and be unable to find some trace, some echo of the divine discourse out of whose wisdom we came to be; equally, there is no point within what we can come to know of God where the steadfast loving-kindness towards the creature is absent. Our existence is always, at some level, 'for God', while God's life is always, in some sense, 'for us'. And if there is, as there surely must be, a mystery in the divine life that our minds can never fathom, then it is a mystery in which our attempts to distinguish between this and that person of the Trinity will also collapse into babble.

In being the bearer of the divine self-communication to human beings, then, Jesus (1) really is that, but (2) in being what and as he is, he also brings to fulfilment what is our own most wondrous human possibility – to be, to live, as friends, as children, as intimates of God. 'The glory which you gave me I have given to them, that they may be one, as we are one; I in them and you in me, may they be perfectly one,' says Jesus in St John's Gospel (John 17.21–2), while Paul speaks of God willing all he calls 'to share the likeness of his Son, so that he might be the first among a large family of brothers' (Rom. 8.29) or, as he puts it elsewhere 'we are being transformed into his likeness with ever-increasing glory, through the power of the Lord who is the Spirit' (2 Cor. 3.18). All of which, we remember, is communicated under the sign of contradiction, the revelation of a glory concealed in rejection and crucifixion. In this respect it is telling that what is often taken as the most characteristic revelation of Jesus' intimacy with God, his use of the 'Abba-Father' form of address, is, on the one hand, most clearly testified in his own prayer of agony and doubt in the garden of Gethsemane and, on the other, is spoken of by Paul as the prayer that, through the Spirit, each Christian may make their own (Rom. 8.15). Even in the moment of maximum fear we are able to say the prayer that frees us from 'a spirit of slavery' to the experience 'that we are God's children, and if children, then heirs, heirs of God and fellow-heirs with Christ' (Rom. 8.16–17).

Even so, it might be objected, if this is our destiny too, then it is ours only in a secondary, derived way, on the basis of election, grace, forgiveness and adoption. It is not, as it was for him, a birthright. We may become taken up into the divine discourse, but he has always been in on it. But what does such a distinction mean this side of the 180° turn in our understanding of creation that is most potently, if counter-intuitively, signalled by Teilhard's image of Christ as the

Omega-Point? If we have once taken to heart the realization that creation was not something that happened once, long ago, in the beginning, but is what it is only as the total process of cosmic and human
becoming, then to speak of Christ as having existed 'before all worlds'
is not to be taken in the sense of some temporal priority but as a sign
that the God-relationship offered in him goes, so to speak 'all the way
down', that what we receive in receiving his Word is 'the real thing',
an initiation into a love that is truly divine, truly infinite, truly the
love from which nothing in heaven and earth can separate us (Rom.
8.38–9), that there is no hidden, wrathful face of God underlying the
mask of love shown in Christ.

We can come at the question from another angle by noting that the
very claim that it is by following this 'sign of contradiction' that we
are welcomed into the divine life must itself affect our understanding of that divine life itself. In Chapter 2, I used Rublev's Holy Trinity icon to sketch a theology of divine glory, speaking as if we did
not have to check every word against the observed realities of time
and history. Even if I had the painterly skills of a Rublev or the poetic
skills of a Charles Wesley, however, the vision of heavenly glory I
would be able to create would be wholly inadequate. And it would
be inadequate for at least two reasons. First, because it would not be
beautiful enough. Even Rublev's painting is not – quite – beautiful
enough. But, second, it could only be a kind of thought-experiment, a
hypothetical projection. For, in fact, we have no possible knowledge
of a heavenly reality that is blissfully unaffected by the traumas we
experience 'here below'. In terms of my experimental theology 'from
above', it seemed almost as if Grünewald's Isenheim altarpiece was a
counter-argument to Rublev's image of Trinitarian circumincession,
almost as if the crucifixion 'disproved' the vision offered by the icon.
If, however, we take seriously the claim that Jesus the Christ is the sign
of contradiction who invites us to the heavenly banquet, then we have,
somehow, to see both pictures together in a kind of double-exposure
or superimposition. The reality of the divine life is misconceived,
if it is conceived only in terms of a theology of glory, as a beautiful
ideal that then, somehow, has to be brought into connection with the
world as we know it. It is rather as if the crucifixion were, somehow,
taken into the Trinity; as if the Trinity were, somehow, revealed in the
crucifixion.

But in what way 'in' the crucifixion?

This question brings us to the question of atonement. From the
earliest days a major theme of Christian faith and devotion has been
focused on seeing the crucifixion of Jesus not as a terrible tragedy, the

inexplicable rejection of God's chosen one, but as the outworking of a divine plan. There have been different versions of this. One early theory was that humanity was in some way held prisoner by the devil, who, however, agreed to let us go on being given God's own Son as ransom. Only what the devil didn't realize was that he only had jurisdiction over sinners. Jesus being sinless, the devil couldn't keep him and, in this way, was completely outwitted, as proved by Jesus rising from the dead (the realm of Satan). A well-known allegorization of this form of the ransom theory of atonement is found in C. S. Lewis's children's story *The Lion, the Witch and the Wardrobe*. Another version, associated with the early medieval Archbishop of Canterbury Anselm, portrays God as resembling a feudal lord whose honour has been outraged by the disobedience of human beings. He longs to forgive us, but simply to do so without further ado would be for him to dishonour himself, by ignoring his own sense of justice, the justice that makes him God. Unfortunately, we are now so degenerate, that we cannot ourselves give satisfaction (in societies governed by codes of honour, only equals can, for example, engage in duels). Therefore only one who was God's own equal could make the required satisfaction by suffering the penalty due to God's justice. This happens in the death of Jesus, who, as God's Son, had the right to do so:

> There was no other good enough
> To pay the price of sin,
> He only could unlock the gate
> Of heav'n and let us in.

Karl Barth, one of the twentieth century's most vigorous proponents of a substitutionary understanding of atonement (where Jesus acts as substitute for us, doing what we cannot do), summed up and reformulated the Anselmian view in the description of what happened in the atonement as 'The judge judged in our place'.[9]

Such an understanding of the saving efficacy of Jesus' death will often be cast in the language and imagery of sacrifice. Where the sacrifices described in the Old Testament or found in other religious systems attempt to atone for human sins, only this sacrifice is really able to do the job and, having done, it makes any further sacrifice superfluous.

> Once, only once, and once for all,
> his precious life he gave;
> before the cross in faith we fall,
> and own it strong to save.

'One offering, single and complete,'
with lips and hearts we say;
but what he never can repeat
he shows forth day by day.

For as the priest of Aaron's line
within the holiest stood,
and sprinkled all the mercy shrine
with sacrificial blood;

So he, who once atonement wrought,
our Priest of endless power,
presents himself for those he bought
in that dark noontide hour. (William Bright)

By means of the definitions of theologians such as Anselm and Barth and through the language of liturgy and hymns, this understanding of atonement has permeated the Christian consciousness. We speak in these terms almost without thinking. But, as many troubled Christians and many critics from outside the Church have pointed out, there are huge problems with such theories. For a start, they often seem simply overelaborate, requiring God to devise complex stratagems for dealing with problems that, if he is indeed as almighty as the theories generally maintain, he ought to be able to deal with in a much simpler way. The Koranic refrain, 'He says "Be" and it is' is, by contrast, refreshingly simple![10] What 'necessity' could compel God to insist on receiving satisfaction before he could forgive an insult to his honour? Why does God have to sacrifice his own Son as a condition of forgiving others (who, in the meantime, have become more guilty than ever before on account of their involvement in putting the Son to death)? Doesn't the whole obsession with punishment reflected in such theories reek of a rather psychologically suspect cast of mind? And, not least, how can we make sense of the idea of Jesus being our 'substitute' if we are convinced that God's will for us is that we should enter the divine communion on the basis of our own free decision to do so, as God's friends?

Yet, whatever their detailed drawback, atonement theories are attempting to deal with an insight that has been at the heart of this chapter, that Jesus' call to us to enter into the divine fellowship and to become what, at Omega-Point, we shall be, is inseparable from his death on the cross. This is also the point of seeing the Rublev Trinity and the Isenheim altarpiece as a double-exposure, as two inseparable facets of the same event. Nevertheless, there remains a clear difference between insisting, as atonement theories typically do, that the death of Jesus was, in some sense, God's will and a part of God's long-term 'plan' for dealing with sin, and saying that God's will is revealed in Jesus *despite* the horror of the cross.

Earlier, I looked briefly at René Girard's theory of sacrifice. Girard saw the phenomenon of scapegoating as the basic form of sacrifice found in all cultures. As such it is always, intrinsically, unjust. The scapegoat is merely arbitrarily singled out as 'guilty' of the violence that, in reality, is the collective responsibility of the whole society. Scapegoating works in the sense that it unifies society ('One man must die for the people'!), but it works only at the cost of a massive collective self-deception, a refusal of the self-knowledge that we are each complicit in and responsible for the violence that the act of scapegoating seeks to purge. Seeing Jesus as the scapegoat who bears our sins and thus takes away the sin of the world is, according to Girard, completely to miss the point of what we actually find in the Gospels. For what we see there is the historically unique witness to the profound injustice of the scapegoat phenomenon and, for the first time in history, a victim who refuses to accept the justice of his death, who, in effect, proclaims that one man should *not* die for the people. For if each person is, in themselves, a reflection of the image and likeness of God and called to fellowship in the divine life, then no act of killing can be 'God's will'. The message of the passion narrative is, then, that in its exposure of the dynamics of scapegoating, it offers a decisive insight into the systemic, structural injustice of the human condition and, through this self-knowledge, demystifies and frees us from the otherwise universal mechanisms of mimetic desire and their inevitable violent outcome. The cross, as witnessed in the Gospels, does set us free. But it does not do so because it is the supreme sacrifice. Rather, it does so because it exposes sacrifice for what it is: murder. If we understand this, then that path is for evermore closed and we are set on the new path of mutual responsibility and care.[11] Where the Church persists in interpreting the death of Jesus in sacrificial terms, however, we may suspect that the lesson has not yet been learned. It is salutary to reflect that the Victorians' preoccupation with sacrifice and atonement provided an all too easy context for the mystification of what happened in the First World War as a Christ-like sacrifice. Only too late did Europe realize that this was not a sacrifice well-pleasing to God but just plain slaughter.

This does not, of course, mean that sacrifice in the sense of renunciation has no part to play in the Christian life. Of course, one

thing often has to be 'sacrificed' for another, not least if we are com-
mitting ourselves to the way of love. If what we are invited to share in
is ultimately fulfilling, it is at the same time an initiation into service.
Grace is free, but not cheap and the grace that saves is likely to cost
everything. But, in this case, it would be less misleading to speak,
simply, of renunciation or discipline rather than of 'sacrifice'.

The atonement thinking of the West has, typically, focused almost
exclusively on the cross. Yet even where this focus has been most
intense, the point of the theory would be lost if it was not followed
through to the resurrection. The resurrection, it seems, is integral to
whatever claims Christians may wish to make about Jesus' identity as
Son of God and to the saving nature of the passion. Yet the resurrection also seems to involve claims about a particular historical event of
a biologically remarkable nature, a body coming back to life after two
nights in the grave. This claim has been at the centre of furious debates
for much of the last 150 years, debates that have often been most
furious when the participants have themselves all been Christians.

At one rather general level all sides are able to agree that the message of the resurrection, whether taken by itself or in conjunction with
the ascension and/or the pouring out of the Holy Spirit at Pentecost,
means that the Word lives beyond its rejection: that the killing of Jesus
as the bearer of the Word has not marked the end of that Word's power
to claim and to transform lives, calling us on to possibilities that belong
no less to the future than to a long lost past. In some sense it means
that Jesus is vindicated, that his death as scapegoat is not a proof of
his culpability but, instead, is a judgement on those who judged him
in this way. This, as Bach's settings of the Passion show, is not to be
taken as referring simply to Pilate and the Jewish leaders but to each
generation that continues to be complicit in sacrificial violence. Or, as
we heard the Muslim writer Khamel Hussein put it, each generation
becomes contemporary with that memorable day. Islam, of course,
does not speak of a resurrection, but it does speak of Jesus as having
ascended to God and so, from another angle, confirms the Christian
claim that, despite his death, Jesus remains our contemporary. In that
possibility there is already a sign that history is redeemable from the
terror of meaninglessness and absolute relativity.

But how far does this hinge on the claim of a literal, physical return
from the dead? St Paul's writings seem to underline rather than to
solve the problem. For although Paul insists that 'if Christ was not
raised, your faith has nothing to it' (1 Cor. 15.17), he also puts his own
encounter with the risen Christ on the Damascus road on a par with
the Easter experiences of Peter and the others (as well as introducing

an otherwise unknown appearance to over 500 disciples, which may or may not be a reference to Pentecost). Yet even in terms of Paul's own description or that found in the Acts of the Apostles, what happened on the Damascus road is entirely interpretable in terms of the kinds of visionary experiences found in many religions. There is nothing in it that compels us to assign what Paul experienced to a resurrected bodily Christ.

Earlier in this chapter I drew attention to how Luke's Gospel speaks of the infant Jesus as a 'sign' and, from there, suggested that, in Jesus' life as the Christ, there is no point at which the Gospels wish to speak of historical events apart from the communicative acts that these events instantiate. Each event, each word in the Christ's life is a word, a calling, an invitation to live with the God who is God-with-us. He himself speaks of the resurrection in terms of the sign of Jonah, thus, in effect, weaving together the scriptural story of Jonah, the events of his own life and the testimony that that life will inspire. And, as we saw, he notes too that even a resurrection will not compel belief in those unwilling to confront the self-knowledge that belief requires. Moses and the prophets would be enough to bring us into fellowship with God, if only we knew how to read them.

The debate about the facts of Easter Day will certainly continue, as will the debate about how what happened on the cross came to be a saving event. But if the call to heavenly citizenship is once heard, can we say that witness of and the witness to Jesus the Christ depends on which side we take? For even on the most literalist view, the fact alone is never enough, nor is the fact itself ever a compelling proof – the devils believe *and tremble* (James 2.19). The fact only leads to faith when it is communicated and received *as a sign* and, as signs, the birth, death and resurrection call us to self-knowledge, to see our lives in the light of his 'Well?' and to hear in this more, far more, than the word of judgement. It is the judgement, the only judgement there is, but it is also, still more importantly, an open door to a new and better life, open for each of us in the unique circumstances of our own time and place. If we insist on explaining just how the door was opened, we risk over-explaining and, indeed, missing the opportunity of entering in. Here, as with other theological debates, we would do well to take to heart what the Elizabethan theologian Richard Hooker wrote in connection with Reformation-era debates about the real presence of Christ in the Eucharist – 'They [the apostles] had at that time a sea of comfort and joy to wade in, and we by that which they did are taught that this heavenly food is given for the satisfying of our empty souls, and not for the exercising of our curious and subtile wits.'[12] For, as

Hooker saw only too clearly in his own time, and as the following century of religious wars more than demonstrated, such 'exercising of our curious and subtle wits' can only too quickly bring us back into a cycle of destruction in which angry words turn to angry blows, and theoretical disputes prepare the way of terror and counter-terror by insurgencies and states alike.

And one thing more. That we can be contemporaries with the life of Jesus the Christ is not solely dependent on what happened 2,000 years ago. It is also, in complex and sometimes distracting ways, tied up with the whole history of the subsequent witness to what happened then. That means that the question of our relation to Jesus cannot be abstracted from the life of the Church, not least from the writings that were produced from within the life of the Church to register once and for all the key elements of the Church's testimony to what it made of the man who was the sign of contradiction.

Tradition

The Gospel and the Church

In his book *The Gospel and the Church*, the French Catholic thinker Alfred Loisy wrote that 'Jesus proclaimed the Kingdom and it was the Church that came'.[1] For a Protestant reader, this might sound ironic, since Protestants would typically see the role given to the Church in Catholicism as diverging from the model of the kingdom found in Jesus' preaching. Loisy, however, was making the serious point that as far back as we can possibly go, the historical testimony to Christ that we have available to us has been shaped by the ongoing life of the Church. Even the most 'primitive' sources of Christian faith, such as St Mark's Gospel or St Paul's letters, are already shaped by questions and concerns that belong to the life of the Church. Even if these sources are shown to contain accurate reports of Jesus' words or actions, the fact that just these words and actions have been remembered while others have been forgotten reflects the way in which the message of his life and work was received. Specifically, Loisy was answering such liberal Protestant theologians as Adolf von Harnack, who argued that we could, in fact, use the Gospel texts to infer the 'real facts' about the historical Jesus, facts uncorrupted by the later accretions and, Harnack would say, distortions of church tradition.

Harnack's aim was, in its way, characteristically Protestant. For the Reformation hinged on Martin Luther's assumption that the plain text of Scripture would enable the believer to get behind what Luther regarded as the corruptions and excrescences that had vitiated and smothered the preaching of the gospel in the course of history and that had become institutionalized in the late medieval Church. Luther's idea was that one could effectively go back to the beginning and start all over again, as if the intervening 1,500 years hadn't happened. Such a tactic led to a massive reordering of priorities in the ordinary life of the Church. Under the slogan *sola scriptura* ('Scripture alone'), the Protestant world saw a wave of new Bible translations, several of which (such as Luther's own translation into German or the English King James Bible) would be virtually unchallenged for many centuries and which thus shaped the emergence of modern European culture itself. Now available in the vernacular, the Bible became the focus both of public preaching and private devotion in a way that was quite distinct from that of the medieval world. Yet this very focus on the Bible led, in time, to the beginning of a radical questioning of the nature of this most singular of books. Scholars became excruciatingly aware of inconsistencies in the text and, as natural and historical science began to develop, of even more troubling inconsistencies between the text of the Bible and what was being discovered about the natural world and about human history. Even within the Church, questions began to be raised as to whether the classic formulae of Christian dogma could really be regarded as a faithful interpretation of the scriptural material or whether they maybe reflected more of the world-view of the Greco-Roman world and the peculiar political situation of the declining and fragmenting Roman Empire. By the nineteenth century, then, the question for Protestant scholarship was no longer how to get back behind the Church to the plain word of Scripture, but how to get back behind the word of Scripture to the historical reality which it represented. This was precisely the line of thinking found in Harnack and other liberal Protestants – and nowhere was the question more urgent than in relation to the Gospels and the figure of Jesus. If only we could get back to the real historical Jesus, theologians believed, we would have an absolute standard against which to measure and regulate the Church, a truly solid rock on which to build the household of faith.

Loisy's riposte – that Jesus proclaimed the kingdom and it was the Church that came – was one of a number of lines of criticism that exposed the naivety of this approach. Even if the movement of modern biblical scholarship has led to an immeasurable expansion in our knowledge of the period in which, in this instance, the New Testament writings came into being, this scholarship itself has increasingly followed Loisy in the insight that it is virtually impossible to draw a simple line between 'Scripture' on the one hand and 'the Church' on the other, or between the 'historical facts' and the way in which these facts impacted on the lives of those who became chiefly responsible for remembering them.

Another way of looking at this is to think about the word 'tradition' itself. Literally it means giving over, often with the connotation of literally handing something over. In this connection we should not overlook the importance of Scripture being a physical object, a book or, in an earlier age, one or more scrolls or manuscripts. Living in an age of mass publishing and in a part of the world where anyone who wants to can just go into their local bookstore and choose from any one of a number of editions of the Bible (old and new translations, illustrated, 'for children', 'retold', etc.), it requires a deliberate effort of imagination to think what the mere possession of a physical 'scripture' meant to the communities making up the early Church. Perhaps we should especially think of what it might have meant for a congregation to receive an original or a copy of one of the works that, over the first two centuries, became incorporated into what we call 'The New Testament'. In the absence of direct acquaintance with any of the other books of the New Testament, the possession and handing over of such a text from one generation to the next or, simply, for copying, would have been a powerful and significant event. And it could only have been 'handed over' to those or to one who would be regarded as an absolutely trustworthy keeper of it. Just imagine the impact on a congregation that, for the first time, received an early version of one of our canonical Gospels, and was able, through the medium of this book, to learn about words and actions by the Lord that they had previously known, if at all, in oral versions.

The point can also be illustrated from the other side: that the same root meaning of 'handing over' lies behind our word 'traitor', a usage originally applied to those Christians who handed over their scriptures to the authorities in the persecution under the emperor Diocletian and who thus, literally, became *traditores* or traitors.

But, persecutions apart, the gradual accumulation of manuscripts into what became recognized as the 'canon' or approved collection of New Testament writings was itself a work of tradition, so we can say that Scripture itself is, in a very tangible sense, a product of tradition. The very fact of its being preserved and made available for faith is, in a very literal sense, dependent on 'tradition', on its having been handled with appropriate care in what was, often, a hostile environment. That this is so is corroborated by the way in which this process involved a complex sifting among texts that, though popular amongst many Christian communities, were not finally accepted into the canon. The identification of Scripture as Scripture, then, is a primary example of the inescapability of tradition in the life of the Church, further illustrating that though this may be rooted in the literal, physical fact of handing over or passing on the community's most treasured writings, it also involves the interpretation and evaluation of those writings in and by the Church.

Nor is it possible to ring-fence this process in an absolute sense. If, in the rhetoric of the Protestant Reformers, 'Scripture' sounds like a rock-solid, self-sufficient edifice, the reality is rather more complex. There is, for example, the body of writings known as the Apocrypha that were books used by the pre-Christian Jewish community but which were known only in Greek, that is, for which there was no Hebrew original. These were incorporated in the Latin Bible but were excised by the Protestant Reformers, although Luther himself translated many of them and allowed them to be printed as an appendix to the Bible, recommending them as non-authoritative but 'useful and good to read', or, as the Thirty-Nine Articles of the Church of England put it, they are to be read 'for example of life and instruction of manners; but yet [the Church] doth not apply them to establish any doctrine'. Today Catholic versions of the Bible also print them separately, though both Catholics and Anglicans use them as prescribed readings in worship.

Even the status of the canonical books is variable – in practice if not in theory. It is already striking that whereas the last book of the Hebrew Bible is the second Book of Chronicles, that place is occupied in modern Christian Bibles by the prophecy of Malachi. This may seem insignificant, but not when we look at the closing verses of these two books. Second Chronicles ends with the decree of Cyrus allowing the Jews who had been exiled to Babylon to return home and to rebuild the Temple in Jerusalem. Malachi ends with the prophecy that before the Messiah comes God will send Elijah again to prepare his way, a prophecy quoted in the Gospels in connection with John the Baptist and in this way taken to be prophetic of the coming of Jesus. In this way the very arrangement of Scripture involves quite far-reaching theological judgements. Indeed, the mere fact that Christians generally speak of the Hebrew Bible as the 'Old Testament' already gives every Christian reader an implicit rule for how to read it, that is, with one eye on its fulfilment in the New, an approach that makes the experience of reading the same text very different for Jews and Christians.

It is, in any case, no secret that any preacher, any Church, will have its own 'canon within the canon'. Texts that play only a marginal role in one tradition are central in others. Luther himself famously spoke of the Letter of St James as an 'epistle of straw', because it seemed to argue against his own preference for faith as against 'works', whereas Kierkegaard made of it one of the defining scriptural points of reference for his whole theological endeavour. Similarly today, where Liberation Theology shows a marked preference for the Jesus of the Synoptic Gospels who is held to have identified himself in word and deed with the poor, the marginalized, women and outcasts, others gravitate to the so-called 'mystical' Jesus who speaks in the closing chapters of St John's Gospel of his union with the Father and of his mission to bring all his disciples into a spiritual friendship with God that is of the same nature as his own God-relationship. What Scripture actually 'is' for any given Church, congregation or individual is, then, far from fixed. If, in the Free churches, the Sunday reading is the minister's personal choice, while, in the more liturgical churches, it is the matter of an official lectionary, the Scripture that provides the basis for preaching is still, mostly, only a small selection of Scripture as a whole.

This basic point takes on a still deeper significance if we also take into account the fact that for most Christians today the Bible exists primarily in translation and, as any translator knows, every translation is already an interpretation. If translation involves elements of science (the translator must, for example, have competence in the relevant languages!), it equally involves elements of art. The translator too – though less literally – is an agent of tradition, handing over the Scripture from one language to another, and in doing so he or she cannot but significantly recreate the text, rather than merely reproduce it. And, one might add, this is especially true of the best translations: a word-by-word literal translation is likely to be unreadable, but a translation in which the translator's own imagination is set free will have far greater potential to convey the power, if not always the letter, of the original. In this perspective one can understand the anxieties of the fundamentalist group known as the King-James-Only-ists, for whom the King James Version of the Bible has a canonical status which they deny to all other subsequent translations. *Only* this translation is the Word of God, they say. This, of course, is something much stronger than merely having the kind of strong preference for the King James Version that many cultural Anglicans (including many non-believers) also express. Yet even if the King-James-Only-ists overstate their own case, they have a point. Each translation is, in a very tangible sense, a *different* work, which brings different aspects of the original to the fore while inevitably losing particular nuances or emphases that are to be found in alternative renderings. These reflections invite the further thought that when it comes to what, for most Christians, are the pivotal texts on which all of Scripture hinges, namely the Gospels, the words of Jesus that we so readily quote are not merely translated words but, even in the text itself, are already translated, since Greek, the language of the text, was almost certainly not the language in which he gave his teaching, even if he might well have had some competence in it.

These remarks do not, of course, mean that there are no constant points in the Church's reception of the Bible, or that all that is solid dissolves into mist. It does not mean that there cannot be enquiry and debate concerning the historical 'facts' or whether one translation or interpretation of any given text is better than another. It means only that the Bible itself, as testimony to a very particular historical experience, also belongs to history and, not least, to the continuing history of the way in which it is ordered, presented, translated and read. It does not stand apart from the time and history of humanity's immersion in the relativity of the profane, historical world and, if it speaks of salvation to those who inhabit this world, it does so in and out of the very medium in which they themselves must think and judge and feel what can be believed on, hoped for and cherished. As a word calling us into fellowship with God it shares the exposure of the Christ, *the* Word, to ambiguity, contestation and offence. Only so can it be genuinely communicative.

The Living Word

For most of Christian history, the main context in which Scripture has been read has not been that of private devotional reading nor yet that of scholarly enquiry. Instead it has been the context of Christian worship. Reading from Scripture as a key part of worship is something that the Church early on took over from the Synagogue – and, in the Gospels themselves, we see an example of Jesus performing the honoured task of reading from Scripture in his home village of Nazareth (Luke 4.16ff.). In this passage, Jesus does not simply read from Scripture, however, he also comments on it and, again from the earliest times, interpreting the meaning of Scripture as well as reading from it became a central part of Christian worship. At the same time, Scripture was present in a variety of ways in each act of worship. Elements of Scripture would be likely to be quoted or alluded to in prayers and hymns, or scriptural psalms were incorporated first into the Synagogue's and then into the Church's own acts of penitence, praise and thanksgiving. Portions of Scripture other than those formally read would be drawn into the exposition of the passage under consideration (and we can see already in St Paul's practice how a skilful preacher could roam freely throughout the whole body of Scripture to find arguments, illustrations and precedents for his case). And, as we have noticed, the worship of the early Church would take on an added intensity of focus when a manuscript of a newly received 'scripture' was read and studied for the first time.

The close link between Scripture and its 'live' exposition in preaching has been one of the most constant features in Christian worship, life and thought. Nor is it any coincidence that the churches of the Reformation, in which the centrality of Scripture was so underlined, developed forms of worship in which 'the word' became dominant at the expense of ritual, art and, sometimes, music. As in contemporary usage, the category of 'word' was, in practice, extended to cover the whole part of worship centred on the reading and interpretation of Scripture, together with the affirmative response ritualized in the saying of the creed, thus 'the ministry of the word'. Within this ministry, preaching has had a particular, if not exclusive, dignity. And if we no longer live in a golden age of preaching, few Christians will not at some point have experienced something of the sacramental dimension of preaching – that preaching, no less than the sacraments more narrowly understood, is a way of God becoming present in time to the believing community. Preaching too can be a way of making-present the 'conversation in heaven' to which God is constantly calling us. Seeing preaching as sacramental in this way goes against the widespread assumption by both preachers and congregations that preaching is primarily a form of teaching, the aim of which is simply to offer an explanation or application of the biblical text, or to demonstrate the logical, historical or psychological grounds for accepting Christian belief. On such a view the purpose of preaching will primarily be to persuade, convince or, simply, argue a point. But when it is seen in these terms, preaching becomes an essentially intellectual activity, even when the 'argument' is clothed in homely illustrations drawn from everyday life (it is telling in this regard that in many Protestant churches, where preaching is especially emphasized, the clergy or ministers wear academic or academic-style gowns and/ or hoods). Like many other features of church life, this is, of course, a self-perpetuating tendency, since once the preacher believes that that is what he should be aiming at then that is what he will produce, at the cost of other models or dimensions of what the sermon could be doing. And this, in turn, will also define for his auditors what is to be expected of a 'good' sermon. This is not simply a matter of preaching coming to be seen as privileging the head at the expense of the heart, though it may also do that, but of the assumptions we make about the kind of communicative act it is.

The controversial theologian Rudolf Bultmann pointed to an alternative basis for understanding preaching when he remarked that the early Church's experience of Jesus Christ's offer of salvation redirected the hearer's attention away from searching for the signs of an imminent end of the world that so preoccupied the authors of the apocalyptic books to something altogether different. Although 'in' history, their experience was not 'the kind of historical development which can be confirmed by any historian. It becomes an event repeatedly in preaching and faith. Jesus Christ is the eschatological event not as an established fact of past time but as repeatedly present, as addressing you and me here and now in preaching.'[2] Preaching, in this perspective, is more than expounding the meaning of an ancient text. It is at its heart the continuation of the movement from creation through incarnation to infinite salvation, the movement of the self-communicating divine presence in history.

That might seem a rather overambitious statement, not least in the light of the British distaste for sermons that last longer than seven minutes and thus interfere with preparations for Sunday lunch or the choir's coffee break. In an age when preachers have begun to come down from the pulpit in order to address the congregation 'eye to eye' rather than remaining 12 feet above criticism, it might seem to open the door for the reinstatement of the most self-deluding forms of preacherly vanity and megalomania. Sacraments, after all, are actions whose performance is, in large measure, independent of the whims and fancies of individuals. Certain elements have to be used, certain things have to be done. In preaching, however, everything would seem to depend on the particular psychological, intellectual, charismatic and rhetorical gifts (or imagined gifts!) of just one individual. Isn't preaching simply too human, too personal, too individualistic really to function as a vehicle of divine self-presencing?

I shall return to this question shortly, but first I shall look briefly at the highly original reflections on the relationship between Scripture, preaching and the Word of the nineteenth-century Danish theologian N. F. S. Grundtvig. Grundtvig was an outstanding hymn-writer (ranked by many Danes as one of their great national poets), translator and educator as well as having been a charismatic preacher. Although many points in his theology now appear rather quirky (and are often expressed in a popular rather than a scholarly form), he was a theologian of worship of unusual range, who mooted a number of important topics that have only more recently worked their way up the theological agenda.

Living when he did in the wake of a century and more of rationalistic theology, Grundtvig was especially concerned that living Christian faith was being ousted in favour of an intellectual, scholarly construct. Something essentially living was, he feared, being turned into something merely bookish. What the Church needed to get back to was the realization that a text such as a letter from St Paul was not to be approached merely in terms of its literal, grammatical or historical meaning. He notes Paul's own formulation that the congregation at Corinth is itself his 'open, readable letter, written not with ink but with the Spirit of the living God, inscribed not in tablets of stone but in the fleshy tablets of the heart'. Really to understand Paul's letters we have to recognize that they are 'as little written on paper as they are inscribed in stone but [they are] impressed upon the heart's fleshy tablets, so that whoever does not recognize the spiritual writing in the heart's inner chamber, the great signature of our Lord Jesus Christ . . . cannot know what the apostle is talking about' and, he adds, this inward spiritual writing in 'the heart's fleshy tablets' is itself the Word of God. And, he continues, it is the same Word of God by which 'all things came to be', it is the Word that became flesh and dwelt among us, and the same Word that 'became Spirit and speaks to us with fiery tongues and seeks to be born again in our hearts so as to burst into flame on our lips and shine forth in our lives and transfigure us in the glory of the only-begotten One'. If this Word or Spirit is absent, then 'the New Testament is only a book and not the letter sent from heaven that the Spirit of God writes with the tongue on the heart's tablets of flesh and . . . the cup of the new covenant is only a memorial to the one who died on the cross, not a spiritual blood-bond with Him who lives unto all eternity'.[3]

Many of Grundtvig's formulations here are, at first sight, fairly conventional, recycling familiar phrases from the Bible itself (as preaching often does). Yet his emphases are distinctive and, as such, the tip of the iceberg. Take the emphasis on the *fleshliness* of the heart. This reflects something that Grundtvig insisted on throughout his writings: that human life is embodied life and that the Christian message is not about liberating an immaterial soul from the shackles of the body but about enlivening the whole, real, actual embodied human being. Though 'inward', the heart is the unifying and centring organ of a being created as those physical, fleshly beings to whom Christ came, himself 'in the flesh'. This 'fleshliness' carries over into Grundtvig's concept of communication itself, which, like many of his ideas, plays on the intertwining of the themes of creation and redemption, of Adam and Christ. For, on his view, the imaginative, pictorial language of Scripture both expresses the embodiment characteristic of human existence and, in so doing, reflects the original language of paradise, in which Adam reproduced in language the true physical image of each creature. Above all this applies to human beings themselves. The word in which we speak our truth is itself an embodied manifestation of the embodied image of God in which we were created. For human beings exist as the image of God precisely as the fleshly, carnal beings they are. Therefore, the language in which our relation to the rest of creation and to ourselves comes to expression is not a kind of ectoplasmic film laid over the materiality of the world, but the reflection, echo or even continuation of the Word of God active in creating a material universe: perhaps literally its *reverberation*. All truthful speaking is thus, in some measure, potentially revelatory of the original image of God impressed upon creation and, above all, upon human beings.

In this connection, we may return to the last-quoted passage and to the way in which Grundtvig speaks of the Spirit writing the Word in our fleshy hearts 'with the tongue', that is, with the living human voice. We cannot underestimate the truth-revealing power of the voice, Grundtvig insists. We, are he says in the sermon 'The Voice of One Crying in the Wilderness':

> . . . as ignorant as animals if we . . . hold in contempt the word spoken by the human tongue, despite the fact that it is clear that everything great and remarkable on earth is carried forward by means of the word, from generation to generation, and, furthermore, originally sprang from a living and powerful word that grips and moves the children of men, thus proclaiming their wonderful kinship with the Word that was in the beginning with God and of which the psalmist sings 'By the Lord's Word were the heavens created, and all their hosts by the Spirit of his mouth' . . . It is only in dead, dull bestial times such as we now experience that it is regarded as peculiar that people flocked in their thousands to hear the voice of one crying in the wilderness, a voice that rang out as a cry from on high, resounding in its hearer in the very depths, in the depths of their hearts, which, like the pool of Bethesda, only works powerfully when, with a word, an angel descends and stirs it. For it is not only by the Jordan, but equally by the Euphrates and the Nile, indeed by the Elba and the Belt and the Sound, that if a word were to ring out like the voice of one crying in the wilderness and like a living resonance of that Creator-Word by which we were formed, . . . all those would gather together . . . [who] need only one dark glimpse of the living word from human lips to feel that we are kin to Him who spoke and said: let there be light, and there was light . . .[4]

The point, then, is that all this depends on the fact that the 'voice' is indeed the living voice of one human being speaking to another in the concrete materiality of his own voice. And this, importantly for

Grundtvig, means precisely the voice that comes most naturally to us, our mother-tongue. The Word must be spoken as a living word, which means naturally, spontaneously, and in a way and a manner that both speaker and listener feel at home in. Here, for Grundtvig, is also the root of the double office of hymnody and preaching in making the Word of creation and redemption present in the worship of the contemporary Church. In speaking to the congregation in his own voice and in its own common tongue, the preacher's greatest achievement is, in fact, to free the voices of the listeners for the poetic song that, on earth, is the highest and best form of the Word. If the sermon breathes – literally breathes – life into the Word of Scripture, the song of praise expresses the upward movement of the Word that has once come to life in us.

Here too, albeit in a far more Romantically-toned version than in Bultmann, we glimpse one way of thinking of preaching itself as sacramental (and, in this connection, it is interesting to note that Grundtvig links word and sacrament extremely closely, as when we heard him say that it is not only the letter of Scripture that is dead without the animating Spirit of the living word, but also that 'the cup of the new covenant' remains 'only a memorial to the one who died on the cross, not a spiritual blood-bond with Him who lives unto all eternity').

If, then, Scripture is to play its sacramental role of making present the divine call into ever deepening fellowship, it will always require the supplement of the living word, the word spoken in our own language and in our own manner. Inevitably, then, the Word of Scripture never exists for us except as an *interpreted* word, a word living and moving in the forward-moving stream of tradition. And we must imagine this process with the utmost concretion. Just as the early Church placed huge value on the handing over of the physical body of holy writings from one congregation and one generation to another, so the living Word is itself physically handed over in the speaking, embodied action of preaching. But – to recur to the charge that such a high evaluation of preaching can only encourage the vanity and megalomania of aspiring preachers – almost the most important thing in this process is not the particular formulations (turns of phrase, stories, illustrations, etc.) that the preacher's individual inventiveness adds to the tradition, but the fact that Scripture is expounded in faith in the mother-tongue.[5] That this happens at all is already a sacramental sign of the faith that the Word of creation and redemption *can* be made present to us in our own time and our own tongue: that it can become *our own* word. The poet Edwin Muir chided the Scottish Calvinism of his upbringing with preaching 'The Word made flesh made word again', but, if we follow the hints provided by Grundtvig, the real movement of preaching is rather a continuation and deepening of the incarnation of the Word. It is the Word entering still more deeply, into the yet finer detail of our embodied, fleshly existence. As such it is both *enfleshing* and, inseparably from that, *envoicing*, in the sense explained by Oliver Davies.[6]

Protestantism, we noted, has tended to contrast Scripture and tradition to the detriment of the latter. In the light of the perspective I have been attempting to develop here, however, we might do better to borrow a phrase from Buddhism and to speak instead of 'written' and 'unwritten' traditions, where Scripture provides the definitive form of the written tradition, and preaching is a paradigmatic instance of the process of unwritten tradition.

Tradition and Truth

Implicit in a much of what has just been said is the idea that the primary locus of Christian tradition is Christian worship itself, the outward, physical, visible gathering of the Church to receive Scripture, to hear Scripture become the living Word of creation and redemption and to respond in songs of praise. This I think is correct, and it is endorsed by what is perhaps the most concise of all New Testament texts with regard to the meaning of tradition, namely 1 Corinthians 11.23–6.[7]

The subject being addressed in this passage is how Christians should conduct themselves when they gather for worship and, in reading it, we do well to recall that the letter itself was, first and foremost, a letter written to a worshipping congregation and would have been read aloud and discussed in the context of a gathering that is at the very least likely to have had elements of worship in it. In these verses Paul lays down as the basis of his argument that 'the tradition which I handed on to you came to me from the Lord himself', which, in order to underline once more the root meaning of 'tradition', we might more literally translate as follows: 'for I received from the Lord what I now hand over to you . . .' This is already an extraordinary claim. One of the few things we know with a very high degree of certainty about the earliest Church is that the man who became the Apostle Paul did not have any significant communication with Jesus prior to the latter's crucifixion. Yet what follows is a most precise rendering of what Paul says were the words and actions of Jesus at the Last Supper (and virtually the only time in all his letters when Paul claims to quote Jesus' *ipsa verba*). Of course, we can easily imagine many ways in which Paul could have got to know this and he did, after all, have personal contact with some of those who were there. Yet he insists both that his account is a 'tradition' and also that it came to him 'from the Lord himself'. Does he mean that it was a part of the revelation to him on the Damascus road, when, as he believed, the risen Christ himself appeared and spoke to him? It seems unlikely since there is no hint of it either in his own references to that event or in the account in the Acts of the Apostles. Does it then mean that he was himself told about it in a context and form that guaranteed the truth that this was indeed a word spoken by the Lord? If so, this would seem to underline the way in which an authoritative and effective communication outside or alongside of the text is an inescapable part of the context in which the text itself comes into being and is transmitted.

There is more than this to our text, however, for what this piece of 'tradition' is about is precisely a very literal handing over, first by Jesus himself and subsequently within the community of believers, of the body and blood of the Lord, of what is figured as the Lord's literal, fleshly being. The passage becomes even more highly charged when we reflect that, as in Mark's Gospel, Jesus, having handed over his body to the disciples, will shortly speak of the hour having come in which 'the Son of Man is betrayed into the hands of sinners' (Mark 14.41), where the phrase 'betrayed into' translates the same verb underlying Paul's 'hand over'. In the light of this we could retranslate Mark as 'the Son of Man is given/handed over into the hands of sinners'. The same verb 'to give over' can, in other words, be used to describe two essentially opposite movements: the faithful or the treacherous handing over of the embodied being of the Lord. In this dual possibility we have an early anticipation of the ambivalence throughout Christian history regarding 'tradition', an ambivalence already glimpsed in the etymological kinship between the 'traitors' who handed their scriptures over to the persecutors and the 'tradition', the process of handing over the faith in the concrete forms of word and, as here, sacrament. In each case we have a process of handing over that is at heart a communicative act, giving the recipient the possibility of making their own what has been handed over. But the very divergent outcomes of such acts of handing over pinpoint the risk of all such communicative action: that each time the Word, or the body and blood of the Lord, are handed over there arises an opportunity for that Word, that body and blood, to be received with faith – or to be rejected, misappropriated and abused (as, indeed, Paul goes on to warn in verses 27–32, where he counsels that anyone eating and drinking 'unworthily' 'will be guilty of offending against the body and blood of the Lord' (v. 27)).

Each act of communication renews both the possibility of receiving the Word and the possibility of being offended by it; over and over again. This dynamic applies equally to word and sacrament, which, in their essence, are two forms of the one creative dynamic, rather than – as sometimes seems to be the case – two distinct and irreconcilable principles vying for supremacy. This mutuality is implicit in Paul's own words, which, while describing how the community is to celebrate the Lord's Supper, call upon the verbal instruction he received 'from the Lord' and, of course, for us the text itself is a part of Scripture, a word 'from the Lord'. In this perspective we can see how the Orthodox theologian George Florovsky could speak of tradition as the accumulation of the acts of judgement made in the life of the Church, since each presentation of Christ in word and sacrament invites the recipient of the communication to judge both what it is that is being offered and what is being demanded of him- or herself. It is, so to speak, the collective memory of a repeated affirmative response to the becoming-present of the self-giving God in our individual and collective life.

But there are two other elements in Paul's text that are central both to the dynamics of word and sacrament and to the phenomenon of tradition of which they are primary forms. One has, in fact, just been touched on: that what is done in the ritual action of eating and drinking the body and blood of the Lord is an act of remembrance, 'in memory' of him. The other is that it also has an essentially forward-looking, future dimension: that, in doing this thing, believers 'proclaim the death of the Lord, until he comes'.[8] Both of these elements clearly bring back into focus the discussion of history in the preceding chapter. Just as the incarnation can be figured as a divine Word spoken towards those falling away from God into the annihilating emptiness of time, so too do the remembering and anticipating dimensions of word, sacrament and tradition serve to arrest that otherwise terrible free fall, restoring to time the possibility of being fulfilled time, time to be lived in and enjoyed as the time needed for fleshing out the divine–human fellowship. Or, to use an expression that has now recurred many times, tradition gives us the possibility of a present, of a time and place to be present to ourselves, present to one another, and present to God. And it does so because the presence that is given us – 'handed over' to us – is the presence of the divine life, creating, redeeming, life-giving and life-restoring, a new creation in the midst of the old, the perpetual motion of eternal novelty, eternal nowness.

Something of what is involved here has been put extraordinarily well by the Russian religious thinker Nicholas Berdyaev, who wrote that 'Tradition is memory which brings resurrection, the victory over corruption, the affirmation of eternal life . . . it is a glimpse of eternity in the mortal flight of time, a union of past, present and future in the oneness of eternity'.[9] Seen in these terms, of course, tradition has none of the connotations of the so-called traditionalism that is one of the favoured categories of journalistic comment on church affairs. 'Traditionalists', according to these journalists, are invariably people who are determined to hold on at all costs to some past state of the Church, whether the Latin Mass (if they are Catholics) or the Book of Common Prayer (if they are Anglicans), or who oppose some change or other in the Church's moral teaching, usually in connection with sexuality. Opposed to such traditionalists are, of course, the progressives (usually, but inappropriately, called 'liberals'), who seem to favour change and innovation merely because it is new. The kind of traditionalism that has been broached here, however, is necessarily 'progressive' and 'dynamic'. Tradition is nothing if it is not a movement through time, repeating and recreating in time the realization of the divine presence in the forms and media of the present and so, in time, counteracting the annihilating and destructive capacities of time. It is not and cannot be an attempt to freeze the flow of time, but, rather, must ever be seeking the deeper rhythm in time itself that makes of time a potential sacrament of eternity. This rhythm is complex and elusive, but there is no reason to suppose that it is not as likely to make itself known in moments of great and intense change as in interludes of apparent calm. What is decisive is not whether time flows more or less rapidly towards the infinite precipice of the future or more or less sluggishly back towards the bottomless source of the past. What matters is what and who, in time, we *are* or *can be*.

Putting it in these terms brings the question of tradition back into the orbit of what, for some, is the more fundamental question of truth. For what is truth? Clearly, this is a question to which many different answers have been given, and it is a question that has been asked with many degrees of either passion or ironic disinterest. One important modern contribution has been that of another Russian thinker, like Berdyaev a part of the great flowering of original religious and philosophical thought at the beginning of the twentieth century, Pavel Florensky.

Florensky took the word 'truth' back to the Greek term *a-létheia*, in which he interpreted the prefix *a-* as a negative prefix negating the root *–lath*.[10] This root, he said, means concealing something, so that what 'truth' negates is concealment or hiding. It is, we might say, openness, bringing or keeping something out into the open. What especially interests Florensky is the form of concealment that is encountered in forgetting, which, in the Greek world, was also intimately connected with death. As Florensky puts it 'The ancient idea of death as a transition to an illusory existence, almost to self-forgetting and unconsciousness, and, in any case, to the forgetting of everything earthly, finds its symbol in the image of the shades' drinking water from the underground river of Forgetfulness, "Lethe."'[11] But forgetting, the obliteration of consciousness that finds its ultimate term in death, was not just some kind of accident in the Greek understanding, Florensky states. It was not the result of the Greeks having had weak memories but of the active power of 'all-devouring time'.

> All is in flux. Time is the form of existence of all that is, and to say 'exists' is to say 'in time,' for time is the form of the flux of phenomena. 'All is in flux and moving and nothing abides,' complained Heraclitus. Everything slips away from the consciousness, flows through the consciousness, is forgotten. Time, chronos, produces phenomena, but, like its mythological image, Chronos, it devours its children. The very essence of consciousness, of life, of any reality is in their flux, i.e., in a certain metaphysical forgetting . . . But despite all the unquestionableness of [this truth], we cannot extinguish the demand for that which is *not* forgotten, for that which is *not* forgettable, for that which 'abides' in the flux of time. It is this unforgettableness which is *a-létheia* . . . Truth is the eternal memory of some Consciousness. Truth is value worthy and capable of eternal remembrance.[12]

This is the Greek view, but, he argues, the Christian concept of truth goes a step further. Drawing attention to the etymological connection of the Russian term *Istina* with words denoting being, breathing and becoming, he insists that what is at stake in the Christian idea of truth is not simply the remembrance of a consciousness or a value but the remembrance, the truth, of an existing, living being or person. Such truth takes historical form as the struggle against time and forgetting, a struggle to keep in remembrance an image of the human person as worthy of truth, as worthy of remembrance, worthy of not being annihilated in death. Such a struggle cannot take its criteria simply from 'how things are in the world' but orientates itself in the light of a hope that transcends the present possibilities of existence and the laws of rational evidence.

The act of judgement that tradition is repeatedly called to make, the judgement by which it itself is judged and which gives it the shape it has, is therefore the judgement as to what is truly worth remembering

and what is truly worth hoping for. Remembering Florensky's insistence
on the *personal* dimension of Christian truth, this is, however, no mere
'what'. For Christian faith, what is worth remembering finds its focus
in 'the light which is the knowledge of the glory of God in the face of
Jesus Christ' (2 Cor. 4.6). Faith does not understand itself as arbitrarily
seizing on its distinctive claims about Christ and defiantly affirming
that *this and only this* is worth remembering. Instead, it experiences
itself as responding to what has presented itself as unforgettable and
worth being a defining part of our human future. And faith holds to
this understanding of itself as response, even when it also remembers
that this is a world in which time is the all-encompassing medium
of existence, and that nothing shows itself on the plane of existence
without exposing itself to the possibility of being forgotten and to the
uncertainty, ambiguity and vertigo of all temporal existence. Nor does
faith deny that placing its stake on just this light as illuminating what
is most worth remembering about human beings is not recoupable
within time, since this stake itself – composed as it is of our deepest,
strongest, boldest, most hopeful and most fearful passions – is also
at every moment liable to tumble down into the emptiness of death
and forgetfulness. Yet, faith maintains, 'we have heard it; we have
seen it with our own eyes; we looked upon it, and felt it with our
own hands' (1 John 1.1). Whatever power tradition has is the power of
this testimony, which can never be the mere testimony of others, as if
one could believe at second-hand, but must be the testimony of each
person who has in some way experienced 'the Word which gives life'
(1 John 1.1), and whatever truth faith may claim for itself is, in the last
resort, dependent on the possibility of this testimony being given, in
time, against time, fulfilling time.[13]

Tradition and Practical Theology

The main thrust of this chapter thus far has been to argue for the
inescapability of tradition as the context in which Christian faith first
becomes possible. In arguing this I have largely focused on the historical dispute between Scripture and tradition and its reflection in
the parallel dispute between word and sacrament. Tradition, I have
suggested, is in fact the most comprehensive of all these categories,
so that we could rewrite many of the familiar antitheses in terms of
written and unwritten traditions, where the unwritten traditions
would also, of course, include many forms of 'the Word', including
preaching itself. The reading of Scripture, preaching and the use of

the sacraments have, as experience and theology both testify, a special prominence in the overall shape of tradition. However, we would have a very abstract and truncated concept of tradition if we left it at that. In the fullness of real life, tradition variegates itself in a multiplicity of forms and media, and I shall briefly sketch some of the most important of these and say a little about the relationship between them. In terms of traditional theology these forms constitute the basic subject-matter of practical theology, which looks at how we 'apply' the 'truths' established by philosophical, dogmatic, biblical and historical theology. In terms of the perspective being developed here, however, this distinction verges on meaninglessness. For if we once reconceive doctrine in terms of a dynamic process of teaching-and-learning, rather than as a set of timeless dogmas that have to be proved and defended, then all of the many ways in which human beings are brought to sense the Word of Life stirring in their own lives belong integrally to doctrine itself, and are not mere adjuncts or applications of it. And if we relocate the issue of the *truth* of faith in the context of the resistance offered by memory and hope to the threat of forgetfulness and obliteration, then this can no longer be treated as something merely theoretical: instead, it becomes dependent on each of the innumerable ways in which human beings feel that they have been in the presence of something worth remembering, something worth hoping for, experiences that involve all the fine detail of life as it is lived.

Some attention has already been given to preaching and worship, which are central elements in the syllabus of practical theology, but over and above these lies a whole raft of topics in which we can see how tradition both forms and takes form in the whole life of the Church. Here we find the questions of Christian instruction, mission, music, pastoral care, spirituality and ministerial function that, often masked by forbidding academic titles (homiletics, pedagogy, ascetic theology, etc.), embrace what many, arguably most, Christians experience as the bread-and-butter issues of everyday church life. If, in fact, they are separated from the central dynamic of the self-communicating, self-presencing life of God in time, then they do indeed become bread-and-butter issues of the most boring and humdrum kind. But, as I have been arguing, they have in principle as much right to be taken into the core agenda of theology as the more conventional heavyweight theological disciplines of Christology, atonement theory, etc. Here, no less than there, the question of who and how God can *be* for us fallible creatures of time, in time, is up for grabs. Nor would it be hard to argue that if, for example, the pastoral care offered by the Church is conceived and carried out in such a way as *not* to communicate anything of the Word of Life, then whatever may have been achieved at the high-level disciplines of Christology, etc. will have been time wasted. It is here, in the daily reality of person-to-person communication that the miracle happens – or not. In relation to how these topics have been treated in the recent history of theology, then, I am arguing for two things. The first is that any separation between theoretical and practical theology will ultimately be to the detriment of both: theory will lose its grounding in the life of faith and fall under the hegemony of one or other alternative academic discipline (whether that is logic, metaphysics, philology, history or, more recently, cultural studies), while practice will fragment into a ragbag of uncritical workaday guidelines for how to do things. In the present social environment, where the Church cannot presume upon majority support, this does, of course, raise particular problems for any theology practised within such public institutions as state-funded universities, which may or may not want to extend their brief outside the purely theoretical or academic domain – but that is a whole further question! The second is that within the conventional range of practical theological subjects, it is absolutely vital to see them not as a series of discrete, self-contained 'disciplines', but in the reality of their constant interaction.

In Chapter 2 I suggested that the Eastern Church's idea of theology as essentially mystagogy, that is, as initiating the practitioner into the mystery of the divine being-with-us, was essentially correct, whether or not our own spirituality can or should model itself on that of Byzantine monasticism. Yet, at the same time, the desire to communicate, to publicize and to make plain the meaning of the mystery also has its rights. In these terms we can imagine the practical theological disciplines as occupying a range of points on a grid marking the tensions, on the one side, between the public and the private, and, on the other, between mystery and clarity. Preaching, for example, would seem to be a quintessentially public act, performed by a duly authorized and accredited person in the context of a collective act of worship and having as its aim the explication of a given scriptural text. Christian pedagogy would similarly seem to be dedicated to explaining Christian doctrine and setting out the rational, historical and psychological grounds for believing. At the other extreme, pastoral care and spiritual direction would seem to be activities chiefly involving the individual, 'under four eyes', often exploring areas of experience – grieving, suffering, religious experience – where rational explanation cuts little ice. Yet these differences are relative rather than absolute. Preaching is not only about explanation. As I have argued in the present chapter, preaching too has a sacramental dimension and may, in the mystery of grace, be the occasion of that mystery itself becoming present to those receiving the Word. At a very obvious level, preaching itself usually begins and ends in prayer and will often have a poetic dimension that goes beyond anything purely pedagogical. Putting it at its simplest, it aims at the heart no less than at the mind. Also, though it is clearly a public activity, directed at the congregation as a whole, preaching has always at the same time been directed at the individual, at moving the heart of the individual and not merely at stirring the crowd. The preacher's ability to do this will, almost invariably, depend on whether he or she is one who, through pastoral conversation, knows the hearts of the ones to whom the sermon is addressed. Conversely, even the 'private' activity of, for example, spiritual direction is likely to involve processes of shared reading, evaluation and reflection that engage intelligence and discernment, however differently from academic study. Moreover, spiritual direction will not usually seek to lead the individual away from the common life of the Church into some supposedly more spiritual isolation, in which the adept can congratulate themselves on not being like the other, merely 'conventional' church-goers. Rather, the process of spiritual direction will draw its resources from the whole life of tradition and will, in the long term, seek to make its fruits available for the community as a whole.

As Howard Clinebell has definitively argued,[14] it is a mistake to think of 'pastoral care' as something that the ordained minister does on the basis of some kind of exclusive expertise: rather, pastoral care is a function of the whole life of a congregation, in which the minister has a key but not exclusive role. Individual and collective are in constant interaction. Where these diverse functions are engaged in a cycle of affirmation, then, we can easily imagine (and, hopefully, have sometimes experienced) that the public, verbal, reasoned art of preaching itself feeds the private, inarticulate, mysterious life of the inner person, while the nurturing of each individual's spiritual inwardness makes it possible for them to understand the preacher's words – and, indeed, the preacher too will only be able to preach effectively in the measure that the words are the product not just of the study but of the 'inmost being' in which the Spirit, as St Paul put it, is at work interpreting our 'inarticulate groans'. Moreover, the interaction between these forms is always both synchronic and diachronic. That is to say, that there is not only a constant and present interaction between, for example, preaching and prayer, but the preaching or teaching of one generation will help shape the prayer life of the next, and vice versa. What we preach today, will be prayed tomorrow and what we pray today will be preached tomorrow.

Something similar could be said of Christian pedagogy. Although teaching processes will instinctively aim at clarifying the matter under consideration, they do not exclude experiences of shared mystery. But teaching also depends not only on its matter and method, it also depends crucially on the relationship between teacher and learner. Here we recall Kierkegaard's observation that in the communication of religious truth the (human) teacher is never 'above' the learner, since, in this regard, only God can truly be regarded as teacher in the fullest sense. Yet, while not excluding God's ability to make some instructive use of educational catastrophes, Kierkegaard's dictum does not rule out – indeed, properly understood, it demands – a relationship of appropriate trust, understanding and respect on the part of both teacher and learner. And here we might also recall that Christian communication is communication of something uniquely and intensely personal, a relationship, a conversation, a trust, a shared life. If this is primarily a matter of a relationship between God and human beings, the personal quality of what is at issue will, normally, inform the processes in which the individual discovers and enters into the inheritance of friendship with God.

In his important study of the role of tradition in the life of the Church, Yves Congar, quoting Thomas Aquinas, pointed out that none of the three founders of the Western world's science, philosophy and religion (Pythagoras, Socrates and Jesus) left behind them a single written word: their impact on history was, in each case, via their immediate influence on a circle of learners, an influence in which their ideas and their personalities were inseparable.[15] At crucial junctures in the history of ideas something similar has repeated itself many times. In modern theology such varied figures as Friedrich Schleiermacher, John Henry Newman, Paul Tillich and Karl Barth would all provide examples of theological teachers whose writings were, in each case, significant in themselves but also effective through conveying the sense of a distinctive spiritual personality. In reading them we are not simply being confronted with ideas, arguments and images, but with the persuasive power of a creative, individual mind.

Of course, it is not only the 'great names' of theological history who have the right to be regarded as teachers in this sense. Many unpublished and unknown figures have exerted an extraordinarily liberating influence on those who have been their students, their teaching activity being poured entirely into their commitment to the actual communities to which they devoted their lives. And, their students are likely to say, although what they taught was important, the really decisive factor was their personality. Some might shy away from anything that could give occasion for a cult of personality, but if, as Barth put it, God could use a dead dog for revelation if he wanted to (poets, of course, might prefer to think of autumn leaves, sunsets or oceans), it would be more appropriate, in normal conditions, for an essentially personal communication to be embodied in media that are not less than personal and, for us, the human person is the most adequate example of such a medium.

Although I have made the point with regard to teaching, it could, of course, be applied to just about any other form of Christian communication. A large part of preaching is dependent on the personal engagement of the preacher – 'It's the way he says it' can be said of the preacher just as well as of the actor, and many sermons that make the earth move in their 'live' setting can seem rather thin when reduced to bare words on paper read after the event. Similarly, a key part of pastoral care will always be simply that someone was there with the sufferer in their suffering, no matter how inept the words with which they attempted to offer comfort. It is in such moments of fulfilled personal communication that Christian doctrine becomes real and even, we may say, becomes 'true' as the actual communication of God's saving presence.

If preaching, the conduct of worship, teaching, pastoral care, etc. can be spoken of as the forms of Christian communication, we should also be attentive to the media of such communication. Where all churches would, in differing mixes, offer preaching, sacraments, pastoral care, etc., there is far less agreement on what are the appropriate media in which these forms can be realized. The bitterest quarrels have centred on the role of visual media, and there have been repeated movements in Church history – early Protestantism being a case in point – where it has been argued that such media are totally inappropriate in the context of Christian communication and that the primacy of 'Word' means that, in the last resort, it is words that are the sole legitimate bearers of the divine self-communication to human beings. Further justification for such a view might also be found in the view that it is in our words, in language, that what is most distinctively human, most truly personal, comes to expression. Even the bodily dynamics of speech might be taken in support of the iconoclastic claim, since, when I speak, the word I utter is formed and sounds within me as it is articulated and, via the medium of external space, resonates also *within your body*. In this way speech performs a passage from the inwardness of the communicator's spiritual existence, via the publicness of articulated discourse to the inwardness of the recipient. Speech lives by means of the breath that many languages identify as the Spirit or life that is in us. In the case of painting or sculpture, however, we are dealing with the action of the hand on some outer medium and, even if the origin of the work of art is taken to be an idea 'in' the imagination of the artist, the image can only come into being by courtesy of a material form that is not itself human.

It is not my intention here to attempt to resolve the ancient quarrel between word and image in Christian thinking. However, it is worth pointing out that though the Bible itself indeed speaks of God as communicating via the Word given to the prophets, etc., it also records many other media used according to circumstance of time and place – rainbows, almond blossom, thunderstorms, earthquakes, solar phenomena, the cycle of the seasons and dreams are all at one time or another taken as belonging to the divine sign-system. Bearing in mind Grundtvig's insistence on the fleshliness of language, it is not hard to see that the biblical idea of 'Word' is larger than that of language narrowly conceived, so that, ultimately, the whole personality, body and soul, of Jesus Christ can be identified in the New Testament as 'the Word'. Certainly a close observation of the actual practice of Christian communication suggests that even in those churches most intensely focused on 'the Word', gesture, posture and intonation are all vital supplements to the formal dimensions of language 'as it is writ'. Nor should one forget the often unnoticed (unnoticed by theologians, that is) accompaniment of music, which, even in its most stripped-down forms, 'says' something more than the unaccompanied word. If we also turn to what is actually said in preaching, this too often turns out to involve appealing to non- or extra-verbal experiences. (I recall hearing a children's address many years ago in a bare, unornamented Calvinist church in the Scottish Highlands in which the preacher began by asking the children whether they had seen anything on the way to the kirk that had reminded them of God. The answer was 'the mountains'. Here, then, is a very ordinary example of how 'the Word' itself plays upon our capacity for seeing and, indeed, for seeing something – the mountain – as somehow more than its bare visual attributes.)

Outside the more determinedly verbal churches of the Reformation, however, we can see that the Christian tradition has made use of a large range of media, in more or less conscious ways. Architecture, painting, stained glass, sculpture, music, drama and dance are just some of the ways in which the central communicative act of the divine self-presentation has been refracted in the manifold of human media. Nor should we think of this solely in the context of public worship or education. Pastoral care, spirituality and even ethical and political reflection may also involve media over and above the written or spoken word, as when, in the past, a dying person would be encouraged to gaze on or hold a crucifix, or an icon, music, a candle or other object is used as the focus of meditation, or dramatic action is used to stir consciences and shake the political agenda. Today the churches are being challenged to discover how they might also use such newer media as film or information technology, and once more questions are raised as to whether one or other medium may, in fact, be more or less inappropriate for communicating the personal truth of Christian doctrine. I shall return to this question in the next chapter, but there is one further issue that needs to be addressed in relation to tradition, namely the relationship between Christian tradition and the larger human context in which that tradition lives.

For much of this chapter it might have seemed as if tradition were being conceived as a more or less self-sufficient movement within human history, the self-constituting story of the faithful few, God's pilgrim people weaving their way through a hostile or indifferent environment. The reality is somewhat different. For the reality is that tradition not only lives out of its own internal dynamics but out of a constant interaction with its environment. From the start I have suggested that God's self-communication is revealed in the structures and forms of our creaturely life in the world, long before there can be any talk of this being given a distinctively 'theological' or 'ecclesiastical' form. If the preacher's word can become a vehicle for 'the Word', it is in part because the conversation of family and friends has already opened us to receiving spiritual challenge and strengthening. Then, once we have entered the sphere of the Church, the way in which the sacraments are celebrated, the Bible is read and the preacher speaks will all reflect the tonality, expressiveness and phrasing of those who share a common contemporary language. This is true both of the way in which language is enacted in being spoken and in the content of that language itself, its images, metaphors and turns of phrase. That, today, friendship may be replacing kingship/subjecthood as a metaphor for the kind of relationship offered in the divine self-communication is just one example of this. It is, I would claim, a legitimate interpretation of tradition itself – but there is no denying that it also reflects changes in social life and political attitudes that have often been formulated in express opposition to the Church. Tradition, then, is not an 'autopoietic' system, that is, a self-generating, self-maintaining system, but an open system whose internal structures and dynamics are continually processing its manifold interactions with its environment. What the Church is, its tradition, is inseparable from its life in the world, and it is to the forms of this life in culture, ethics and the political that we now turn.

6

Formation

Culture

If we wish to see what is going on in the dynamic, God-communicating life of tradition (i.e. Christian doctrine), we must also take into account the environment in which the tradition finds itself. At a number of points I have alluded to general features of the human condition that are of significance for the form and manner in which we find ourselves called into the divine fellowship – that we are embodied creatures, subject to time and finitude, yet open to the sacramental epiphanies of God in nature and in those elements in our own lives determined by nature, above all the passages of birth, reproduction and death. But if, like every other mammal, human beings are products of nature, they are also beings whose behaviour, consciousness of the world and sense of self is importantly modified by their participation in a common social life. This means that we are not only creatures of nature, we are also creatures of culture, taking the term in its broadest sense. Many contemporary theorists would take this observation so far as to say that, in fact, there is nothing in us that is not culturally determined and therefore relative, though psychobiologists would strongly disagree. But one does not have to subscribe to the extreme view of cultural determinism in order to acknowledge that until we have taken the shaping spirit of culture into account we will have only a very abstract notion of what a human being is. In many theories of culture the word 'shape' itself plays a crucial role. The German term *Bildung*, for example, implies the formation of the human being into a certain determinate image, or *Bild*. According to the philosophers of *Bildung*, each age and each nation is marked by a distinctive combination of scientific, aesthetic, moral and religious knowledge and sensibility, it has a distinctive world-view that comprises both the picture we have of the external world and also our image of what a human being can and should strive to become. In these terms, culture was conceived both in terms of the individual internalizing the dominant image of humanity handed down by cultural tradition and in terms of the individual creatively transforming that same cultural inheritance. A cultured person was both someone shaped by the great tradition of arts, letters and science as well as someone able to contribute to the further development of the sphere of culture itself. Even the creative innovator, however, will be marked by their time and place, such that the unique contributions to culture of a Shakespeare, a Goethe, a Picasso or a Shostakovich are each marked by their distinctive cultural context, not least their nationality, as well as the impact they themselves made on that context.

The religious person, no less than others, would seem necessarily to be shaped by his or her participation in the culture of the day. An educated European believer of today, for example, will share many of the cultural presuppositions of other educated Europeans, including views about the origins of the cosmos and of human beings themselves, what artistic activities are worth cultivating and what moral and political values are most worth defending. If being or becoming religious means having somehow to slough off our cultural heritage then this will plunge us into bitter and intractable disputes, as debates about the teaching of creationism in schools illustrate. What, then, should be the stance of the believer in relation to culture? Is religion itself a form of sub- or counter-culture, more or less comfortably nesting within the larger stream of our collective cultural life? Or is there a basic continuity between religion and culture such that, as Tillich sometimes put it, culture is the manifestation of religion, religion the essence of culture?

Tillich wrote here out of his own background in the German tradition of *Bildung*-philosophy, in which the early nineteenth-century theologian F. D. E. Schleiermacher had been a prominent figure. Schleiermacher himself formulated the continuity between religion and culture in terms that we today might find surprising. He wrote that 'The highest purpose of the Church is the shaping of an artistic inheritance, through which the feelings of each individual are given shape and to which each individual in turn contributes.'[1] This may seem startling in an age such as ours when, after a century and more of modern art, it has become clear that, whatever religious aspirations individual artists may have, art generally finds itself happy to be free of religion and when religion, for its part, seems to want to focus more on peculiarly religious activities, rather than 'the shaping of an artistic inheritance'. The counter-intuitive nature of Schleiermacher's claim is deepened when he goes on to argue that the distinction we make between sacred and secular is not ultimately sustainable. Whereas the ancient world's conception of religion required the careful delineation of sacred and secular (to the point where, as in the Bible, those who trespassed unlawfully on the Holy Mountain, could be put to death), the modern world knows no such distinction. For us moderns, Schleiermacher says, it is not a matter of 'holy things for holy people' but 'every single profane thing has the potential to become the material of the religious, and that if anything profane were really to be irreligious, then it would be equally unsuitable for use by art'.[2] In other words, there is no final division between sacred and secular. There is nothing that cannot become the bearer of religious meaning. There is no art that does not have the potential to contribute to our religious formation.

Does Schleiermacher go too far in conflating religion and culture? Is there any real difference between his view and the opinion widely held among our own cultural elite that while religious motivations and beliefs might have had an important role in the past in stimulating the production of such great 'works of art' as the Sistine Chapel, Bach's *St Matthew Passion* or the icons of Russia, these are now part of culture rather than religion, and can be experienced and understood without our having to share the beliefs of those who produced them? Schleiermacher's contemporary, the philosopher Hegel, made the point rather memorably when, speaking of the great works of Italian Renaissance art, he stated that 'no matter how we see God the Father, the Christ and Mary so estimably and perfectly portrayed: it is no help; we bow the knee no longer'.[3] Whatever these works might have been in the past, they have become mere art, a part of the cultural inheritance, and no more. We certainly do not expect to see visitors to an art gallery venerating the pictures hung on the walls, praying, singing and weeping before them.

That is, of course, *our* view. An alternative approach is hinted at in the recent film *Russian Ark,* in which the viewer is taken on a tour of St Petersburg's Hermitage Museum by the ghost of a nineteenth-century French diplomat, the Marquis de Coustine, a historical personage, known for his traveller's letters from Russia. In the course of the film we find ourselves in different eras of the Museum's history (it was a royal palace before it became a museum), encountering various emperors and empresses, as well as present-day visitors and ending in a grand nineteenth-century ball. At one point the Marquis encounters a modern teenager looking at El Greco's painting of Saints Peter and Paul. De Coustine genuflects and crosses himself as he approaches the picture, before launching into a cross-examination of the hapless teenager. Do you read the Gospels, he asks and, when the boy admits that he doesn't but had merely heard that it was a good painting, de

Coustine asks him how he can possibly understand what human beings have it in them to become, what the founders of 'our Church' were as men and what they mean for our own existence. Gesturing towards a vividly realistic painting on the neighbouring wall that depicts a butchery, dominated by a large and bloody ox carcass, he challenges the boy to say what stops us from taking that image of dead meat as a truer image of the human condition than the painting of the apostles. Our capacity to respond to art itself is, in other words, intertwined with our readiness to face up to fundamental questions about the nature and possibilities of being human. Merely to 'see' El Greco as 'art' without being open to this deeper challenge would, then, be radically to foreshorten our vision of the art itself.

There are, then, very diverse ways of reacting to the question as to how far or in what ways cultural creativity can express the religious sense of the divine calling. The most widely used taxonomy of the various kinds of responses was set out by Richard Niebuhr in his 1951 study *Christ and Culture*. Here Niebuhr lists five possible forms that the relationship between Christ and culture might take.

The first is what he calls Christ *against* culture. Examples of this approach are found in Christian thinkers as diverse as Tertullian and Tolstoy, who call upon believers to separate themselves from the dominant forms of culture in order to live the Christian life in its absolute purity. Against this extreme position, Niebuhr points out that if the Christian is nevertheless to bear witness to Christ in the world, then, at the very least, that means using the words and ideas in which alone the message can be understood even if they are changed by being assumed into Christian usage. At the same time he points out that such an approach has a tendency to legalism and undervalues grace, since, it would appear, we have to do it all ourselves, not, in Tillich's phrase, accepting that we are accepted, but trying, through world-denial, to make ourselves acceptable to God.

The second position is what he calls the Christ *of* culture, where, among other examples, he locates the kind of cultural Protestantism derived from Schleiermacher. Here, he notes, the Christian task was no longer conceived in terms of overcoming the world but of humanizing or spiritualizing our natural, biological nature. Looking back from the twentieth century this is easy to criticize, not least with regard to the way in which it often seemed to do little more than cast a sentimental halo around the bourgeois family, but we should also be aware that that even the criticism of this kind of easy, established Christianity may owe as much to culture as does what is being criticized. One might think of the kind of Bible Belt fundamentalists who, as portrayed in a film such as *Elmer Gantry,* let rip at fast-talking, East Coast, city types, with their cynical attitudes and belief in evolution, not realizing that they themselves are living out a particular cultural form, rather than articulating a realistic response to the Bible. A readiness to extol the Bible and 'old-time religion' has become as much a cultural marker as it is the sign of a religious commitment.

A third option is that of Christ *above* culture, which Niebuhr sees in Thomas Aquinas and the Anglican Joseph Butler. Aquinas's saying that grace perfects rather than destroys nature sums up this approach. More nuanced than either of the preceding positions, Niebuhr finds it nevertheless a little bit too optimistic, emphasizing nature at the expense of grace.

The last two possibilities are both more drastic and more complex. The first is that of Christ and culture 'in paradox', which Niebuhr sees in Paul, Luther and Kierkegaard. Here the Christian must continue to live in the world though not being 'of' it. Yet there is no real interest in the creative possibilities of culture in their own right. By way of contrast, the Christ who *transforms* culture has a similar sense for the irresolvable paradox at the heart of the relationship, but, at the same time, places a positive value on cultural creativity. Niebuhr cites Augustine and F. D. Maurice as examples of this approach. Here the presence of God in time is given its full significance, and eternal life is understood not so much in terms of life with God 'after' time as a dimension of existence in the here and now.

It is, of course, often a problem with such categorizations that real-life thinkers or positions do not always readily fit them. I would want to argue that, in many respects, Kierkegaard belongs more to Niebuhr's last category than to that of 'Christ and culture in paradox', although I can also see evidence that would point to him being grouped with Tertullian and Tolstoy as world-denying. One could have similar debates about a number of the figures I have referred to in this book – Tillich, Teilhard, Grundtvig and even Schleiermacher himself are all figures who have traits of several different Niebuhrian positions. Catholics and Anglicans might want to argue that Aquinas and Butler were transformers of culture, rather than merely sublimating it in a complacent religiosity. Perhaps, however, the point is not or should not be to use such a schema as a way of simply tucking this or that thinker into this or that pigeonhole, but rather as a means of alerting us to the constantly moving pattern of possible relationships that are always in play when the issue of Christ and culture comes up. Moreover, there is a real sense in which the question of culture is itself culturally coloured. For the modern world this question often crystallizes around the possibility of a unitary culture, in which all of humanity's diverse spheres of action – religion, art, economics, politics, etc. – are somehow harmonized. Perhaps modernity can even be defined by its sense that it has irrevocably exited from such a culture, whether this sense takes a feeling of liberation or of nostalgia and regret.

Already in the 1790s, the poet and thinker Schiller famously analysed the stresses and strains of modern life in terms that have become almost routine: in the modern world, he argued, the division of labour has brought about the division of head and heart, feeling and intellect, individual and society; alienated and fragmented, the modern person finds him- or herself in an emotional and intellectual vacuum, which, left to itself, will lead rapidly to despair. Schiller's own counter-proposal was for an 'aesthetic education', a cultural formation that, primarily through art and poetry, would reconnect what social and scientific progress had put asunder. Schiller not only adumbrated a critique of society that remains current to this day, he also anticipated a tendency to turn to the past for alternative models. In his case, that meant an idealized version of Ancient Greece, but for many Christian thinkers, artists and ordinary believers it meant a revival of interest in the Middle Ages, which, having been scorned in the period of the Enlightenment, were now endowed with the accolade of having been the great Age of Faith. As this ideal medieval world took shape, it presented a picture of a society in which all the arts, sciences, industries and politics of the age had been synthesized into a great religio-cultural unity.

One of the great exponents of this view of the Middle Ages was the French philosopher Jacques Maritain, who wrote of the relationship between art and the Church in the following, glowing terms:

In the powerfully social structure of mediaeval civilisation the artist ranked simply as an artisan, and every kind of anarchical development was prohibited to his individualism, because a natural social discipline imposed itself upon him . . . He did not work for society people and the dealers, but for the faithful commons; it was his mission to house their prayers, to instruct their minds, to rejoice their souls and their eyes. Matchless epoch, in which an ingenuous folk was educated in beauty without even noticing it, as perfect religious ought to pray without being aware of their prayers; when doctors and painters lovingly taught the poor, and the poor enjoyed their teaching, because they were all of the same royal race, born of water and the Spirit![4]

This attitude, albeit in a somewhat more subtle form, continues to be encountered today, and a distinguished Catholic Church historian such as Eamon Duffy can eloquently commend the late medieval world as one in which the humble ploughman learns his paternosters through the art, the music, the drama and the great festivals of the Church's year in a way that was far more humane and far more thorough than the merely intellectual cast of Christian instruction in the Post-Reformation world.

Whatever is to be said for or against this as a historical assessment of the medieval world, there is no doubt that the ideal played a massive and paradoxical role in the modern world itself and, in particular, in determining the cultural profile of religion itself. Perhaps the clearest example of this is the phenomenon of the Gothic Revival which, in the nineteenth century, effectively came to monopolize church architecture in England. With roots in the eighteenth century and, arguably, links with a lingering living tradition of Gothic architecture, the Revival found a brilliant advocate in the young and colourful architect Augustus Welby Pugin who, tellingly, had first made a name for himself as a stage designer, producing much acclaimed sets for a dramatization of Sir Walter Scott's *Ivanhoe*. In such works as *An Apology for the Revival of Christian Architecture in England* and *Contrasts* (in which he contrasted the glories of medieval architecture with the absurdities and abominations of its degenerate modern descendant), Pugin insisted that the only possible architectural form for an English Christian Church was that found in Gothic:

> If we worshipped Jupiter or were votaries of Juggernaut, we should raise a Temple, or erect a pagoda. If we believed in Mahomet, we should mount the crescent and raise a mosque . . . If we denied Christ we should reject his Cross. For all these would be natural consequences; but, in the name of common sense, whilst we profess the creed of Christians, whilst we glory in being Englishmen, let us have an architecture, the arrangement and details of which will alike remind us of our faith and our country – an architecture whose beauties we may claim as our own, whose symbols have originated in our religion and in our customs . . . [5]

It was one of the extraordinary results of the success of Pugin's propagandizing on behalf of Gothic, followed by the zealous campaigning of the Camden Society, that while the seventeenth and eighteenth centuries had seen church architecture developing forms that matched those of contemporary secular architecture (Wren being

undoubtedly the supreme example of such a 'modern' church architect), nearly all of the new churches built in Britain from the 1840s
onwards reverted to a Gothic style. The impact of this on the whole
mission of the Church in modern society cannot, I think, be sufficiently emphasized. Apart from what one might think of its aesthetic
virtues (and Kenneth Clark's judgement that the Revival 'produced
so little on which the eye can rest without pain' is still worth pondering, even though he himself came to judge it over-severe), it was
simply an astonishing and, I believe, nearly suicidal move on the part
of the Church to allow the church buildings being created for the ever-
growing populations of the new industrial cities to be constructed in
a deliberately archaic style. Even before the organist played the first
note of the prelude, even before the preacher uttered the first word
of the sermon, the very building itself declared in no uncertain terms
that the Church had chosen *not* to engage in what Niebuhr would
call the creative transformation of culture, but had, instead, chosen
to opt into the mode of counter-culture, to separate itself out from the
new industrial and technological society that had grown up around it.
Paradoxically – but predictably – a move that was designed to reinstate
a unitary religious culture actually served to deepen and sharpen the
cleft between Church and society, underlining the Church's increasing marginalization and out-of-dateness in the modern world.[6] And,
in retrospect, the Revival demonstrated that *if* the ideal of an unitary
religious culture as idealized by Maritain is desirable, it cannot be
reinstated merely by a 'revival', by a return or an attempted return to
a past form of the Church's life. The Church, as we have repeatedly
seen, cannot and need not attempt to shake off its own saturation in
the flood of historical change, and the very concept of tradition itself
requires an attention to, and a responsiveness to, the specific opportunities as well as the specific problems of the present. Engagement with
culture is not likely to – and should not – lead to the identification of
the Christian message with any one cultural form, even though the
communication of that message can never occur except in a form that
is 'cultural'.

Image and Word

One question which the absorption of many Christian writers, artists
and thinkers in the Middle Ages did serve fruitfully to bring back to
the fore of the Church's consciousness, however, was that of the media
of Christian communication. Again we have to be wary of the trap of

over-simplification into which many of the admirers of Gothic have repeatedly stumbled. Yet there is some justice in the view that the Middle Ages was in a very distinctive way a visual religious culture that, in its own terms, was extremely effective.

The origins of Christian art and the extent of its role in the Church prior to Christianity becoming the official religion of the Roman Empire are obscure and debated. Clearly there were some places with traditions of painting tombs of saints or places of worship (sometimes the same) from at least the second century onwards. But there are also stories of images in churches causing outrage, as when the fourth-century Bishop Epiphanius of Salamis tore down an image painted on a curtain in a church (but then he is described in Cross's edition of the *Oxford Dictionary of the Christian Church* as a man of 'unbending rigidity' with a 'want of judgement' and a 'complete inability to understand any who differed from him'!). By the beginning of the fifth century, however, there was a large and rapidly growing body of Christian art that was developing its own distinctive style and not simply recycling previous pagan styles (as in some early Roman Christian art). The great storms of the Iconoclastic Controversy (which lasted a little over a hundred years, from 730 to 843) and the incursions of Islam naturally curbed this growth, although these did not affect the Western Church in the same measure. From the end of the Iconoclastic Controversy, however, the creation of a great cultural inheritance of religious art flourished virtually unchecked in East and West, until the Reformation, although, at least in the West, there was a continuing undercurrent of criticism in some monastic and radical movements. Yet, in the main, the language of religion in the Middle Ages was very much a visual language, a situation endorsed in the then universally quoted (actually misquoted!) saying of Pope Gregory the Great that images were 'poor men's books' or 'books for the unlearned', who, of course, were the vast majority of believing Christians.

In terms of the comments in the last chapter about the way in which the various forms of the Church's communicative life can each employ a variety of media, the Middle Ages provide many examples of how images played a central role in public worship, private devotion, teaching, penitential practices and, indeed, the whole range of religious activities. One example nicely illustrates both the multifaceted and subtle nature of this language. It is the image known as the Mass of St Gregory. One of the most widely disseminated images of the fifteenth century, its importance was such that anyone saying five paternosters, five Ave Marias and one Creed before any reproduction of it could receive 32,755 years' remission from purgatory. The image itself shows a miracle supposedly connected with Pope Gregory I himself.

The legend is that one day, while Gregory was saying Mass, Jesus himself appeared on the altar in the form of 'the man of sorrows', scourged and bleeding. But although Gregory in fact lived in the second half of the sixth century, the story first appears about 1400. Art-historically, it is intimately connected with one particular image, an icon that originated in the Eastern Church but, partly through the agency of the legend of the Mass of St Gregory, became widely disseminated in a variety of versions in the West. More specifically, it is an image of the dead Christ, shown with discoloured skin, his hands folded over his chest, revealing the imprint of the nails, and his head drooping to one side. The origin of the legend is associated with a mosaic icon made in Sinai in about 1300, brought to Rome in 1380 and installed in the Church of S. Croce i Gerusalemme, where the popes were accustomed to say Mass on Good Friday.

That the legend appears shortly after this time and, in the earliest illustrations, the manifestation of Christ clearly reflects just this particular icon, alerts us to the fact that we are looking at a powerful synthesis of themes around the authority of the pope, the root of that authority in the sacrificial death of Christ, and the role of the Mass in communicating the benefits of that death to the believer. Nor is it coincidental that this image developed within a context in which the doctrine of transubstantiation had begun to shape the whole liturgical consciousness of the Church. For the belief that through the words of consecration spoken by the priest the communion host became, literally, the body of Christ, led to an intense visualization of eucharistic practice. In this period begins the elevation of the host, so that all can *see* the Lord's actual body, altars become more brightly illuminated to further facilitate such viewing and a new verb comes into usage, 'to sacre', meaning to gaze upon the transubstantiated host. In the feast of Corpus Christi ('the Body of Christ') this transformation found its ultimate expression in the great ritual processions that often involved not only the clergy but town guilds performing *tableaux vivants*, and in which the carrying of the host in a monstrance (quite literally, a vessel in which the object contained is 'shown forth') was the central feature. However, against the Protestant view that this visualization of religion meant the neglect of preaching, it should be added that Corpus Christi became in many places one of the principal occasions for important public sermons, a function especially associated with the Dominican Order.

It was perhaps a testimony to the sheer power of the medieval world's visual culture and to the way in which this did not merely illustrate doctrine but was intimately tied up with the very meaning of the doctrine that the Protestant Reformation rapidly became marked by hostility towards visual art. Luther himself was not completely hostile to images, and was happy for his translations of the Bible and for catechetical works to be illustrated. Yet, in the main, the century and a half from Luther to Cromwell saw a massive emptying of images of all kinds from churches in Protestant areas, England, for all our self-image of moderation, having been one of the most iconoclastic of all Reformation countries.

It would be easy to interpret this Protestant iconoclasm as marking a simple, black-and-white hostility to culture, an illustration of the first of Niebuhr's categories: Christ *against* culture. This would be how some Protestant iconoclasts themselves would have understood it, since, in their terms, the visual culture of the Middle Ages exemplified the state of a Church that had been choked and overwhelmed by the values and practices of the world. But this would be to see only half the picture, so to speak. For neither early nor later Protestantism was ever simply *without* culture. Rather, it incorporated a whole new cultural movement in which a new medium arose to take the place of the medieval image, namely the book. It would, of course, be wrong to imply that Catholicism was unaffected by the culture of the book, but it is, equally, no coincidence that the Protestant Reformation was able to ride the wave of the discovery of printing, which enabled the rapid and mass circulation of the new translations of the Bible produced by the Reformers, as well as a multitude of biblical commentaries, theological tracts and polemical pamphlets.

The advent of the book not only impacted on the dominant visual language of religion, it also inaugurated important new approaches to knowledge and communication in a wide variety of ways. In this regard the work of Walter J. Ong is of especial interest, not least because of the way in which Ong's point of departure is precisely the border between philosophy, on the one hand, and the cultural phenomenon of the printed book, on the other. In his earlier work he produced an important study of the sixteenth-century logician Pierre de la Ramée, often referred to in his own time and subsequently by the Latin form of his name, Petrus Ramus. Teaching in the University of Paris, Ramus revolutionized the teaching of logic, breaking with the then dominant interpretation of Aristotle and encouraging a much greater clarity in the forms of argument and presentation. His conversion to Protestantism and his death in the massacre of St Bartholomew's Day, led to him acquiring the status of a martyr among many Protestants, in addition to his intellectual reputation. Among other things, Ramus encouraged the dividing up of each subject into a series of subordinated headings, rather than, as seen in Aquinas, a sequence of more or less laterally arranged subjects distributed along a common level. The interesting connection between this and the rise of print is evidenced in the emergence of the kind of layouts that one can see, for example, in Robert Burton's *Anatomy of Melancholy* – admittedly an extreme example, which some commentators suspect of being an essentially ironic take on the pretensions of the new knowledge. These kinds of layouts would not, of course, be impossible to produce manually, but the advent of print made them far more feasible when it was a question of producing multiple copies. Ramus's thought was also strongly influential via English Puritans in the early academic culture of New England and, through such institutions as Harvard, had a powerful role in shaping American intellectual development. Although some of the more specific traits of Ramism soon passed into the history books, the kind of hierarchical, systematizing tendencies he encouraged can be seen in the sort of organization of subject-matter one encounters in German idealism and which still influences the conceptualization and organization of academic syllabuses in many (especially European) universities.

All – or much – of this, Ong claims, would be inconceivable without the agency of print. The more specific characteristics of Ramism aside, Ong offers many examples of how print changed the organization and presentation of knowledge. Indexes now became regular features of scholarly works (manuscripts could rarely if ever be produced with precisely matching pagination across hundreds of copies!), as well as standard illustrations, especially important in this period in scientific works (as, for example, in Robert Hooke's beautifully illustrated *Micrographia,* a book devoted to the wonders of nature discoverable through the microscope). The age of the dictionary now gets into full swing and, as Ong points out, it was not until the 1961 edition of *Webster's Third New International Dictionary* that compilers of dictionaries fully accepted the principle of including usage not found in printed sources. In other words, from the seventeenth to the twentieth centuries, the dictionary movement attempted to define the language primarily in terms of its printed form. Printed editions also greatly facilitated standard quotation practices, shadowed by the rise of copyright and complex legal issues about the ownership of a text.

Despite the presence of a strong literate minority in Europe before the sixteenth century, Ong emphasizes how, before the rise of print, the vast majority still inhabited what was an essentially oral culture, and he is painstaking in describing the differences between such an oral culture and the book culture that replaced it. The use of language in oral culture is largely determined by the principle that 'You know what you can recall.'[7] The need to make ideas and narratives memorable is served by 'heavily rhythmic, balanced patterns, in repetitions or antitheses, in alliterations and assonances, in epithetic and other formulary expressions, in standard thematic settings (the assembly, the meal, the duel, the hero's "helper", and so on), in proverbs which are constantly heard by everyone'.[8] Other features he enumerates are that oral style is additive rather than subordinative, aggregative rather than analytic, redundant or 'copious', conservative or traditionalist, close to the life-world of the 'immediate, familiar interactions of human beings',[9] agonistically toned, empathetic, homeostatic (i.e. filtering out what is not immediately relevant), situational rather than abstract. I shall not go into the details of what all these distinctions, some of them couched in rather opaque terminology, mean, but the first provides a nice and theologically relevant example of the kind of shift Ong is describing.

That oral style is additive means that, instead of subordinating a sequence of clauses or sentences to one overarching idea defined by the paragraph, each clause or sentence has an independent status. Ong illustrates this with the difference between the early English translations of the first five verses of the Bible and their modern successors. He uses the Catholic Douay and the New American (1970) Bibles to make the point, but it is equally clear if we compare the King James Version with any contemporary translation. King James reads:

> In the beginning God created the heaven and the earth.
> **And** the earth was without form, and void; **and** darkness was upon the face of the deep.
> **And** the Spirit of God moved upon the face of the waters.
> **And** God said, Let there be light: **and** there was light.
> **And** God saw the light, that it was good: **and** God divided the light from the darkness.
> **And** God called the light Day, **and** the darkness he called Night.
> **And** the evening and the morning were the first day.

I have placed the additive (rather than merely connective) 'ands' in bold type to emphasize the point. Where King James has ten of these, the Revised English Bible has only five, and many other modern translations have fewer still. Ong argues, persuasively, that the early translators, though clearly men of high educational achievements, lived in and from a culture where language was still permeated by oral patterns and that they quite naturally reproduced them in their own English usage. Nor was it only the Bible that reflected these patterns. Several years ago I saw a production of *A Midsummer Night's Dream* in a middle school in the heart of rural England. The young boy who played the 'rude mechanical' Nick Bottom made a point of giving exaggerated emphasis to the word 'and' every time it cropped up – and it soon became clear that, to the audience's modern ears it cropped up an amusingly large number of times. We cannot doubt, of course, that Shakespeare had the best of ears for the speech patterns of his own, largely oral environment, nor that those of his audience who regarded themselves as better educated would not relish such a way of underlining the 'rudeness' of the barely literate 'mechanicals'! And one might add that it is possible that the residual hold that the King James Version and Cranmer's Prayer Book still have on many contemporary Anglicans is not so much to do with their precision or elegance but their innate sense for the orality of language, an attribute particularly favourable to texts that are designed to be read aloud.

Certainly printing was decisive for the way in which the Bible came to be used in Protestant churches and spiritual life, when, as printed texts became steadily cheaper, the ideal of a Bible in every home came close to realization. The same might be said of the manifold catechisms produced by the Reformation churches, often illustrated; of collections of sermons for personal reading (beginning with Luther himself); and, by the time we reach the nineteenth century and the rise of a genuine mass market, of the proliferation not only of Bibles but of the 'lives of Jesus' that, in more or less fantastic ways, supplemented the believer's 'picture' of the historical Jesus. Nor was printing less significant for Protestant missions and the Bible Societies and organizations such as the Society for the Propagation of Christian Knowledge that combined publishing, missionary and educational activities.

If the monastic cell of the ancient and medieval Church had often functioned as a place of study (as the iconography of Saint Jerome and Saint Barbara, among others, shows), the Protestant minister became intimately associated with his 'study', rather than the oratory, and would be expected to hold a private library – although, in his chapter on 'The Parson's Library' George Herbert programmatically states that 'The Country Parson's Library is a holy Life.'[10] But, then, Herbert was perhaps presciently aware of the danger in this development: that scholarship – 'book-learning' – could easily come to dislodge piety as a defining trait of public ministry. Of itself, of course, there was no intrinsic reason why being learned should not be compatible with being pious (and Herbert himself provides a good example of how they might be combined), but the possibility was always there. I began this book with an anecdote concerning how, when I was first getting interested in Christianity and approached my parish priest, he gave me a book to read. I wasn't at all surprised that he should. It seemed somehow an accepted part of the role of the parish priest that he *should* be able to lend out or to recommend suitable reading for those interested in particular religious issues. It is only when one steps back that one realizes that this is a very specific, culturally determined expectation.

In rejecting the visual culture of the Middle Ages, Protestantism was only rarely, in practice, able to reject culture as such. On the contrary, it became the flag-bearer of a new wave of culture, the culture of the book, of universal literacy, of the Bible in every home, or, putting it another way, it made of this culture the dominant form of its own religious practice.

Today, of course, we find ourselves in the midst of a new cultural revolution, in which many are predicting the demise of the book as new cultural forms engulf us. There is not scope here to develop a full discussion of these, only to flag that this is an area which deserves probably more theological reflection than it is currently getting. For, as we have seen, cultural media are never simply neutral transmitters of communicative acts, but the medium undoubtedly shapes, colours and informs the message, even if we hesitate to go all the way with McLuhan and say that 'the medium *is* the message'. Two of the new cultural forms that should be mentioned, however, are cinema and the electronic media.

Cinema has, throughout its short history, had an ambivalent relationship with Christianity. The Bible provided the subject-matter for some of the very earliest films, but, on the other hand, many perceive cinema as having been the most powerful vehicle for the saturation of modern society with images of sex and violence. If one thing is clear, however, it is that many of the directors who have ventured into the area of religious and, especially, biblical subject-matter, have not sufficiently reflected on the tensions between the materials they are using and the nature of the medium. In many respects, most of the films that have dealt with biblical topics have done so in the manner of the nineteenth century's scholarly or literary 'lives of Jesus'. In other words, they have attempted to portray the events of, say, the Gospels as if they made up a coherent narrative. But, by the beginning of the twentieth century, as the age of cinema itself was dawning, most theologians were having to concede that trying to get a coherent, harmonized narrative out of the Gospels was unachievable, if only because they were not that sort of text, they were not potted biographies of Jesus.

Yet film directors have rushed blindly ahead, trying to link materials from different parts of the gospel into a single, simple narrative. But worse, the modern demand for psychological and social motivation has meant that they have had to add all sorts of extraneous material to make the narrative credible. The realism of the medium itself cruelly exposes the flimsiness of such constructions, and it was only too easy for *Monty Python's Life of Brian* to pillory such efforts. In fact, some of the worse sequences of George Stevens's *The Greatest Story Ever Told* or Zeffirelli's *Jesus of Nazareth* could almost be from the *Life of Brian*. This is not because they are incompetent works, but simply because they are based on entirely false premisses.

Much more successful are those works that show a certain reflexivity in relation to the text, alerting us to the fact that what we are seeing is not 'how it was for Jesus', but is an artistic representation of a text. *Jesus of Montreal*, for example, does this by the conceit of a group of actors attempting to revitalize a passion play only, as they do so, their own lives come to be shaped by an analogous drama, ending with them being excluded from the church where it is being performed and the death of the troupe's leader. In this way the film does not attempt to show us anything like historical verisimilitude, but invites us to reflect on what this story can mean for us today in 'Montreal'.

Although Piero Paolo Pasolini's *The Gospel According to St Matthew* may at first look like another historical costume drama, it too avoids the gaffes of many other Jesus films. The title itself warns us that what we are seeing is not history but the film of a book, and by keeping close to the text the film refuses to stray into the kind of psychological fantasy that has Jesus and Peter staring into each other's eyes with deeply meaningful expressions or that invents complex sub-plots explaining Judas's betrayal. The use of music from many periods, including Bach, blues and Russian church music, and costumes that are more Italian renaissance than first-century Palestine also underline that this is not a narrative spectacle but something that demands our interpretative activity. The same, in a very different way, could be said of *Jesus Christ Superstar*. Mel Gibson's *The Passion of the Christ* avoids some of the problems of earlier Hollywood-style film Christs by its sharp focus on the passion and by the sustained violence that pre-empts any sniggering at the absurd contrivances of plot and dialogue that mark other films of this type. Its closeness to the Stations of the Cross also gives it a liturgical feel that helps distance it from a simple historical chronicle. On the other hand, the flashback scenes, though interesting as an idea, show how hard it is to shake off the sentimentality of the genre, while, as in many other cases, the Judas sub-plot degenerates into absurdity.

Of course, there are other, more subtle, more indirect ways of treating fundamental religious questions in film that do not involve the direct treatment of biblical material. A director such as Lars von Trier (in *Breaking the Waves* and *Dogville*) creates allegories of aspects of Christological doctrine, while the Russian director Andrei Tarkovsky perhaps went further than any in creating films that achieve something like a sacramental communication of spiritual truth. But what is important here is not so much the rarity of such achievements, but the fact that they are possible.

Nor should we be too exclusively high-brow: in a wonderful episode in *Hannah and Her Sisters*, Woody Allen's familiarly anguished Jewish New Yorker is pondering the existential meaninglessness of life and wondering whether to convert to Catholicism. But then he goes into a cinema and sees a Marx Brothers' movie, and, as the waves of laughter roll over him, he realizes that life is, after all, good. Though this might be taken as an *anti*-religious moment, it is in its own way profoundly expressive of the sacramental power of film art to transform our living self-awareness. What yet remains to be done in cinema is unknown, but we cannot presume to have fully explored its potential as a medium of religious communication.

More recently, we have witnessed the rapid exodus of knowledge, information and the word from off the pages of the book (and, for that matter, off celluloid) into the universal and invisible medium of electronic communication. We speak glibly of 'Information Technology', yet it is striking that Ong gave his study *Orality and Literacy* the subtitle *The Technologizing of the Word*. We should not forget, in other words, that the rise of print and the book as we know it are themselves 'technological', no matter how different, aesthetically speaking, the experience of handling a beautiful, leather-bound seventeenth-century tome and tapping in a couple of key words to a search engine. The old book may, in its way, also be a work of art, but it too was a technologically determined product. As the Church begins to orientate itself to the new situation, then, it is not a question of whether Christian communication is 'for' or 'against' technology as such, it is a question of the particular possibilities and limitations of particular technologies. Just as most Christians today probably sense that there was some loss involved in the jettisoning of the medieval visual culture, so too there is likely to be some loss in the transition from the age of the book to the age of electronic communication. Under the universal limitations of history, each age, each culture, can only bring to expression a limited range of communicative possibilities, and these will be accompanied by the equally inevitable omission of others that, in another age and another culture, may be or might have been the most highly regarded. At the same time, few if any Christians today would wish to erase the contribution of the printed word from the overall life and development of the Church. Nor is it likely to happen. Just as the advent of the book did not mean the end of visual media in the life of society at large, nor even in the Church, so too the advent of the Information Revolution is likely to leave important scope for the book, although the function of the book will very likely develop into something quite different from what it has been for the last 500 years or so. It is perhaps typical of the situation we are in now that the quotation I took from the King James Bible – that masterpiece of an early printed book – was downloaded from the internet into what, at this moment, is an electronic document but which, by the time you read it, will be a book! Ong speaks of the new technological revolution as ushering in what he calls a 'new orality', although, as he also remarks, this will be something very different from the old or original orality.

In all that I have been saying about doctrine as the process of communicating Christian truth, I have been arguing that it is helpful to see this process as the communicative event of a call, an invitation, an opening by which we are given the possibility of being drawn into the process of the divine life. I have variously described this process as a conversation, a dance, a play, friendship or fellowship with God, a spiralling advance from glory to glory but, in all these forms, I have underlined that it is experienced and understood as a communion of persons and, therefore, from our side, the matter of a free and creative response. Many of the anxieties that Christians have about the communications revolution, I believe, arise precisely from their sense that there is something about the new media of email, the mobile phone and the internet that intrinsically leads to the diminishment of the personal element in communication. In this connection it might be seen as no coincidence that, in literary theory, the same movement that, from the 1960s onwards, has proclaimed 'the death of the book' has also proclaimed 'the death of the author'. Where knowledge is broken down into 'bits' of information and conversation fragmented into the staccato, infinitely-repeated catchphrases of text messages, something very precious seems to be going missing. In the speed of contemporary communication, there seems no longer to be space to think, to *be*. Try it – just once in a while write a letter to someone with whom you usually keep in touch by email or the mobile phone. You will surely find that it is a very different process, bringing very different parts of your own personality into play. Unless you are happy to send a completely messy letter, not too many words or sentences can be 'deleted' as you go along, so you will have to think very carefully about what you are saying and be committed to it in a far greater degree. It will, at one level, be far more 'you'. In the case of the mobile, however, and as the advert for one mobile phone company put it, with my mobile I can be 'where I want, when I want, even when I'm not'. Such an aspiration seems to be the epitome of a world that has altogether lost the possibility of 'presence', of being ourselves where and when we are and thus open to a God-relation in which God too is, however mysteriously, 'present' (theologically, of course, we would want to say that it is precisely this divine self-presencing that is the ground of our being able to be present to ourselves). Seen in the perspective of such suspicions, dumbing-down is not an accidental by-product of the changes we are going through, it is of their essence. Here – and this returns us to the questions which, in Chapter 1, we saw being raised by such contemporary humanist thinkers as Habermas – it would seem to be the fundamental challenge of contemporary reality that it stifles, routinizes and organizes out of existence not only the freedom of moral and political action, but also the creative freedom that, in its deepest roots, is simply incompatible with such a seamless global systematization of knowledge and, along with knowledge, power. The internet, it could be added, is not only the perfect symbol of such a systematization, it is also its expression and medium.

We are, of course, still too much in the middle of these massive upheavals to have any detached, objective view as to what they really mean. We should, however, note that the kind of suspicions being voiced here can be paralleled in the case of the other media we have been considering. Many Protestant iconoclasts believed that visual media were necessarily tied to sensuous representation in such a way that cultivating them would lead to the occlusion or dissipating of human beings' spiritual possibilities. Your God is that on which you set your heart and which, in turn, defines who you are, argued Zwingli. If, then, you make your God a visual image, so too will your sense of who you are be limited to whatever can be represented in two dimensions. But, equally, we noted George Herbert's beautifully indirect word of warning against allowing book-learning to take the place of cultivating holiness. Each age, each culture, each form, each medium of Christian communication has its perils, and each must be recognized and reckoned with in their own terms. And we must also remember that, if we are duly attentive to what is implied in Kierkegaard's doctrine of 'the sign of contradiction', there never has been and never can be a sign, or system of signs, a medium of meaningful communication, that is able altogether to break out of the ambiguity, uncertainty and paradox that marks every facet of the human God-relationship in time and history.

The recognition of this essentially unstable element in any symbolic representation of the divine–human relationship has itself been a major factor in iconoclastic and other anti-cultural movements, as if one could get rid of the problem by getting rid of the symbols when, in fact, the problem lies much deeper. As we have just seen, while it was possible for the Protestant Reformers to break the power of the visual culture of the medieval world, it was not, in fact, possible for them simply to step out of the sphere of culture altogether. They simply chose different cultural forms that, in their judgement, better served the needs of Christian communication at that historical juncture. Whether or how far they were correct in that judgement continues, of course, to be debated. But putting it like this is not to say that all cultures are more or less the same, all have their pluses and minuses and, therefore, we should simply stick with the one we've got. In terms of the view of tradition developed in the last chapter, the Church, and each believer, is constantly in the midst of a moving landscape of symbolic communications that require interpretation and require a response. We cannot – and do not – simply hold ourselves aloof, suspending judgement, but are – and should be – constantly engaged in sifting, evaluating, interpreting and, finally, judging. Sartre wrote that we are condemned to be free and, as the essentially communicative beings we are, we may equally well say that we are condemned always to be interpreting, reinterpreting and responding to (and therefore also transforming) the words, images, symbols, forms, media that make up the whole milieu of our communicative life.

The element of transformation in this process points to the last of Niebuhr's categories, Christ the *transformer* of culture, though, one might add, some element of transformation, no matter how slight, belongs to every genuine cultural event. This possibility also points to how, over time, one might see the emergence of a distinct Christian culture, as the whole range of cultural possibilities are gradually transformed through their interaction with a dynamic and vital religious tradition. This might equally well be in the form of the visual culture of the Western Middle Ages or the book culture of at least some Protestant countries in the period from the seventeenth to the nineteenth centuries. In this way, as Schleiermacher stated, religion can itself produce an inheritance of cultural works, institutions and values that are saturated with possibilities of communicating the things of God to those who have ears to hear. Whether such a possibility might emerge out of the present communications revolution is and has to be an open question. However, we should also ask whether, if possible, it is also desirable or what it would mean if it could be achieved. For the same dynamics of interactive transformation that allow for the emergence of a Christian culture mean that instability is already built into the process and that what emerges will also dissolve back into it. Such a culture can itself be no more than a provisional and temporary expression of a communicative dynamic that, sooner or later, will see it swept away with all the other products of human history. No such culture will ever be the kingdom of God on earth, except in so far as that kingdom accepts its own ambiguous and paradoxical character. Now that we have the historical sense to recognize in advance that that is how it is, we are perhaps less inclined to postulate such a unitary religious culture as the 'highest' goal of our religious striving, whether in its Catholic or its Protestant forms. More realistically, we might be inclined to acknowledge that, in the longer course of its development, the dynamics of Christian tradition will bring about the alternating predominance of each of Niebuhr's categories, as the Church repeatedly has to make its exodus from a cultural Christianity that has lost its vitality and, in manifold ways, both transform what it has inherited from the past as well as discerningly taking up what it judges to be the best of the possibilities presented by the new.

Ethical and Political Postscript

The Ethical

The shape acquired by Christian doctrine in the process of creative communication between God and world is not exhausted by the cultural forms into which it enters or which it generates. No less important are its ethical and political forms. Indeed, many would see these as being of far greater importance than 'mere' cultural formation, since, they believe, ethics and politics engage with reality at a more fundamental level than cultural activity. Culture, it is felt, is a kind of luxury item compared with the basic decisions that confront us as we struggle with basic issues of good and evil or with socially institutionalized injustice. Society in general confirms this feeling by the way in which leading church figures are far more likely to be invited to comment on the burning moral and political issues of the day than on, say, the latest controversies in the world of culture and the arts. 'Personal morality' in particular is seen to be an area in which religion is an important stakeholder. People look to the Church, it is said, for moral guidance or moral leadership. And, although there are considerable variations in attitudes in different countries – even within Western Europe – no one is too surprised if bishops speak out on matters of war and peace, poverty, racism or injustice: they do not, however, expect to see a bishop or theologian sitting on the panel of a late-night arts programme, unless the topic is some work of art likely to cause offence to religious believers.

This being said, it is not always easy to draw a sharp line between issues of culture and of ethics. Many social and cultural theorists see culture as something far more pervasive than 'culture' in the narrow sense of 'the arts'. On this larger view, culture embraces, shapes and expresses every aspect of human sensibility and, therefore, many areas that Christians have traditionally regarded as ethical. Perhaps the most divisive issue in many churches today is that of homosexuality, and one of the reasons why it is so divisive is precisely because there is a general failure to agree on whether it is a cultural or a moral issue.

For the traditionalist or conservative,[1] it is, plainly, a moral issue, and whether one sees the roots of morality in divine law (biblical pronouncements against homosexuality) or natural law (some supposed universal law that homosexual acts are against nature), there is a clear question of right and wrong. Some liberals accept this framework, arguing that the biblical proof-texts adduced by the conservatives need to be interpreted in a more sensitive or complex way or that the testimony of nature is less clear than has been assumed.

But the difficulty of reaching any agreement is compounded by the fact that many on the liberal side of the argument simply do not see it as a moral issue in that way. As they see it, sexuality is no less 'culturally' determined than, say, eating with table cutlery or fingers. James Allison, for one, sees the question as being on a par with St Peter's discovery (as recounted in Acts 10) that Jewish dietary laws could not be a universal condition of welcome into the divine fellowship.[2] Different cultures do it differently, and that's all.

Many traditionalists are, of course, quite comfortable with the idea that Christianity can and should be 'enculturated' in a myriad of different forms, and that the social mores of the European should not be imposed on the African or Asian in the way that missionaries tended to do in the past. But they do not accept that the question of sexuality is merely one of culture in this sense. Equally, the liberal would probably not accept that (say) the admissibility of torture is something that can be regarded as a matter of cultural variability. The liberal is likely to insist that Christians should oppose torture wherever it is found. An 'ought' is in play, putting the argument on a whole different footing to arguments about culture. One cannot argue about matters of taste, but one can and must argue about matters of right and wrong, because there is a right and a wrong outcome. Then again, there are matters that a broad consensus today accepts as matters of culture (and therefore legitimately variable), but which were argued passionately in the past, as issues on a level with the gravest moral questions. This is most obvious in the case of debates about the role of images in religion, or in the shift from oral to book cultures, or from Latin to vernacular liturgies (and in the complaints of some evangelicals that rock-and-roll is intrinsically 'devil's music', though older generations of Puritans said the same about the use of the organ to accompany singing).

One can therefore allow that there is a difference between culture and ethics, while acknowledging that there is considerable scope for disagreement as to where exactly the line between them should be drawn. This obscurity lies at the root of one of the paradoxes of society's attitude to religion. On the one hand, the disorientating pace of cultural change is cited as a factor driving many to seek guidance or help from the Church, but that change itself makes it difficult for us to agree on what exactly the Church is or isn't competent to speak on. Even in the area of personal morality, there is increasing hostility in wide sections of society to church leaders making any significant pronouncements at all, if these deviate from an assumed consensus. And even within those church communities that officially espouse the idea of a leadership competent to give clear and authoritative guidance, there is widespread evidence that whether it concerns issues of birth-control or war-making the laity simply ignore the guidance that they themselves call for.

Yet it remains a deep conviction in both conservative and liberal circles that, whatever else it does or doesn't do, Christian faith must impact on the way in which we engage with the great and inescapable moral questions that confront us on our journey through life. Many Christian apologists (and, for that matter, those of other faiths) have also argued that religion is one of the chief pillars of morality itself and that without religion, society would not stay moral for long. The half-way house of many late twentieth-century secularists abandoning belief in God but holding on to moral ideals such as the good (Iris Murdoch might be taken as a sensitive recorder of this position) is judged to be no more than a temporary solution.

The case that morality without religion simply cannot be strong enough to stand up to the demands made upon it was, in a sense, implied in Nietzsche's attack on both morality and religion. Whereas an earlier secularist such as Feuerbach deemed it possible to let go of faith in God but still hold on to belief in humanity and in love, Nietzsche argued that such ideals were mere echoes of the old theology. Once we realize that God is dead, he said, we realize that all values are relative and that we are entirely free to choose whatsoever values we like or, to put it in more Nietzschean terms, whatever values we are courageous enough to stand up for. Such convictions, restated in the mid-twentieth century in Jean-Paul Sartre's existentialist philosophy, have continued to reverberate on into our own time. Nor is this simply an academic philosophical debate. On the contrary, it impacts on the very way in which we think of being human. Much counselling practice, for example, Christian as well as secular, reflects the key intuitions of Carl Rogers, one of the seminal figures of the modern counselling movement, whose view of what counselling aims at is decidedly Nietzschean. Counselling, Rogers says, is to lead the client to become the self that he or she truly is by moving 'away from "oughts"', 'away from meeting expectations', 'away from pleasing others', and 'towards self-direction'.[3] In other words, being truly one-self means regarding oneself as unconstrained by any moral or social expectations that come from others. As individual selves, we are free to be whatever and however we like. This, fairly concisely, mirrors the popular wisdom found in soap operas, when those facing life-changing decisions (whether to have an abortion, leave a partner, or undertake some self-sacrificial act) are told by their friends, 'Don't let anyone else tell you what to do,' 'You have to decide what's best for you,' etc.

But whether it is a matter of intellectual consistency or simply personal courage, such a reinvented private morality would seem to be vulnerable in ways that traditional morality, that is, morality backed up by religion, was not. If the human penchant for underwriting our actions and commitments in terms of their being 'right' or 'good' is less easily disposed of than Nietzsche thought, the fact that the content of such moral judgements is so infinitely stretchable makes morality an increasingly emptier dimension of human life. And that, almost inevitably, makes it even harder for individuals to commit themselves to principles or to actions that may turn out to have only a relative and not an absolute content. Nietzsche's own fate might be taken as offering a parable of just this situation. Having derided the virtues of pity and compassion in many of his philosophical writings, his last act before being overwhelmed by insanity was to rush out into the street and to throw his arms round the neck of a horse being beaten by its owner – a scenario that recalls several passages in Dostoevsky where such incidents are used to symbolize the fundamental need for pity and compassion in the face of suffering. Having rejected these Dostoevskian values (with specific reference to the Russian writer), Nietzsche now seemed to be acting them out in his life, crushed by a pity whose existence he intellectually denied. And so we find ourselves asking: if the sole basis of moral values is simply our own will-power, is that ever going to be powerful enough to sustain a reliable moral framework through the course of a lifetime?

Perhaps it is a sign of the weakness of such moral self-invention that even those who are moral relativists in one area are rarely as consistent as Nietzsche and are more than likely to reinstate general morality in new ways. Where the vast majority of my parents' generation (includ-ing many advocates of so-called permissiveness), saw homosexuality as, in some way, 'wrong', the majority of my children's generation, including those who are actively heterosexual, tend to regard it as 'wrong' to be prejudiced against someone on the basis of their sexual orientation. Even more paradoxically, the soap-opera character who takes a decision on any basis other than what's best for him- or herself is acting 'wrongly'. The categories of morality survive the transformation of their content. When the self-styled Satanist Aleister Crowley restated the Rabelaisian principle that 'Do what thou wilt shalt be the whole of the law', he was, paradoxically, turning absolute freedom itself into a new law. Moralism lives on in the rejection of morality.

What can or should be the role of religion in this situation of moral vulnerability and paradox? Is it to offer clear moral judgements to the confused and wavering faithful? To teach us about right and wrong? Appealing as it may be to church leaders to cast themselves in the role of arbiters of societal values, and clamorous as some of the voices may be that call on them to take on that role, this is arguably not the most creative response to the situation. This is not because what the Church has to say is necessarily wrong. The guidance offered by a wise pastor may be the best available guidance there is. Nor is it because, as things stand, most people are likely to ignore it anyway if it doesn't chime in with what they themselves want. More profoundly, the problem has to do with the dynamics of ethical communication itself.

At the start of this short course we examined Kierkegaard's theory of ethical and ethical-religious communication and his insistence that, when it comes to ethical communication the best we can do is to act the part of a Socrates. Precisely because the thrust of ethical teaching concerns the freedom of the learner, a good outcome is only possible when the learner learns to think, choose and act freely, that is, *not* to think, choose and act on the basis of someone else's say-so, but because they themselves have reached a decision as to what it is best to do. Something similar, we saw, is found in the secular thinker Habermas, who also insists on ethical communication being communication that involves all parties in a dialogical search for understanding.

But doesn't this simply return us to the situation of the contemporary anomic individual who operates on a 'what I want is the whole of the law' basis? Not exactly, because although Kierkegaard and Habermas both assert the freedom of the learner as jealously as a Nietzsche, they also make clear that the learner, as Kierkegaard put it, shares a 'situation' with the teacher, or, in Habermasian terms, both are engaged in a common social enterprise. Supplementing their terminology with the idea of friendship, I attempted to underline how we should not be looking solely at the outcome of the communicative process – the individual's 'discovery' of their freedom – but much more at the communicative process itself and how this process embraces teacher and learner and their interaction in a reality that is larger than any of its parts. It is, with the benefit of hindsight, analogous to the divine Trinitarian life itself, a process in which persons come to be what they are through the communicative movement between them. As a 'moral' community (which is not, of course, all that it is), the teaching thus becomes a community of learners, who are also friends in the slow, difficult discovery of their mutual freedom and responsibility. Or, to put it another way, the Christian community (or *a* Christian community), is one in which the mutual solidarity of love must always precede the distinctions that arise on the basis of morality.

Yet we also had early occasion to note that we are not actually – or only rarely – in anything like an ideal speech situation and that there are considerable obstacles in the way of our achieving such a thing. The greatest of these obstacles is, simply, human beings themselves, and, on the basis of what we know of human beings, the difficulty we have in being confident that what they are seeking really is the good or, if they are genuinely seeking the good, whether they have the strength to realize it. In order to do the good, it seemed, they (we!) need not just to be helped but to be redeemed, reborn, re-created even. The idea of Christ as a sign of the divine presence among us, a sacramental communicating of just such a possibility of a new beginning, was offered as a way of countering the discouragement and even despair that we experience in the face of our own *in*capacity for the good. Yet if Christ too is one who wants 'friends' and not 'disciples', there is something Socratic even about a Christ-given redemption. True, there is something more than the merely Socratic relation here, since the friendship this 'Socrates' offers is the possibility of being drawn into the divine conversation itself, until we reach the point where the truth of our being is lost in the unfathomable mystery of the divine life, 'hidden with Christ in God'. The discovery of the freedom to be who we are is not an act of sheer invention, it is a mystery given to us, opened to us.

This recontextualizing of the ethical question in the theological question of human freedom in divine mystery underlines the fact that, whatever else it is, ethics can never be a science, the demonstration of something knowable. I can never know that I am doing the right thing, I can only trust and hope and pray that I am. Ethical rules cannot be extrapolated from a double context of relationship, divine and human, in which it is not knowledge but the mystery of love that counts.

But what does this mean, practically speaking?

For the believer, it means that the whole experience of the Church, on earth and in heaven, is a constant, if usually implicit, part of moral decision-making. The actual experience of Christ-centred friendship does not give immediate answers to difficult moral questions, but it empowers me to confront and address those questions. The point is something like that made in Bonhoeffer's writing on ethics: that the aim of Christian ethics is not knowledge of good and evil but the shaping and forming of our whole lives in conformity with our experience of God in Christ.[4] Strikingly, the key German term translated as 'formation' in Bonhoeffer's *Ethics* is the same word, *Bildung*, often translated as 'culture'. It is the experience of the Christian life *as a whole*, in its sacramental, worshipping and praying *culture*, and not just its 'ethical teaching', that is most significant for our experience and discovery of freedom, responsibility and obligation (the core concepts of ethical life according to Bonhoeffer).

Something similar is suggested in more recent forms of 'narrative' Christian ethics. The best-known representative of this approach, Stanley Hauerwas, writes that

> The nature of Christian ethics is determined by the fact that Christian conviction takes the form of a story, or perhaps better, a set of stories that constitutes a tradition, which in turn creates and forms a community. Christian ethics does not begin by emphasizing rules or principles, but by calling our attention to a narrative that tells of God's dealing with creation.[5]

Hauerwas is not, of course, saying that it is *just* a story. As he sees it, 'story' is a basic mode of our life in the world. We live in and through the stories we come to tell about ourselves, individually and collectively. And, as the passage quoted also suggests, the stories we tell are inseparable from our experiences of the communities in which we live. Christian ethics, then, is not a matter of isolating a number of ethical rules from, say, the Ten Commandments or the Sermon on the Mount, but of allowing our decision-making to be shaped by our Christian stories and the Christian community life in which they are embedded. Stories of the Exodus or of the ministry of Jesus do not tell us what to do in specific situations, but they set a horizon that will make our Christian way of responding to situations significantly distinctive from that of the average secular person.

Important emphases here are shared with a significant strand of contemporary philosophical ethics, namely, the so-called 'virtue ethics'. Here too, often with reference to Aristotle and to the Catholic Thomist tradition of moral reasoning, more stress is placed on the formation of character (virtue) than on specific moral rules or attempting to find Christian 'answers' to one or other question of the

day. Both Hauerwas and such representatives of virtue ethics thinking as Alasdair MacIntyre see this as a way out of the dead-end of the
moral individualism in which all do what is right in their own eyes.

To some extent the path that we have travelled through this short
course would seem to endorse such an approach. Here too we have
stressed the primacy of the lived experience of divine love in the
manifold life of tradition over the abstraction of particular 'doctrines'
or 'moral principles' from the totality of the communicative process
– and, we may add, what is story-telling if not a singularly powerful
form of communication? Doesn't this story- and community-oriented
approach fit rather well with the general thrust of my argument thus
far?

Certainly, I have no wish to underrate the importance of stories in
the communicative practice that is Christian doctrine. Just to speak of
creation and redemption is already to employ some kind of emplot-
ment, to see faith in terms of a journey through time that is more than
a sequence of haphazard events but a narrative, in some strong sense.
Once we think of life as temporal or historical, the category of story
seems unavoidable. What has been said about remembrance in the
last chapter might also be understood in narrative terms. But there are
a number of qualifications that should be made to the kind of privileging of story and community found in Hauerwas and typical of much
contemporary theology.

First, it is important to remember that the dynamic process of tradition, as described in the last two chapters, is never and can never
be entirely self-enclosed. The Jewish story and the Christian story
and other religious stories developed out of many-sided and many-
levelled encounters between individuals and communities. Quite
often in Christian history, pagan or secular stories have been taken
up and transformed into Christian ones. Christian stories of fallen
women redeemed by love (Mary Magdalene), have been transformed
into secular stories, *La Traviata* or *Pretty Woman*, which, in turn, may
or may not be suitable for reworking by Christian apologists (probably not in this case!). Islamic legends concerning Jesus often deviate
significantly from the Christian community's own stories, yet they
also often have or can be given a powerful Christian meaning.[6] This
is not a question of reducing Christianity to its cultural background
in the Hellenistic world (as some earlier history of religions theorists
tried to do), but simply of recognizing the ubiquity of the interaction
between Church and culture in the shaping of Christianity itself. As
communicative action, Christian doctrine can never be isolated from
its world.

Second, what I am given by my participation in the life of tradition is not only nor even primarily a set of life-shaping stories. It is also a body of experiences of a pre-narrative kind. That someone sat with me in my hour of need and maybe said nothing but just held my hand, that someone visited me in prison, even though all we talked about was football, that I came to the altar with a hunger that obliterated every thought about what it was hunger for – such experiences are no less important than the narratives that the pastor, the visitor, the sacramental minister use to contextualize and explain them. The simple act of holding the hand of the sick or the dying says as much (and sometimes more) than any stories we might remember or tell. The whole pastoral and fellowship life of the Church comes to the fore in such situations in as wide a multitude of ways as there are forms of human interaction. 'Story-telling' picks out one element of this manifold experiential life, but only one.

Third, and following on from this, such core ethical values as the freedom, responsibility and obligation flagged by Bonhoeffer,[7] place Christian ethics on a ground recognizably common to all human beings, no matter what their cultural background. This is not to claim that there are universal ethical norms or values, but, to recur to Kierkegaard's terminology, that the ethical task is always situated in some specific way. The teacher and learner must share a common situatedness as the presupposition of genuine moral teaching and learning. As a rich Westerner, I cannot talk about the virtue of self-denial or fasting to one who doesn't have enough to eat. Equally, when I learn a lesson about life from my secular neighbour who cuts my lawn when I'm too ill to do so, I am also learning a lesson *within* the process of my Christian development.

Although hostile to Kierkegaard (whom he misunderstood), the modern Danish theologian Knud Løgstrup seems to have argued something similar to this in his attempt to identify a fundamental ethical scenario rooted in the most basic patterns of human interaction. According to Løgstrup, the 'ethical demand' (to use his chosen phrase) is already implicit in such an ordinary situation as striking up a conversation with a stranger on the train. With my very first word, I place myself and my fate in his hands, I make an act of pre-reflective trust that he will accept the claim that my words make. I 'hand myself over', as Løgstrup puts it, in words which should by now have an added resonance for us, since it was just such a 'handing over' that we found at the heart of the dynamic of tradition. Such an act is a primal expression of trust in life itself.[8] Løgstrup does not say that this is already 'ethical', but it is, he suggests, the taproot, the basic possibility of more specifically ethical relations arising in human life. Already in such a basic exchange, such a basic act of communication, issues of freedom, responsibility and obligation are set in motion, if not yet articulated.

Fourth, and perhaps crucially, we do not have to subscribe to fully blown existentialist ideas about the motiveless nature of choice to acknowledge that in actual situations which demand a moral decision, we typically find ourselves unprepared, taken by surprise, stretched beyond our resources. To act morally will, minimally, involve my engagement as a free agent. It cannot be the automatic application of a learned rule or habit. That social life would be intolerable if we did not act habitually (stopping my car when I see a red light, for example), is not an issue. Of course that is the case. But no more than do principles or rules, can habits and virtues cover all the ground that lies before me when I have to act ethically. And the more important, the more pressing the choice, the less likely my story, my community, my principles or my virtues are to offer assistance.[9]

One might see this in terms of an inescapably tragic dimension in ethical life, where the choices we often have to make are not simply choices between a clear good and a clear evil (such that the issue is only whether we are brave enough to do the good and suffer the evil), but where good and evil lie on both sides and precedents fail. In the First World War a well-known Church of England army padre got into serious trouble with his superiors as a result of an incident in which he took charge of the surviving troops in a combat situation, following the deaths of all the officers in his unit, an action which was clearly against the rules of conduct for army chaplains. Perhaps there is not and never can be a clear-cut answer as to whether he was right or wrong to do so, and perhaps he himself (or another individual in a similar situation) might never become clear as to whether he acted rightly or wrongly. Yet he acted, and had to act, in a space for which neither his church experience and 'narrative' nor his own previous life-experience could ever have adequately prepared him.

A similar point is perhaps being made by Iris Murdoch when she writes that 'The only genuine way to be good is to be good "for nothing" in the midst of a scene where every "natural" thing, including one's own mind is subject to chance . . .'[10] When I act ethically, or am called upon to make any moral decision, then I am more likely than not to be in a situation where there is at best only a balance of probabilities and never a cast-iron certainty as to the right thing to do. In terms of Christian doctrine, we can never cultivate morality in such a way as ever to presume upon our own rightness or clear-sightedness.

Once more, all we can do is to trust and hope and pray that we have received grace to do the right thing. What redeems the situation from that of intolerable moral torment is simply the further trust, hope and prayer that if we are mistaken (as we are many times likely to be), then God's power to renew his covenant with us is not thereby exhausted. Not knowing what we do, the hope of forgiveness is always possible.

It is in this context that many modern theologians, from J. G. Hamann in the eighteenth century, through Kierkegaard in the nineteenth and, recently, David Tracy, have privileged the fragment rather than the story as a mode of Christian communication, for the fragment, incomplete, uncertain, and open to varying interpretations, may best figure the open-endedness and inscrutability of these most challenging situations of moral decision-making, as well as best hinting at the unfathomability of the divine grace by which we are empowered to engage them.

The Political

I have already remarked that there is a general acceptance in Anglo-Saxon society that church leaders are likely to speak out on matters of national and international politics. At the same time, there is always a potent opposing voice that makes itself heard whenever these pronouncements are too controversial, and we hear warnings that 'the Church shouldn't meddle in politics'. Certainly in Britain, while it is widely accepted that the churches are, in important ways, stakeholders in debates about poverty, social justice, education and some other areas, whatever is said in the name of the Church should not go too far into the area of politics narrowly defined as party politics. Throughout the period of Mrs Thatcher's prime-ministership, church leaders regularly warned of the possible consequences for the poor of her government's policies but nearly always stopped short of telling voters not to vote Conservative![11]

In the Roman Catholic Church too there is a long and powerful tradition of political involvement of very varying kinds. In our own time the role of the Roman Catholic Church in resisting communism in Poland has illustrated one side of this, although many commentators remarked a possible inconsistency when John Paul II vigorously discouraged priests such as Ernesto Cardenal from getting involved in the left-wing liberation movements of Latin America (in Cardenal's case this included accepting a ministerial post in the Marxist Sandinista government of Nicaragua). Other traditions are markedly less political.

Although the situation in Germany has changed radically since the experience of Nazi dictatorship, it was a long-standing Lutheran tradition to stay outside the political sphere. Luther himself propagated what has become known as a 'two kingdoms' doctrine, according to which the peaceable laws and methods of the kingdom of God cannot be practised in a world subject to the violence of sinful men, who must be restrained from the worst excesses of sinfulness by whatever means the worldly power finds appropriate. Thus, where Anglicans, Catholics and Calvinists are all likely to believe that political processes should be formed in various ways by Christian beliefs, Lutherans have tended more to emphasize the inwardness, hiddenness or other worldliness of Christ's kingdom. This was, famously, the background to the kind of anguish experienced by Bonhoeffer when confronted with a regime (Hitler's) towards which it was no longer possible for the Christian to maintain a stance of detached neutrality. Yet although the phenomenon of the Third Reich significantly undermined the more complacent version of the two kingdoms doctrine, many North European Lutheran Christians today would argue that whatever may have been the case in the past, the advent of democracy now provides an avenue along which the Christian citizen can freely pursue his or her political objectives. In this situation the Church qua institution should remain firmly in the background and focus on its spiritual tasks. Perhaps if some such threat as Nazism or Apartheid were to arise, then things might be different. But within a democratic society the Church will necessarily appear as a heteronomous power if it in any way attempts to bypass or overrule the processes of democracy itself.

It might be added that Orthodoxy, especially in its Russian form, has also tended to take a quietistic approach towards political life in modern times, influencedpartly by Peter the Great's adoption of a model for Church–State relations derived from Swedish Lutheranism. Many of these fundamental tendencies have re-emerged in the United States, albeit transformed by a situation where there has never been an 'established' church, as in most of the European countries.

Clearly the background to these various views is rooted both in theology and in experiences over many centuries of complex and often violent struggles, as in the Reformation struggles in England that, effectively, took nearly 150 years to resolve, and encompassed several rebellions and one major Civil War. Seen in the light of this long, often tragic and frequently discreditable history, it would be very hard today to say with any great confidence what the 'correct' Christian approach to politics should be. Many Christians today are inclined to sneer at the supposedly easy-going tolerance promulgated by the Enlightenment, but we should not forget that part of the appeal of such tolerance was the sheer scale of the devastation and cruelty wrought on Europe in the name of religion (specifically the Christian religion!) in the sixteenth and seventeenth centuries, a history from which virtually no major Church emerged with unbloody hands. It is perhaps a part of the appeal of many new religious movements in the West that they are free of such historical baggage and are able to focus exclusively on the spiritual dimension of life in a way that the rambling structures of the mainstream churches with their complex historical and institutional involvements in the body politic cannot. But it is not only our difficult past that makes caution an attractive option, it is also the sheer complexity of the present global social and political situation, in which rapid technological, economic and cultural change and an as yet unresolved realignment of power blocs and alliances make any kind of diagnosis (let alone prognosis) extremely problematic. The Christian voice is not only encumbered by its past, it does not have any obvious claim to read the signs of the times better than any other institution or movement. In the equally uncertain and obscure period after the end of the Second World War, Tillich advised that it was best to regard the present time as a time of waiting,[12] and Christian leaders and theologians today might also be advised to wait long and listen hard before they venture to assume the prophetic mantle.

Yet it would be as irresponsible as it is impossible for the Church entirely to refrain from involvement in political life. Why so?

There is, of course, the pragmatic reason that, as a matter of fact, the churches have all manner of responsibilities in such areas as education, the care of the elderly and other forms of social work that are affected by and sometimes call for legislative change and, therefore, require political involvement. In Germany, the churches are the second largest employer after the State. Even in England over a fifth of state primary schools are church aided or controlled. However obliquely, churches in these situations cannot but have some responsibility in the relevant political discussions.

Similarly, if it is once conceded that the churches have a stake in contemporary ethical issues, then it is hard to rule out a further political dimension. For just as culture and ethics are only with difficulty to be disentangled, so too are ethics and politics deeply intertwined. Whether it is a matter of abortion, gay marriages, racism or the production and maintenance of a nuclear deterrent, the moral question is inseparable from the legal and political framework that affect the individual's options. If we imagine the position of a Roman Catholic Christian who follows the papal view on abortion, it is clearly possible for such a person to accept that, in a modern democratic society, the Church can only offer counsel to individuals and cannot overrule any given legal framework. Yet even if a society has once opted to allow the freedom of individual choice regarding the termination of pregnancy, the Church might still, in its own terms, legitimately question whether the neutrality of the State is a genuine neutrality, or whether educational, welfare and other policies might actually be generating pressure on vulnerable women to have terminations when this might not be their most favoured course of action. Or there might be issues around the employment conditions of medical staff who might for reasons of conscience not wish to participate in performing these operations. Or, in another context, what of the scientist or worker who might not wish to be involved in any work related to the development or construction of nuclear or other weapons, when technological change itself means that it is no longer so easy to compartmentalize different domains of production (so that high-level computer or engineering research might equally well be applied in a variety of domains)? What kind of rights of refusal can such workers claim in a democratic society with a free labour market?

Yet this kind of defence of Christian political involvement might easily seem to be missing the main picture, treating politics as if it were merely an accidental by-product of, say, educational activity or ethics. Hasn't the church involvement in the liberation struggles of Latin America, in the overthrow of Apartheid, in the opposition to the nuclear arms race or, most recently, to the Anglo-American invasion of Iraq taught us that something much larger is at stake than securing the social context of the Church's domestic affairs? Haven't many of the most powerful Christian voices of recent times been those that named the 'principalities and powers' that have presided over oppression and disorder for what they are? From Bonhoeffer, through Martin Luther King, Daniel Berrigan, Gustavo Gutiérrez, Desmond Tutu and, it could be claimed, John Paul II himself, the Church has shown itself at its best in confronting worldly evil in political form. In terms of the theme of Christian doctrine as communicative action, such voices are precisely resonant communications of the possibilities of hope, freedom and love in situations dominated by destructive social and political forces. What could be more important?

At the same time we should note the importantly contextual character of many of the heroic moments of Christian political witness. If there are occasions where confrontation with the political powers-that-be becomes an unavoidable issue for the Christian conscience, the extreme situations of Latin American military dictatorships in the 1960s and 1970s or of Apartheid in South Africa are not readily translatable into the horizons of a Western European democratic society. This is not to say that issues of poverty and racism can be ignored by wealthy Christians, whether these come to light within European society itself or in the global network of societies interlinked with Europe. The chronic problems of sub-Saharan Africa are not problems anyone can safely ignore. But we cannot abstract ourselves from the concreteness of our own situation, and the fact that whatever confronting such evils may mean for us, it will not have the same political form as it arguably had (and has) to have for the front-line victims of violence and oppression. If we do not match the reality of our responsibilities with an awareness of the real limits of our actual situation, we risk reducing Christian politics to the most empty form of gesture politics. If the communication of life-affirming hope requires opposing institutionalized violence, injustice and vice by political means, the nature of these political means will, in practice, vary from situation to situation, even within the common time-frame of the present. No one anywhere can simultaneously engage with all the issues that might justifiably claim their attention, and their effectiveness will almost certainly be in proportion to the appropriateness of their focus on the actual possibilities of their given situation. If Christian morality cannot be condensed into the shorthand of a table of moral laws, the Christian engagement with political life cannot easily be fitted in to any simple political programme. But just as Christian faith serves ethics by awakening the possibility of courageously embracing the freedom and responsibility required for moral action, so too it offers encouragement to the Christian who wishes to engage in political life without prescribing how that is to be done – for it is of the essence of genuinely political life that it expresses the free and responsible decisions of those who participate in it.

Faith cannot be, as it is often said to be, simply a 'private matter'. If the decision for faith must flow from (or at the very least through) the depths of the individual's subjectivity, the life of faith, as a life of friendship and dialogue, will have a public form and, therefore, a legitimate place in the public sphere. If the idea of the public sphere is today under attack and, arguably, much diminished in comparison with the recent past,[13] the life of the Church would seem to offer a pre-eminent example of a public institution, positioned somewhere between the privacy of individual and family life, on the one hand, and the great business of the State, on the other. As such it might also perform a significant, if humble, political role simply by being the public body that it is and thereby helping to keep alive a social space that many commentators believe to be crucial for the survival of genuine political liberty. For political life itself can only flourish if the space between the individual and the State is a space of rich diversity in opinion, social practice and cultural function. Only so can the individual acquire a sense of their own life having a stake in that of society as a whole, and only so can the State (or supra-political institutions such as the larger international media corporations) be made responsive to the openness and vitality of social reality.

It is not my intention to imply that this public role of the Church requires anything like, for example, the continuation of Church of England bishops sitting in the House of Lords. There is no such parallel in other European countries where the churches nevertheless exercise at least as effective a role as constituents of the public sphere. Although my remarks about being attentive to the concrete particularity of our own actual situation might offer one line of defence for this 'local' tradition, it is not my view that the present relationship between the Church of England and Parliament really helps either much. The Church could well remain an effective public body without this aspect of establishment. What I am arguing for, in other words, is something very different from the 'back to the catacombs' kind of Romanticism found in some proponents of disestablishment. The challenge for us today is neither to cling on to an absurd form of establishment nor to go all out for a Christian counter-culture, but to negotiate the transition from establishment in such a way that the era of establishment will not be seen as a Babylonian captivity but as a historically enriching experience we can now leave behind. What is most 'enriching' in this experience will then be precisely the sense of the Christian's public responsibility. Although I am making this point with specific reference to the current situation of the Church of England, I believe that the crisis of the public sphere today is a global crisis, and that analogous issues are confronting churches in many other countries, as well, of course, as the other churches within Britain itself.

I conclude with some comments on what has become one of the most challenging political issues of our time, or, rather a knot of issues that have been brought into the sharpest focus by the so-called 'War on Terror'. It is possible that by the time this book is published events will have moved on and the political rhetoric around this unfortunately named 'War' will have changed dramatically. But it is scarcely likely that many of the deeper issues involved in it will have been resolved.

What might this 'War' have to do with Christianity, and what might 'Christianity' have to say about this 'War'? For the Christian pacifist or the Christian advocate of human rights, there are many specific issues that the 'War' has thrown up. Certainly these issues are to be faced and debated. But the underlying conceptualization underlying some views of this 'War' are also worth the attention of Christianity. In an important article, followed shortly afterwards by an extremely influential book, the American political analyst and Harvard professor Samuel P. Huntington argued that the fall of communism did not mark the global triumph of liberal capitalism and the 'end of history' propounded by Francis Fukuyama.[14] What we are experiencing instead is the advent of a new age of irreconcilable civilizations, for many of which modernization did not necessarily mean Westernization, and that liberal democracy and free markets could only hope to go so far in making inroads into them. Huntington wrote that

> In sum, the post-Cold War world is a world of seven or eight major civilizations. Cultural commonalities and differences shape the interests, antagonisms, and associations of states. The most important countries in the world come overwhelmingly from different civilizations. The local conflicts most likely to escalate into broader wars are those between groups and states from different civilizations. The predominant patterns of political and economic development differ from civilization to civilization. The key issues on the international agenda involve differences among civilizations. Power is shifting from the long predominant West to the non-Western civilizations. Global politics has become multipolar and multicivilizational.[15]

The major civilizations identified by Huntington are Western, Latin American, African, Islamic, Sinic, Hindu, Orthodox, Buddhist and Japanese. Four of these, at least, are defined in terms of religion: Islam, Hindu, Orthodox and Buddhist. What about the West? Huntington is coy about this, but sometimes he does refer to 'Western Christian' civilization, and, certainly, some have taken 'West' to mean also 'Christian'.

It is certainly appealing in a superficial kind of way to see the 'War on Terror' in terms of a clash of civilizations between Islam and the West. The Taliban and al-Qaeda abroad and debates about the wearing of the hijab or veil by Muslim women here in the West make the conflict between Islam and the West a matter of everyday consciousness. Of course, the leaders of the West have never identified Islamic civilization as 'the enemy' and, indeed, take pains to emphasize that Western action in Kosovo, for example, was in defence of a Muslim minority. But, uncomfortably, the main enemies in the War on Terror, that is, the terrorists against whom action is actually taken, are, fairly uniformly Muslim and it is unfortunate that this conflict has, on several occasions, been referred to as a 'crusade', a word which, if one is a Muslim, does not conjure up heroic images of noble knights, but rather orgies of genocidal violence perpetrated by barbaric Western thugs. And, of course, from the other side, al-Qaeda itself is more than happy to paint its war as part of a clash of civilizations.

Huntington himself, it should be said, is on record as opposing the invasion of Iraq. Nevertheless, there is an important element in his theory, over and above the rhetorical possibilities of a phrase such as 'clash of civilizations', which makes it particularly easy to portray the real differences between Islam and Christianity as exemplifying the irreconcilability of Christian and Islamic civilizations. This element concerns Huntington's treatment of religion itself. As has been noted, he sometimes takes religion as a defining characteristic of a civilization and other times not. This is connected, I believe, with his repudiation of a distinction between culture and civilization that, he claims, was only ever made by some nineteenth-century scholars in Germany and to which no one today holds. This is too simplistic, however.

It is clear that there are times and places where religion is so interwoven with the whole fabric of life that it seems appropriate, even unavoidable, to talk of a Christian (or Islamic or Hindic) civilization. In Western Europe, in the Middle Ages, religion was not merely a matter of church attendance. It permeated every feature of life, from the coronation of monarchs and the delimitation of their powers, to the names of wayside flowers. Architecture, sculpture, painting, music and literature were shaped by the requirements of the Church and, even when they showed a secularizing tendency, such as the love-songs of the troubadours, often contained many religious allusions. No feature of life seems to have been left untouched. From hunting, ploughing, sowing and harvest, to childbirth, marriage, sickness and death, religion was present in one way or another. Yet, if I am correct, although religion remains an important part of our surviving public sphere we could only with difficulty talk about the West today as a Christian civilization in the same sense that we might call the Middle Ages a Christian civilization. The rise of a highly differentiated scientific and technological society has instituted a civilizational shift, while leaving religion to continue as a vital cultural force, taking the word 'culture' here in a sense that embraces also the ethical and political dimensions that have been the subject of this chapter.

If this is true of Christianity, is it or can it also be true of Islam? There are many commentators who say it cannot. The theocratic nature of Islam, it is argued, means that Islam can never be happy to sink down to the status of a mere expression of culture. It must always aspire to shape society as a whole. Yet Huntington's conception of civilization is something larger than society and larger even than a given political order. 'Civilization', I suggest, better describes the global network of scientific and technological practices, practices to which most Islamic societies are now as committed as the West. To sustain this technological civilization – the internet, energy supplies, air travel, industrial production, mass media, etc., etc. – certain core educational and social structures and disciplines are required. There is no Islamic or Christian aircraft maintenance, only safe aircraft maintenance; no Islamic or Christian way of processing spent nuclear fuel rods, but only a properly managed technological way of processing them. Fukuyama, I suspect, was partly right, though not in the directly political or economic terms in which his argument was couched. We are entering an era of a largely uniform global civilization, but that is neither Western nor Islamic. It is technological. Nevertheless, this all-encompassing civilizational unity may still remain host to a variety of cultural, ethical and political formations, among them such religions as Christianity and Islam. To harden these differences into civilizational differences is, rhetorically at least, to invite seeing them in terms of conflict and, ultimately, of military conflict. To see them in terms of cultural, ethical and political differences, however, while not immediately taking the sting out of current antagonisms, opens a better prospect towards dialogue and cohabitation between religions. On this model, the various religions each have their part within a global public sphere. This allows plenty of scope for argument, debate, conversion and counter-conversion, but it minimizes the drive towards a permanent state of emergency engendered by the prospect of an endless clash of civilizations.

Christianity should and will testify to its sense of the dynamic presence of God in creation, incarnation and redemption by the courageous championing of the poor, the oppressed and the afflicted. But it will also communicate something no less important for human flourishing by remaining vigilant against being identified with the cause of one or other civilization. This, today, must be one of its most urgent political tasks.

Further Reading

In addition to the works referred to in the notes, the following titles may be helpful to those seeking to take further one or other of the themes dealt with in this short course.

For a clear introduction to the theoretical debates involved in the development of doctrine on the Patristic period, J. N. D. Kelly, *Early Christian Doctrines* (San Francisco: Harper, 1988). For subsequent developments, see Alister McGrath, *Historical Theology: An Introduction to the History of Christian Thought* (Oxford: Blackwell, 1998). For the impact of the revolution in ideas in the modern period, see Don Cupitt, *Sea of Faith* (London: SCM Press [new edition], 2003) – even if one does not agree with Cupitt's radical views, he offers an excellent presentation of issues and debates. On the twentieth century, see David Ford (ed.), *The Modern Theologians* (Oxford: Blackwell, 1997).

The understanding of theology in this book is indebted to many 'classic' modern authors, among them Paul Tillich, Karl Rahner and David Tracy. Their theology can be further explored in, for example, Paul Tillich, *The Courage to Be* (London: Fontana, 1962); Karl Rahner, *Foundations of Christian Faith* (London: Darton, Longman and Todd, 1978); David Tracy, *The Analogical Imagination* (London: SCM Press, 1981). See also John Macquarrie, *Principles of Christian Theology* (London: SCM Press, 2002). For an introduction to the so-called 'postmodern' theology see G. Ward (ed.), *The Postmodern God: A Theological Reader* (Oxford: Blackwell, 1997) and John D. Caputo, *The Prayers and Tears of Jacques Derrida* (Bloomington: Indiana University Press, 1997).

The important influence of the Eastern Church is represented by the texts by Lossky and Schmemann indicated in notes. The Trinitarian theme can also be explored further through some of the works indicated in notes, especially Oliver Davies, *A Theology of Compassion: Metaphysics of Difference and the Renewal of Tradition* (London: SCM Press, 2001) and C. M. LaCugna, *God for Us: The Trinity and Christian Life* (San Francisco: HarperCollins, 1973). See also D. Brown, *The Divine Trinity* (London: Duckworth, 1985) and J. Moltmann, *The Trinity and the Kingdom of God* (London: SCM Press, 1981).

Helpful works in relation to Christology include L. Boff, *Jesus Christ Liberator: A Critical Christology of our Time* (London: SPCK, 1980); J. Hick, *The Metaphor of God Incarnate* (London: SCM Press, 1993); E. Schillebeeckx, *Jesus – An Experiment in Christology* (London: Collins, 1979) and *Christ – The Experience of Jesus as Lord* (New York: Crossroad, 1988).

On the encounter between theology and culture, see D. Jasper, *The Study of Literature and Religion* (Basingstoke: Macmillan, 1993) and W. Hamilton, *A Quest for the Post-Historical Jesus* (London: SCM Press, 1993). Gesa Thiessen (ed.), *Theological Aesthetics: A Reader* (London: SCM Press, 2004) is a useful compilation of 'classic' texts in Christian theological approaches to questions of art and beauty.

There also exist many helpful series offering further material on many of the thinkers (e.g. the *Cambridge Companion* series), movements and topics (e.g. the *Blackwell Companion* and *SCM Dictionary* series) discussed here.

Notes

Chapter 1. From Saving Knowledge to Communicative Action

1 See, for example, J. Habermas, tr. T. McCarthy, *The Theory of Communicative Action*, Vol. 1, Boston, Beacon Press, 1984.
2 Habermas himself focuses on this example in his book, tr. J. Shapiro, *Knowledge and Human Interests*, London, Heinemann, 1972, esp. Ch. 10–12, pp. 214–300.
3 These are available in English in H. V. and E. H. Hong (tr.), *Søren Kierkegaard's Journals and Papers*, Vol. 1, Bloomington, Indiana University Press, 1967, pp. 267–308.
4 Philosophers such as Kant and Habermas are, of course, concerned to provide an account of the conditions that guarantee that these beliefs are not merely wilful but rational.
5 This is not to be confused with his more popular *Mother Courage and her Children*. Based on a story by Gorky, *The Mother* was also filmed (in German) in 1958.
6 N. Berdyaev, tr. D. Lowrie, *The Meaning of the Creative Act*, London, Gollancz, 1955, p. 98. In a different theological tradition, some interesting remarks on the value of human creativity are also found in E. Gilson, *Painting and Reality*, Cleveland, Meridian, 1957.
7 Berdyaev, *Meaning of the Creative Act*, p. 99, italics in text.
8 Berdyaev, *Meaning of the Creative Act*, p. 100.
9 I take this latter example merely because it was a debate in which Kierkegaard himself played a leading part in student circles in 1830s Denmark. See A. Hannay, *Kierkegaard. A Biography*, Cambridge, Cambridge University Press, 2001, Ch. 1.
10 See especially F. Dostoevsky, *Notes from Underground*, various translations.

Chapter 2. The Movement of the Mystery

1 It has, for example, recently been used in a manner largely parallel to the way in which I shall use it here by Oliver Davies in his *A Theology of Compassion: Metaphysics of Difference and the Renewal of Tradition*, London, SCM Press, 2001, pp. 256ff. Rublev's life was also interpreted filmically by the Russian director Andrei Tarkovsky, whose eponymously titled film ended with a powerful transition from the black and white in which the narrative of the film had been shot to colour, allowing the camera slowly and lovingly to explored the nuanced brilliance of Rublev's masterpiece. The Soviet leader, Leonid Brezhnev, it might be added, had walked out of a private screening long before this point, since Tarkovsky used Rublev's life as a fairly transparent allegory of the sufferings of a spiritual artist in the Soviet Union. For my own commentary on the painting see my *Art, Modernity and Faith*, London, SCM Press, 1998, pp. 128–30.

2 See K. Barth, tr. G. Bromiley, *Church Dogmatics I/1*, Edinburgh, T. and T. Clark, 1975, p. 370. The more 'dynamic' understanding of *perichoresis*, with emphasis on the image of dance, is found in, among others, C. M. LaCugna, *God for Us: The Trinity and Christian Life*, San Francisco, HarperCollins, 1973, pp. 270ff. and R. Kearney, *The God Who May Be: A Hermeneutics of Religion*, Bloomington, Indiana University Press, 2001, pp. 109ff.

3 N. Berdyaev, tr. G. Reavey, *The Meaning of History*, London, G. Bles, 1936, p. 45.

4 Berdyaev, *The Meaning of History*, pp. 48–9.

5 However, see the last three chapters of my *Short Course in the Philosophy of Religion*, London, SCM Press, 2001.

6 This particular story can be found in H. Arendt, *Eichmann in Jerusalem. A Report on the Banality of Evil*, Harmondsworth, Penguin, 1994 edn, pp. 49–51.

7 See Davies, *Theology of Compassion*, pp. 262ff.

8 See M. Buber, tr. W. Kaufmann, *I and Thou*, Edinburgh, T. and T. Clark, 1970. Buber discusses the convergence of the 'everyday' experience of the 'Thou' with the 'Thou' of the God-relationship in Part Three.

9 See, for example, V. Lossky, *The Mystical Theology of the Eastern Church*, Cambridge, James Clarke, 1957, Ch. 3, 'God in Trinity' and John Zizioulas, *Being as Communion*, London, Darton, Longman and Todd, 1985, Ch. 1, 'Personhood and Being'.

10 See M. Bakhtin, tr. C. Emerson, *Problems of Dostoevsky's Poetics*, Minneapolis, University of Minnesota Press, 1984, p. 287.

11 Quoted from A. M. Allchin, *N. F. S. Grundtvig. An Introduction to his Life and Thought*, London, Darton, Longman and Todd, 1997, p. 165. The phrase is also used by Allchin to summarize one of the five major

themes of Grundtvig's thought. We shall return to other aspects of this in subsequent chapters.

12 See Brother Lawrence (Nicholas Hierman), *The Practice of the Presence of God*, London, Allenson, 1906 (translator unknown).

13 R. Otto, tr. J. W. Harvey, *The Idea of the Holy*, Penguin, Harmondsworth, 1959.

14 See Barth, *Church Dogmatics I/1*, pp. 162ff.

15 P. Tillich, *Systematic Theology*, Vol. 1, Welwyn, James Nisbet, 1968 (One volume edition), p. 121, from the section 'Revelation and Mystery'.

16 It is characteristic that Karl Rahner, one of the defining Catholic theologians of the twentieth century, saw 'man's basic and original orientation towards absolute mystery' as the presupposition of any more articulate or thematized knowledge of God, philosophical or dogmatic. See K. Rahner, *Foundations of Christian Faith*, London, Darton, Longman and Todd, 1978, p. 52 (and, in fact, the whole of Ch. 2, 'Man in the Presence of Absolute Mystery').

17 See Lossky, *Mystical Theology*, 'Introduction: Theology and Mysticism in the tradition of the Eastern Church'.

18 G. Marcel, tr. G. S. Fraser, *The Mystery of Being, Vol. 1*, London, Harvill, 1950, Ch. 10, 'Presence as a Mystery'.

19 See Zizioulas, *Being as Communion*, p. 92.

20 For the influence of this work (including, importantly, the nativity as well as the crucifixion panel) on Karl Barth, see Reiner Marquand, *Karl Barth und der Isenheimer Altar*, Stuttgart, Calwer, 1995.

21 See Christopher Browning, *Ordinary Men. Reserve Police Battalion 101 and the Final Solution in Poland*, New York, HarperCollins, 1992.

Chapter 3. The Sacrament of Creation

1 J. Moltmann, tr. M. Kohl, *God in Creation. An Ecological Doctrine of Creation*, London, SCM Press, 1985, p. 98 (the translation is my own from the German original).

2 S. McFague, *The Body of God. An Ecological Theology*, London, SCM Press, 1993, p. 130.

3 For a more extended discussion of Ruskin's theology of art, see my *Art, Modernity and Faith*, London, SCM Press, 1998, Ch. 4, 'Christian Theoria'.

4 See A. Wessels, tr. J. Bowden, *'A Kind of Bible'. Vincent van Gogh as Evangelist*, London, SCM Press, 2000.

5 D. H. Lawrence, ed. B. Steele, *Study of Thomas Hardy and other Essays*, Cambridge, Cambridge University Press, 1985, p. 140.

6 See, for example, Gormley's contribution 'Still Moving' in Bill Hall and David Jasper (eds), *Art and the Spiritual*, Sunderland, University of Sunderland Press, 2003, pp. 11–17.

7 A. Schmemann, *The World as Sacrament*, London, Darton, Longman and Todd, 1966. Strikingly, an important modern Catholic encyclopaedia of theology also took the title *Sacramentum Mundi* [the Sacrament of the World], indicating the fundamental importance of this idea to its whole theological project.

8 Pierre Teilhard de Chardin, *Le Milieu Divin. An Essay on the Interior Life*, London, Collins, 1960, p. 123.

9 Teilhard de Chardin, *Le Milieu Divin*, pp. 122–3.

10 Teilhard de Chardin, *Hymn of the Universe*, London, Collins, 1965, p. 20.

11 Teilhard de Chardin, *Le Milieu Divin*, p. 50.

12 Schmemann, *World as Sacrament*, p. 10.

13 Schmemann, *World as Sacrament*, p. 14.

14 Schmemann, *World as Sacrament*, p. 15.

15 It is perhaps not irrelevant that his own intellectual development was marked by his engagement with the thought of the Romantic philosopher F. J. W. Schelling who was a major figure of Romanticism in Germany, developing a highly spiritual philosophy of nature, which also influenced S. T. Coleridge, among many others.

16 Paul Tillich, *Systematic Theology*, Vol. 3, Welwyn, James Nisbet, 1968 (One volume edition), p. 128.

17 Tillich, *Systematic Theology*, Vol. 3, p. 128.

18 Tillich, *Systematic Theology*, Vol. 3, p. 128.

19 Tillich, *Systematic Theology*, Vol. 3, p. 129.

20 Tillich, *Systematic Theology*, Vol. 3, p. 130.

21 Tillich, *Systematic Theology*, Vol. 3, p. 130.

22 D. Brown, *God and Enchantment of Place: Reclaiming Human Experience*, Oxford, Oxford University Press, 2004.

23 It is, of course, true that artists from Mayakovsky through Warhol and on to conceptual, modernist and postmodernist art celebrate the eclipse of nature and the triumph of the infinitely mediated reality of the contemporary technological world. The contemporary balance of forces on this issue is hard to read, and probably depends on which artists one looks at, which journals one reads, which exhibitions one attends or which genres one is interested in. The film trilogy of *The Lord of the Rings* is, of course, a very ambiguous example, because it celebrates non-technological values in a highly technicized medium.

24 In M. Heidegger, tr. A. Hofstadter, *Poetry, Language, Thought*, New York, Harper, 1971, p. 172.

25 Heidegger, *Poetry, Language, Thought*, p. 172.

26 J. Macquarrie, *Paths in Spirituality*, London, SCM Press, 1972, p. 89.

27 Macquarrie, *Paths in Spirituality*, p. 89.

Chapter 4. The God in Time

1 See especially M. Eliade, *The Myth of the Eternal Return or Cosmos and History*, Princeton, Bollingen Paperback, 1971.
2 The quote is from Hölderlin, freely translated.
3 Girard's theory is set out in R. Girard, tr. P. Gregory, *Violence and the Sacred*, Baltimore, Johns Hopkins University Press, 1977 and in many subsequent works.
4 See E. Schillebeeckx, *Christ the Sacrament*, London, Sheed and Ward, 1963.
5 R. Haight, *Jesus, Symbol of God*, Maryknoll, Orbis, 1999, p. 11.
6 P. Tillich, *Systematic Theology* , Vol. 1, Welwyn, James Nisbet, 1968 (One volume edition), p. 265.
7 In G. A. Studdert-Kennedy, *The Unutterable Beauty*, London, Hodder and Stoughton, 1927 and subsequent editions.
8 K. Hussein, *City of Wrong. A Friday in Jerusalem*, London, Geoffrey Bles, 1959, pp. 3–4.
9 See K. Barth, tr. G. W. Bromiley, *Church Dogmatics, IV/1 The Doctrine of Reconciliation*, Edinburgh, T. and T. Clark, 1956, pp. 211–83.
10 See, e.g., Surah II, 'The Cow', 116–17.
11 For Girard's interpretation of the passion, see, amongst other works, R. Girard, tr. Y. Freccero, *The Scapegoat*, London, Athlone, 1986; R. Girard, tr. J. G. Williams, *I See Satan Fall Like Lightning*, Leominster, Gracewing, 2001.
12 R. Hooker, *The Laws of Ecclesiastical Polity*, London, Everyman edition, 1907, Vol. 2, p. 322.

Chapter 5. Tradition

1 A. Loisy, tr. C. Home, *The Gospel and the Church*, Philadelphia, Fortress Press, 1976.
2 R. Bultmann, *History and Eschatology*, Edinburgh, Edinburgh University Press, 1975, pp. 151–2.
3 N. F. S. Grundtvig, *Christelige Taler eller Søndags-Bog*, Vol. 2, Copenhagen, 1828, pp. 528–30.
4 Grundtvig, *Christelige Taler*, Vol. 1, pp. 36–7.
5 On the recent resurgence, in a feminist context, of 'mother-tongue theology' see Jeff Astley, *Ordinary Theology*, Aldershot, Ashgate, 2002, pp. 77ff.
6 See page 36 above.
7 The reflections that follow partially reprise my discussion in S. Platten and G. Pattison, *Spirit and Tradition. An Essay on Change*, Norwich, Canterbury Press, 1996, pp. 47ff.

8 On the forward-looking aspect of the Eucharist see G. Wainwright, *Eucharist and Eschatology,* London, Epworth Press, 1971.

9 N. Berdyaev, tr. O. F. Clarke, *Freedom and the Spirit,* London, G. Bles, 1935, pp. 330–1.

10 See P. Florensky, tr. B. Jakim, *The Pillar and Ground of the Truth,* Princeton, Princeton University Press, 1997, p. 16. Some readers will recognize an intriguing similarity to the reworking of the idea of truth in the work of Martin Heidegger. This is commented on by R. Slesinksi, *Pavel Florensky: A Metaphysics of Love,* New York, St Vladimir's Seminary Press, 1984.

11 Florensky, *Pillar and Ground of the Truth,* p. 16.

12 Florensky, *Pillar and Ground of the Truth,* pp. 16–17.

13 Taken together with my comments on the theme of friendship, this does, inevitably, have important implications for the way in which the normativity of doctrine takes shape in the Church. For to the degree that what I am arguing for is valid, then the truth of doctrine can no longer be construed as something to which one group or stratum within the Church has privileged access apart from the whole process of conversation in which all are engaged. A recent proposal on the discipline of the Church of England clergy in relation to doctrine stated that 'the Church has to exercise th[e] guardianship of doctrine through particular persons or bodies charged with the responsibility of so acting', adding that it is the House of Bishops that has the 'role as guardians of the Church's faith and teaching' (The Archbishops' Council, *Clergy Discipline [Doctrine],* London, The General Synod, 2004, pp. 25–6). Apart from the fact that this special role for the bishops practically contradicts the massive emphasis on the shared ministry of the whole body of the Church that has been so central in recent years in Church of England teaching and liturgical reform, it ill accords with the idea of a community of friends that one group within that community is in a unique way the 'guardian' of the truth of the conversation as a whole. One might think of the analogy with those self-appointed 'security services' that stand outside the democratic process yet see themselves as the true 'guardians' of the truth of, for example, Britishness. It would be a great pity if the Church's testimony to the freedom and maturity that is offered in Christ were to be obscured by such an institutionalization of immaturity. God will look to his own, and we have to attend to the authenticity of the truth that we speak to one another concerning the divine things we believe ourselves to have received. Clearly, if this view is accepted then the future will be a lot less uniform than the past, but one can only say to those who fear such pluralism in the Church that (a) it better accords with the nature of our fellowship in Christ and (b) that the attempt to impose theoretical uniformity on the mind of the Church has, as the historical

record shows, been deeply divisive, even when it has not been backed up by the use of imprisonment, torture and execution.

14 See H. Clinebell, *Basic Types of Pastoral Care and Counselling*, London, SCM Press, 1984.

15 See Y. Congar, *Tradition and Traditions*, London, Burns and Oates, 1966.

Chapter 6. Formation

1 F. D. E. Schleiermacher, ed. H.-J. Birkner, *Ethik (1812/13)*, Hamburg, Felix Meiner, 1990, p. 122 (§213).

2 Schleiermacher, *Ethik*, p. 123 (§219).

3 G. W. F. Hegel, tr. T. M. Knox, *Lectures on Fine Art*, Oxford, Oxford University Press, 1975, p. 11.

4 J. Maritain, *Art and Scholasticism*, London, Sheed and Ward, 1933, pp. 21–2.

5 A. W. Pugin, *An Apology for the Revival of Christian Architecture in England*, London, 1843, p. 9.

6 A very different – and, arguably, no less appreciative – relation to the medieval heritage was that of an architect such as Le Corbusier who, in his book *When the Cathedrals were White (Quand les Cathedrales étaient Blanches: Voyages an Pays des Timides*, Paris, Plon, 1937), hailed the great works of medieval architecture as prototypes for his own modernism.

7 Walter J. Ong, *Orality and Literacy. The Technologizing of the Word*, London, Routledge, 1988, p. 33.

8 Ong, *Orality and Literacy*, p. 34.

9 Ong, *Orality and Literacy*, p. 42.

10 George Herbert, 'A Priest to the Temple' in *George Herbert's Works Vol. 1*, London, Pickering, 1846, p. 233.

Chapter 7. Ethical and Political Postscript

1 I am using the terms 'traditionalist', 'conservative' and 'liberal' here in the sense in which they are used in newspaper discussions of these debates. Whether they are really helpful is a whole other question.

2 J. Allison, *On Being Liked*, London, Darton, Longman and Todd, 2003, pp. 101–2.

3 Carl Rogers, ' "To Be That Self Which One Truly Is". A Therapist's View of Personal Goals' in *On becoming a Person. A Therapist's View of Psychotherapy*, London, Constable, 1961. This is, arguably, an ungenerous selection from Rogers's list of therapeutic goals, and

it is true that he does offer some balancing goals, such as 'Towards Acceptance of Others'. Yet, in relation to the preceding moralistic approach to personal life-problems, Rogers's basic concept – and the practice of many therapists – clearly requires if not the abolition then certainly the suspension of making key life-decisions on the basis either of what we take to be moral rules or of obligations towards others.

4 See D. Bonhoeffer, ed. E. Bethge, tr. Neville Horton Smith, *Ethics*, New York, Macmillan, 1955.

5 S. Hauerwas, *The Peacable Kingdom. A Primer in Christian Ethics*, Notre Dame, Notre Dame University Press, 1983, pp. 24–5.

6 See, e.g., T. Khalidi, *The Muslim Jesus. Sayings and Stories in Islamic Literature*, Cambridge, Mass., Harvard University Press, 2001.

7 See Bonhoeffer, *Ethics*, 'The Structure of Responsible Life', pp. 224–54.

8 See K. E. Løgstrup, *Den etiske fordring*, Copenhagen, Gyldendal, 1991, p. 24. I am tempted to say that what Løgstrup is aiming at is a rearticulation of what the eighteenth-century Anglican theologian Joseph Butler dealt with in terms of 'benevolence'.

9 I am not saying that habit is antithetical to freedom. Clearly, in approaching a red light I remain free to override my habitual inclination to stop, and to this extent habit itself rests upon the constant exercise of freedom. But imagine that you are driving at speed on the motorway and the car immediately in front of you goes into an uncontrollable spin. Although certain driving habits may help in this situation (especially if you have developed the habit of keeping a safe stopping distance between yourself and the car in front!), these habits are not of themselves sufficient to decide your response, which will also have to take into account a variety of other factors (other vehicles, weather, etc.).

10 I. Murdoch, *The Sovereignty of Good*, London, Routledge and Kegan Paul, 1970, p. 71.

11 Of course, there were many prominent Conservatives who shared those anxieties, but believed they could be addressed within the framework of Conservative philosophy and policies.

12 P. Tillich, 'Waiting' in *The Shaking of the Foundations*, London, SCM Press, 1949, pp. 147–52. It is relevant to comment that in the period leading up to and immediately following Hitler's seizure of power, Tillich had been one of the few prominent Lutheran theologians calling for active political opposition to Nazism.

13 See Alastair Hannay, *On the Public*, London, Routledge, 2004.

14 See F. Fukuyama, *The End of History and the Last Man*, Harmondsworth, Penguin, 1992.

15 Samuel P. Huntington, *The Clash of Civilizations and the Remaking of the World Order*, London, Simon and Schuster, 1997, p. 29.

Subject and Name Index